Why Have You Come Here?

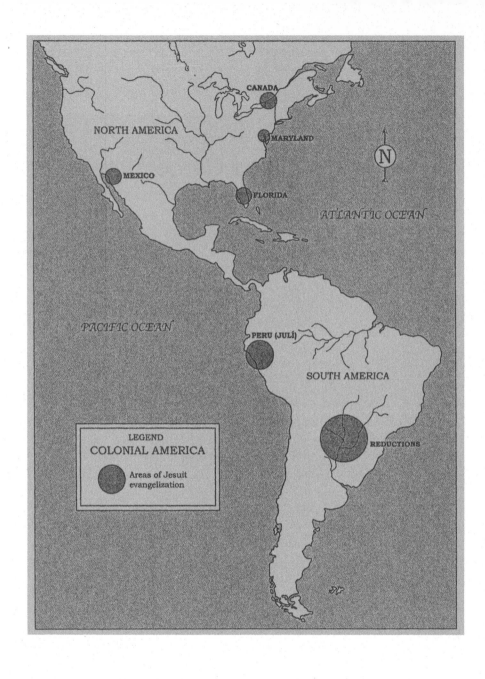

Why Have You Come Here?

The Jesuits and the First Evangelization of Native America

NICHOLAS P. CUSHNER

OXFORD
UNIVERSITY PRESS

2006

OXFORD
UNIVERSITY PRESS

Oxford University Press, Inc., publishes works that further
Oxford University's objective of excellence
in research, scholarship, and education.

Oxford   New York
Auckland   Cape Town   Dar es Salaam   Hong Kong   Karachi
Kuala Lumpur   Madrid   Melbourne   Mexico City   Nairobi
New Delhi   Shanghai   Taipei   Toronto

With offices in
Argentina   Austria   Brazil   Chile   Czech Republic   France   Greece
Guatemala   Hungary   Italy   Japan   Poland   Portugal   Singapore
South Korea   Switzerland   Thailand   Turkey   Ukraine   Vietnam

Copyright © 2006 by Oxford University Press, Inc.

Published by Oxford University Press, Inc.
198 Madison Avenue, New York, New York 10016

www.oup.com

Library of Congress Cataloging-in-Publication Data
Cushner, Nicholas P.
Why have you come here?: the Jesuits and the first evangelization of native America/
Nicholas P. Cushner.
p. cm.
Includes bibliographical references and index.
ISBN: 978-0-19-530801-3
1. Jesuits—Missions—North America—History.   I. Title.
BV2290.C87 2006
266'.27—dc22   2005031829

Printed in the United States of America
on acid-free paper

". . . [the white man] does not understand our customs, just as we do not understand his. We say he is foolish because he does not know our ways, and perhaps he says we are foolish because we do not know his. Let him go away."

—Chinua Achebe, Things Fall Apart

Preface

The response of indigenous America to the European attempt to re-organize religion was eclectic to say the least. Motivation, a difficult driver to interpret, ran the entire continuum of factors. Besides trying to figure out why Native America did this or that, the problem of sources and their interpretation persists. In the present book I view indigenous American cultures through specifically European Jesuit spectacles, thus creating the problem of accuracy. The concern is not so much with the interpretation of what the European saw but, more importantly, with the objective accuracy of *what* they saw. The cultural filter might well have so blurred the object as to turn it into something else. Thus, a healthy skepticism seasoned with a good dose of caution must accompany any attempt to enter the mind of a sixteenth-century European or Indian.

The quincentenary in 1992 did not produce a deeper understanding of what the agent of cultural change attempted or accomplished. Recent studies of the Indian-European encounter in North America include detailed insights about the failure or success of European missionaries who tried to change the social practices and religion of Indians groups. Nevertheless, little has been done on a comprehensive basis to investigate the effects of Jesuit cultural change, which partly justifies the comparative nature of this book. How, why, and to what degree was the European successful in altering the religion of the Native American? If we define culture as "how people do things," the questions to be asked are how and why the initial European-Indian encounter changed the religion, beliefs, attitudes, and ideas of Indian societies.

The organization of the book follows fairly standard lines. An analysis of the book's major theme falls within a rough chronological framework. The European missionaries were initial front-line contacts with indigenous cultures throughout North and South America. These Europeans were the bridge between Native American groups and the Western culture introduced to the New World. The first chapter, "Two Worlds Meet," discusses basic questions about American Indian groups and the motivational and cultural forces working in the psyche of the European agent of religious change. What had the individual European brought to America in *his* cultural baggage? What were his expectations of the American landscape, the American Indian? What did he hope to achieve? How did he expect to do it? And finally, how was he prepared for the task? An examination follows of how these agents of change acted and the responses they received.

Florida was the first stage on which the clash occurred, followed by Mexico, Peru, Paraguay, and New France. Maryland was the last. In each the European encountered Indians. In each they attempted to change religious behavior as well as social habits.

Acknowledgments

I have become indebted to many while preparing this book. The National Endowment for the Humanities allowed me to visit Archives in Rome and Spain in 1991, one of many visits over the past decade. The Mellon Foundation provided support for a stay at St. Louis University in order to use the Vatican Film and Jesuit Archives material in the Pius XII Library. I first presented part of chapter 1 at a conference on the Church in Colonial America at Tulane University in 1987. In 1992 I spoke again on the Jesuits as cultural agents at the International Congress of Americanists in New Orleans. I was especially helped at the conference by long discussions beneath the golden arches of McDonald's with Dan Reff of Ohio State University and Fr. Gerald McKevitt of Santa Clara. Walter Nugent of Notre Dame University looked at the outline of the book in its earliest stages and made many helpful suggestions about its organization. Eugene Lyon of the St. Augustine Foundation looked at chapter 2 and Gerald Fogarty of the University of Virginia had the patience to read chapter 9. I risked losing the friendship of Dan Reff by asking him to read the entire manuscript. He did; we're still friends. Many changes in the book followed. Sensitive to my time constraints in Rome, Hugo Storni of the Jesuit Historical Institute allowed me to use the institute library in the fall of 1996 during times when it was closed to researchers. F. J. de Cock, S.J., put at my disposal the rich holdings of the Jesuit Archives. Prof. John A. Larkin, of the History Department, SUNY Buffalo, friend and historian, helped me immensely to sharpen the vague ideas I had about evangelization in the Americas. State University of New York/UUP grants enabled me to employ expert technical assistance in producing the final manuscript from a hodgepodge of software programs, which I used on different computers in different countries over the past ten years.

Contents

Abbreviations

AGI	*Archivo General de las Indias*
AGNBA	*Archivo General de la Nación, Buenos Aires*
AHSI	*Archivum Historicum Societatis Iesu*
AM	Archives of Maryland
ARSI	*Archivum Romanum Societatis Iesu*, Rome, Italy
CA	*Cartas Anuas*, Bancroft Library, UC Berkley, CA
JR	*Jesuit Relations and Allied Documents*
MAF	*Monumenta Antiquae Floridae*
MM	*Monumenta Mexicana*
MNF	*Monumenta Novae Franciae*
MP	*Monumenta Peruana*
MPA	Maryland Province Archives, Georgetown University

Why Have You Come Here?

Introduction

The purpose of this book is to explain and interpret how one belief system replaces another. What variables come into play? What has to take place during the interaction to ensure that one system effectively overcomes the other? Can or does the host religion ever completely disappear?

Modern cultural anthropologists object to the idea that one belief system should actually replace another. However, even before the sixteenth and seventeen centuries (the general temporal frames of the present investigation), proselytizing cultures believed that it was their right and duty to change the existing fabric of societies. The introduction of Christianity by the Benedictines into the remote corners of the Roman Empire was simply the logical consequence of the earlier substitution of a monotheistic Christian deity in place of the Roman gods. Islam's sweep over the Middle East in the seventh and eighth centuries was as much political as religious. The Crusades of the twelfth and thirteenth centuries were warnings of the intransigent nature of evangelical Christianity. The discoveries of the New World simply rerouted Europe's crusading spirit to the East and not to the South. Therefore, a formal state religion was the traditional structure in societies from fifth-century B.C. Mesopotamia to fifteenth-century A.D. Europe.[1] The idea of "tolerance" or allowing belief systems to exist side-by-side does not enter Western consciousness until Locke, Hume, and the American and French revolutions popularized the notion of democracy in the seventeenth and eighteenth centuries.

In the present book, the encounter or collision of Christianity with Native American religions is examined. Christianity prevailed. Why it became the dominant religion is this book's subject matter. Why did it happen and what was the process of substitution? How did the agents of religious change go about the task of substitution? What variables were at play? What were the circumstances permitting success (how does one define success?) in Mexico, Paraguay, or Peru, but failure in Florida and Maryland?

Was there a correlation between the weather and success in evangelization? And by success is meant the development of sustained ecclesiastical institutions. It seems that temperate weather systems insured a reliable cycle of farming accompanied by reliable conversions. When North American aborigines set out to hunt during the winter snows, the European missionaries were flabbergasted. But what was the Native American to do? He might have stared from his long house, watched the snow pile up, and waited. But hunger soon overcame him. No crops grew in the snow! So he would hunt for winter prey. In less hostile zones, missionaries were more successful. Their Christian converts were even more authentic. In Mexico, Paraguay, and Julí, the conversion rate was higher. Added to this was the bond, the partnership-loyalty connector, that Jesuit and Guaraní forged when the European Jesuit assumed the role of broker of Guaraní-grown Jesuit tea. "We will make more money for you," said the Jesuit, and from that time on, a new relationship was formed, the loyalty became deeper, and their religion became more acceptable. This could only have been accomplished where the weather was favorable and the people remained in one place. In Maryland political circumstances trumped ideas and the formation of such bonds, while in Florida the Spanish soldiery who fed off Indian supplies merely drove the Indian away.

This is not to underestimate the effectiveness of the tools of conversion, as outlined below: coercion, the devil, and agriculturalist versus hunter-gatherer. The agents of religious change were Christian missionaries, but to narrow the scope I am mainly concerned with the early Jesuit missionaries in the Americas. Of course, there were other missionaries besides Jesuits. But because of the Jesuits' particular position in the Spanish imperial scheme of things and because they were meticulous record keepers and writers (as well as the suppression of the Jesuits in 1773 that resulted in many of their records being placed in national archives), the documentation on the Jesuits and their interaction with Native America is abundant.

Although the first Jesuits in America were Portuguese missionaries who worked with the Tupinambá of Brazil as early as 1559, Florida is the first site chosen for the study of early Christianization activity in North America. The missionary record there is full and documentation available. From the records about Florida, we can gather what the Europeans in North America expected to encounter and achieve. Furthermore, we can ask how their experience in Florida affected their future encounters with Native Americans in Mexico, Peru, Maryland, and in the rest of North and South America?

Changing religions was merely part of the European effort at cultural change. A series of violent cultural clashes occurred in sixteenth- and seventeenth-century America, whose effects were more penetrating and long lasting than people anywhere had ever experienced. Soon after the Europeans discovered that Columbus's landfall was not the Far East but a landmass blocking his way to India, groups of Spaniards, Portuguese, Frenchmen, Dutchmen, and Englishmen descended on America in search of precious metals, land to till, resources to exploit, and a new world to inhabit. Trouble was, the new world was already inhabited. So for the first time in the history of the West, intensive contact between its culture and other cultures began to occur. Traits of Western culture were transferred to the Native American and vice versa. For the European, culture became an expression of social solidarity, a means of separating oneself from the "uncivilized native," and later a barometer of loyalty to the mother country.

A related question concerns the reliability of the reporters. Jesuit missionaries were the bridge between Europe and the New World. Who were these "men on the spot"? Does the fact that they were present at a particular event entitle them to the mantle of reliability? Were they too biased to be neutral observers? And what did they observe, or think they were observing?[2] Or did these sixteenth-century observers actually possess and project a renaissance self-fashioning concept that enabled them to appreciate or at least collect a series of parts that could be admired and one day placed into a collective whole?[3]

In the early years of the encounter Christian missionaries sought to impose a set of cultural modifications on the Indian, but they did so with limited success.[4] Only gradually did they realize that Native Americans were selective in their acceptance of European traits. And their motives for doing so were varied.

Chinua Achebe's novel, *Things Fall Apart* (1959), confronts this issue directly, probing the enigma facing adherents of the old religion vis-a-vis the new. The African called the white missionary and his tiny band of local followers "the excrement of the clan," whose crazy ideas were given no chance of survival. The Christian belief in a god who had a son but no wife, who was the creator of everything, even the "evil forest," whose followers allowed the outcasts to enter their church, was a kind of "mad logic" that was allowed to survive because the village elders thought that it would soon disappear. But there was something intriguing about the stories the new religion told. They reached deep, so deep that the people called the stories the "poetry of the new religion." And before they could organize against it, Christianity had grown with new and powerful members. Along with the new church came government, courts and trials, prison, and the white man's laws. The feeling that "there was something in it after all" attracted more adherents.[5] When Ajofia upbraids the missionary, Rev. James Smith, for thinking that the structures he had so meticulously created would continue, the Englishman, uncompromising in his belief, cannot understand what the elder is talking about. Smith cannot fathom that his law, government, and religion could collapse under the weight of the other's cultural heritage. There is a point in the dialogue when neither understands the other. The words are comprehensible but the meaning is lost. Ajofia's anger is partly directed at himself. Smith uses an interpreter, never having learned the African's language. Ajofia has become the bridge between the two cultures. On some level, he realizes that his world is collapsing. It is falling apart. Obierika spoke for the clan when he said "he [the white man] has put a knife on the things that held us together and we have fallen apart."[6]

Although Chinua Achebe wrote about nineteenth-century Biafra, the sequence of events accompanying the clash in America was similar. Granted that the initial encounters in Florida, New France, and Maryland were not accompanied by the same degree of military violence that Mexico and Peru witnessed, the actions of the major players were remarkably the same. The presence of the Europeans was initially tolerated because it was not perceived as a threat; after the missionaries converted a handful of Indians, government, laws, courts, and the white man's culture followed shortly thereafter. Resistance to the new order of things was thereafter deemed unlawful insurrection. The linkages between imperialism, culture, and Christianity demonstrate how the agents of one supported the other. The key colonialist ideas of authority and submission were imbedded within the concepts of Spanish Catholicism, a major factor accounting for the different approaches to the Native American exhibited by the English, French, and Spanish. Cultural technologies as well as force of arms sustained the colonial empire.[7]

A corollary to this, of course, is what Native Americans understood when the concepts of Christianity were presented. In what way did they relate to and grasp the notions of king, loyalty, submission, and how did they understand the key ideas of faith, Church, Trinity, the Virgin Birth, or other elements of the Christian belief system? By substituting the concrete for the abstract, the European was able to circumvent obstacles to appreciating his perspective. But this could be taken only so far. Greg Dening describes how Captain Cook's words were processed and understood by his South Pacific audience in a way the Englishman never intended.[8]

The Columbus quincentenary in 1992 offered the occasion to examine in greater detail the European-Amerindian encounter. Most studies focused on how Europeans conceived of the Native American, on how Old World pathogens wreaked havoc on the native population, and on the train of social and economic consequences set in motion by the Columbus discoveries.[9] These recent studies provide a framework of postulates around which any study of European-Indian relations must be set. For example, Dobyn's demographic analysis of the Florida Indians is essential for assessing early Spanish attempts to occupy the Florida coast, and Milanich's most recent work on the European-Florida Indian conflict brings to bear the latest anthropological and historical research on the area.[10] While the Caribbean and Mexico were the principal recipients of this scholarly largesse, some of the broader studies encompassing North America are useful in trying to get into the mind of the early colonists. Medieval and renaissance beliefs about the "Wild Man" of the forest enhance our understanding of European expectations. Popular European culture equated the Wild Man with the Native American. The expected encounter with vast spaces, towering mountains, and enormous rivers allowed the European to substitute freely between the real and the fantastic. The studies of Pagden, Stannard, Todorov, Chiappelli, Dobyns, and Richter and Merrell to mention only a few, have called attention to key theoretical and practical aspects of the early European-Amerindian contact and have enabled subsequent researchers to piggyback on their work in order to add a few more brush strokes to the early American canvas.[11]

Through the process of European-Amerindian contact in sixteenth-century America, a thread of deceptively unified themes runs clearly. Coercion was present, as was the devil, identified as the ultimate agent responsible for opposing European culture.[12] The agriculturalist versus hunter-gatherer dichotomy also emerges as a prominent feature of the European-Amerindian encounter. These strands that run through the early encounter carried a special importance for the European Jesuit, but they also had a broader significance for the relationship between colonist and Indian. In Michener's *Hawaii* the Congregationalist minister, Abner Hale, is stunned when his native assistant, Keoki, marries according to his traditional rites. "It puts you outside the pale of civilized . . . ," shouts Abner. He could not finish the sentence. And so it was for most Europeans in the Americas. Marrying or even sympathizing with a native non-Christian was tantamount to becoming an uncivilized pagan. It meant turning one's back on the culture from which one came. Such rejections

occurred but not too often.[13] The agents of religious change viewed such oc-
currences as anomalies, deviations from the norm caused by temporary insanity or the devil.

Coercion

The history of the conquest and colonization of America is rich with literature
that describes what Europeans did when introducing Christianity and the Native American response. At one pole is the sweeping replacement of native for
European forms as a metaphor for cultural change. At the other pole is the
idols-behind-the-altar resistance that sees acceptance of foreign cultural traits
as a cloak concealing the retention and practice of the old ways.[14] In Mexico
and the Andean world, elements of the totally integrated pre-Hispanic past
persist to form essential parts of Native American culture. The Christian saint
is treated like an anthropomorphic deity, the old gods are propitiated at moun-
tainside caves, and drunkenness has become part of the religious fiesta.[15] Because religious beliefs and practices of adults are the least likely to change, and
when they do, they do so very slowly, the agents of religious change targeted
children. These agents realized that native religious instruction took place during adolescence or early youth.

In spite of the persistent efforts of Europeans on several levels to effect
conversion, Native American groups were able to shield, protect, and interject
key aspects of their cultural systems into the new culture presented to them.
The overwhelming preponderance of European symbols proclaiming the destruction of the old affected segments of the native population in various ways.
But enough of the old survived to give credence to the suggestion that much
of it managed to survive.[16]

Europeans used several techniques to influence the will of Native Americans to act in certain ways. Brute force was rarely if ever used to change habits
of behavior. Only if the custom so clashed with Western mores, such as the
practice of human sacrifice in Mexico or the continued worship of idols in
Mexico and Peru, and only if the Europeans exerted government control, was
physical force used to bring an end to a practice. Otherwise verbal criticism
from missionaries, and in some cases from civil officials, was the weapon of
choice.

But the most effective weapon in the Western arsenal was the power of
indirect persuasion. Reff has shown that on the frontier of Northern Mexico
Jesuits pointed out to Indians that they were not touched by the diseases rav-
aging the native populations because the god of the Europeans was stronger.[17]

Therefore, he and his agents should be obeyed. The conquest of Mexico and Peru by the Spaniards produced an almost catatonic effect on the native populations. Their gods had abandoned them and the god of the White Invaders had replaced them.[18] The Indian mind was ripe for domination and persuasion. Furthermore, economic benefits accrued to those who joined the conquerors. Visibly accepting the ways of the conqueror and actively supporting their goals made one eligible for the rewards they distributed. The pull toward the new ways was often irresistible. In Peru and Mexico, the Spaniards erected social structures that paralleled pre-Hispanic society but allowed only Christians to enter the new arrangement. The French and English in North America exerted similar influences even though they did not possess direct control over Indian social structures. When the Pequot Indians along the Connecticut River resisted, militia captain and Puritan John Mason attacked the terrified victims and burned their wigwams, praising God "who had laughed at his enemies and the enemies of his people, . . . making them as a fiery oven."[19] Later, European colonists would not have to resort to warfare. They pitted one Indian group against another by offering rivals new hunting, fishing, and household equipment that promised to make the life of the Native American much less arduous. The iron fishhook did not readily break, the iron pot lasted far longer than the bark kettle, and the bullet silenced the enemy much more efficiently than an arrow.[20]

Coercion was not new to Western proselytization. Biblical passages and stories were partly at the source of Western religious and cultural aggression. "Go, make disciples of all nations,"[21] and the parable of the king who prepares a feast to which no one comes causing him to tell his servants to "force them to come in,"[22] gave Westerners a religious rationale to use forceful means in the name of God.

Europeans in America did not have to go too far back in their history to find a precedent for using force in achieving cultural uniformity. Boswell maintains that fourteenth-century Europe was the watershed dividing a period of tolerance from one of increasing bigotry.[23] Spain's seven-century struggle with the Muslims reinforced the notion of intolerance that culminated in King Ferdinand and Queen Isabella reversing a long tradition of tolerance by expelling the Jews and Muslims in 1492.[24] A "corporate" view of society saw religious differences as a cancer that unless excised would infect the entire body.

Europe shared the renaissance conviction that Western culture had reached the pinnacle of human achievement. But its moderating ideas had little effect on those who believed in waging God's war. While Florentine artists busily mixed their paints, Spanish warriors sharpened their swords and lances for battle with the Muslims. And Capt. John Mason, who led a Puritan army

against the Pequots, would probably never have admitted to being these warriors North American equivalent, even though Spaniard and Puritan were
equally certain that God was on their side. The intellectual baggage of the
seventeenth-century European contained the truculence of the *reconquista*—
re-conquest of Spain from the Muslims—and the self-assuredness that renaissance culture was superior to anything the New World indigenous
populations could offer.

In New Spain coercion was evident in the methods the Franciscan missionaries used in their mission stations. Robert Ricard's classic study refers
frequently to mass baptisms and the forcible suppression of indigenous religious practices.[25] Patios of churches became makeshift schoolhouses where
Christian doctrine was taught and acceptable manners were inculcated. Physical punishment awaited those absent from evening meetings.[26] However, Stafford Poole's study of Indian-white relations in New Spain emphasizes the importance of physical geography rather than physical coercion. Violence was
more likely to be manifest among those closest to military action while in
remoter areas settlers and traders tended to affect a more pacific native response.[27] Louise Burkhart takes Nahuatl-European relations to another level,
showing how language affected the emerging belief system.[28] The relationship
between European and Native American was conditioned not only by the sword
and musket but also by the language that the newcomer used.

The French and English were unable to use physical coercion to bring
about a change of religion and behavior. Persuasion and the threat of everlasting punishment in hell was the furthest that the agents of religious change
would go. For those inclined to accept Western ways, isolation in one of the
French-controlled "reductions," or in one of the English "Praying Towns," provided safe havens for religious converts.

The Devil

Another common theme that runs through early reports about the Native
Americans is the presence of the devil and his human associates, Indian priests
or shamans. Opposition to Western religion is concretized in the person of the
hechicero in Peru or *jongleurs* in New France. The Jesuits who made early contact
with the American Indians were convinced that the ultimate cause of native
resistance to their ideas was the devil who bitterly resented the intrusion of the
Christians. The figure of the devil as described by early missionaries evoked
pre-Hispanic supernatural figures.[29] For the European, the devil was the major
opponent in the battle for the Indian soul. Georges Baudot has shown how the

use of the Nahua terms for devil and demons may have inadvertently led to the affirmation of native beliefs.[30]

The obsession with the devil is tied to the folk Catholicism of the Europeans. Pío Baroja's work on the role of the devil in popular European Catholicism explains how the concept of the Evil One became a central feature in the Old World belief system.[31] The European Jesuit who had been educated to believe that forces of evil waged a continual struggle against the forces of good easily translated Native American opposition into Satan's handiwork. They were unable to imagine any other reason for the Native American's refusal to accept Christianity along with major features of European culture. Witches or *brujos* were the servants of the devil. Thus, the fiesta in which individual saints were honored as protectors against the devil were important spiritual as well as social activities. European iconography placed Satan in a pivotal position whose manifestations became ubiquitous.

Agriculturalist versus Hunter-Gatherer

Just as upsetting to missionaries was the reluctance of the Native American to "settle down." Hunter-gatherer societies and groups who spent part of their time away from village centers puzzled the Europeans. The Hurons in New France who combined both agriculture/horticulture and hunting to support themselves offered the Jesuits a major challenge because the Europeans were unable to continue an immersion-type indoctrination through the hunting season. On the other hand, the Jesuits in Julí in the Peruvian Andes were thoroughly satisfied with their agriculturalist/pastoralist parishioners. Their activities were predictable, determined by the rhythm of the agrarian cycle.

Beneath the difficulties with hunter-gatherers was the Western prejudice against anything that differed from stable agricultural life, considered to be the civilized way to live. The hunter-gatherers were considered to be primitive, backward, savage, and undeveloped.[32] The bias toward agriculturalists was reflected in Western concepts of land ownership.[33] The fence, whether the stone barrier of New England or the natural boundary lines so often described in Latin American land documents, reveals the Western bias toward stable, inalienable, fixed property rights, determined by legal means, not to be infringed on. On the other hand, there exist examples of missionaries who came to appreciate the positive characteristics of hunter-gatherer life after traveling with hunter bands. Food sharing, hunting techniques, social interactions, quality cooperation, and displays of goodwill and affection caused Europeans to question the supposed primitiveness of hunter-gatherer life.

However, missionaries in general were convinced that social stability and village life were essential for effective evangelization. Control and indoctrination were keys to success. Besides the reductions of Paraguay, the town of Julí near Lake Titicaca and the reservations near Montreal were considered ideal places for religious indoctrination. Separation from the pagan masses and corrupting influences of traders and merchants was considered essential for producing European-like Native Americans.

One of the most powerful tools used by missionaries in the destruction of key aspects of Native American religion was the *Confessionario*. This was a bilingual handbook that the confessor used in auricular confession to question the penitent about behavior and beliefs.[34] Since confession was a sacrament considered essential for receiving the Eucharist, which in turn meant acceptance into the full Christian community, it became the bulwark against whatever was considered at odds with Christian doctrine. A great deal more than doctrinal beliefs fell into the wide net of Christian doctrine. The penitent was questioned about birds, fish traps, lightning, snakes in the road, dreams, ceremonies of war, abortion, sex, and other topics considered related to authentic Christianity. And at the end of it all, the penitent was told: "Son, all of these abuses and tremors of the body and signs of birds and animals, none of it is to be believed."[35] Or to herbalists, midwives, and sorcerers: "Leave that evil prayer because it is perverse, cure only with medicine."[36] The confessor held the keys of eternal life, and if the penitent wanted to enter, he or she had to accept what the confessor believed to be genuine, pure Christianity.

These three themes, coercion, the devil, and agriculturalist versus hunter-gatherer provide a framework for discussing how Christianity became the dominant religion in the Americas.

I

Two Worlds Meet

Soon after Columbus landed on Hispaniola, Spanish attention
shifted to Mexico. Cortés's conquest of Tenochtitlán in 1521 and the
subsequent flood of settlers arriving through Havana provided the
Old World with detailed accounts of Mexico's native peoples. Contacts between the Old and New worlds occurred north and south of
Mexico City and along the east and west coasts of Florida. Slowly the
physical map of the Americas took shape in the European mind. It
was completed long before the Europeans understood the cultural
profile of the inhabitants of the lands they invaded.

Native America

The values, beliefs, and insights held by peoples of the Americas
contrasted sharply with those of the Europeans. It is presumptuous
to attempt to sum up the cultures of the peoples of the Americas in
a few pages. The millennia that followed the original entrance of
Asians into the Americas by land across the Bering Strait and by
boat along the Pacific Coast witnessed multiplex culture development in North, Central, and South America.[1] Nevertheless, certain
common elements were shared by native peoples allowing for variations caused by differing physical environments.

One major shared attitude was their relationship to the natural
world. The natural environment, whether trees, mountains, the soil,

the animals inhabiting the forests, the forest itself, was endowed with a sacredness stemming from the particular spirits who dwelled in them. To disturb the balance of the environment, whether by overhunting the beaver or destroying the forest, meant that the spirit of the place or thing was disturbed and would bring harm to the perpetrator.[2]

Whether the Tupinambá of Brazil, the Calusa of Florida, the Hurons of New France, the Aymara of Peru, or the Sonorans of Northern Mexico, all saw a manifestation of the divine in the environment that surrounded them. Within every object dwelled a force that governed its existence. The animate and inanimate were virtually indistinguishable. Humans, animals, plants, stones, as well as dreams, emotions, and ideas were regarded as having indwelling spirits, forces pervading all objects, ultimately responsible for good and evil in the world. This belief of recognizing a supernatural force in the natural world clashed with the Western notion of man as ruler of the natural world. The book of Genesis gave humans domination over the land, seas, and animals of the universe.[3] God did not dwell in nature but ruled over it and he gave to man, his creation, the power to do with it whatever man wished. Western man even took this a step further declaring that key elements of the earth could be owned if acquired legitimately. Land, soil, water, forests, lakes, could be private property and disposed of according to the will of the owner. The Native American belief in the absolute integration of the divine within the natural world was not interpreted by the Western invaders as a form of "God's presence in all things," as medieval and early modern theologians would hold, but as a form of pagan animism that endowed the material world with supernatural powers it in no way possessed.

Closely linked to the Indian beliefs in the supernatural were the rites through which the group or individual achieved harmony with the spirit world. These generally revolved around animal sacrifices performed as propitiatory offerings to a particular spirit. The sacrifices were often associated with harvest, planting, hunting seasons, or to mark a special event in the life of a community or a group member. One such event in the yearly cycle of the Huron Indians was their celebration of the Day of the Dead. Jean de Brebeuf's lengthy account of Huron burial practices was mixed with empathy and revulsion. "Our savages," he wrote, "are by no means savages in so far as their natural respect for the dead is concerned."[4] On the Day of the Dead, he continued, the burial grounds were "an image of hell. The great open space was filled with fires and flames and the air filled with screaming shouts of the barbarians."[5] Brebeuf sketched a scene of diabolical frenzy worthy of a Pieter Brueghel painting. But did he understand what he saw? The only interpreter of the scene in front of him was the filter of his European mind set: the dead should have been remembered in the manner of European Christians, namely by silent prayers, the laying of garlands near the gravesite, or by a vigil on the eve of All Saints Day.[6] Fire, flames, and screaming smacked too much of pagan rituals.

While Europeans derived attitudes about marriage and sex from their religion, Native Americans saw no such connection. Marriage for the Native American was primarily a socioeconomic phenomenon essential for a community's survival. If the partnership proved dysfunctional for whatever reason, it was dissolved. The prevalence of pre-marital sex and polygamy was viewed by Europeans as major obstacles to full adherence in the Christian community.

At the root of the issue was the role of women in Native American society. Most Indian societies were matriarchal with inheritance passing through the mother. This meant that a woman's role in society was not simply one of handmaiden or keeper of the house. Land ownership, clan decisions, and clan policy were often a woman's prerogative. The European was accustomed to a society in which the male played the lead role. Thus, interpersonal relationships within kinship groups in which the woman played a major role puzzled Europeans. Marriage between cousins or between consanguineous adults while not forbidden but strongly discouraged by the Catholic Church was viewed as close to incestuous. Francisco Pizarro's kangaroo court condemned Atahualpa to death because he allegedly slept with his sister. And the Jesuit missionary, Jean de Brebeuf, was skeptical of the Huron males ever committing themselves to Christianity because of their unwillingness to stay with one wife.[7]

The European World

In sharp contrast to the values of native Americans, the Renaissance European missionary was in the middle of a movement that asserted man's control over nature, masculine rule over the household, and a Christian religious fundamentalism that alleged certainty in everything. These core values clashed head-on with Native American beliefs and living conditions.

The Jesuit missionary carried these values with him to the remote corners of North and South America. The Jesuits who first came to Florida in the 1560s did not imagine that a special preparation was required for the work they envisioned.[8] In true renaissance fashion, they thought that they were sufficiently equipped both intellectually and spiritually for the task that lay ahead. Since evangelization was primarily a spiritual activity, the best preparation, it was thought, was to hone the spiritual dimension of the Jesuit. Ignatian principles, a basically Tridentine theology, the recognition of the perfectibility of the American Indian, and a model of missionary behavior formed the basic intellectual and spiritual preparation for the Jesuit going to America. But it did not take long for Jesuit administrators to realize that theology, philosophy, and classical studies were neither the only nor the best preparation for evangelizing the American Indian.

What Bernard Cohn analyzed and determined to be the "cultural techniques of rule"[9] as opposed to the military and economic, are strikingly compatible with what the Jesuits perceived and developed as necessary tools for religious evangelization. Although their primary focus was the transference of their belief system to Native American societies, Western values and behavior were linked to religion as essential by-products. The writing of grammar texts, historical treatises, and the recording and critique of native religion became part of the modus operandi of the Jesuits in America. These writings and analyses were a logical consequence of the classical formation required of all who aspired to be Jesuits. The predisposition to the world of knowledge became a pillar of colonial control in America.

In the fifteenth and sixteenth centuries, Western Europe was in the laborious process of modernization. The medieval world's focus on religion and the church as the ultimate answer to man's problems was being replaced by a vision that located man at the center of the world. Confidence in man's inherent goodness and ability for self-improvement was at the root of the movement and the recently invented printing press spread the new ideas with unimagined speed. European man's concept of the physical world and his place in it was changing. New worlds across the seas were discovered. Clergy were interested because the gates of salvation could be opened to uncounted souls. Secular rulers could have new realms to conquer that would furnish precious metals and exotic resources. Meanwhile, Luther and Calvin shook the foundations of the church. A massive administrative machine concerned with making money and international politics had separated itself from the body of Christendom. The church itself was divided between higher clergy, an aristocratic and aloof hierarchy, and a lower clergy composed of village priests who were impoverished, ignorant, and angry. Luther's movement begun in 1519 was a logical consequence of decades of resentment. The Council of Trent, convened in 1545, was the Roman Catholic response to all of this. The Jesuit founder, Ignatius Loyola, saw it as another opportunity to choose between the banner of the Good King and the banner of Satan—Muslims against Christians, the devil against humanity, darkness against light. He and his followers would serve beneath the banner of the pope.

The spiritual principles that the European Jesuit brought with him to America in the sixteenth century were rooted in the life and struggles of Ig-

natius Loyola. These were adjusted to the pronouncements of the Council of
Trent (1545–1563) and transmitted to indigenous America.[10] The Council of
Trent's (a city in northern Italy) doctrinal statements, its reformulation of ideas
about what human nature with God's assistance or grace was or was not, and
above all, an almost new spirit of Catholicism, at once truculent and uncompromising, had a direct effect on how the Roman Catholic agents of change
perceived America and on the belief system they imparted.

The Council of Trent was convened to reform the practice and restate the
theology of the Roman Catholic Church. The theology of Trent was a restatement of doctrine, but the restatement was combative in tone. The issues raised
by Martin Luther and the reformers were major targets of the council. One
that had important consequences for Indian America was the reformulation
of the question of justification, or how man and God did or did not cooperate
in sanctification and salvation.[11] The Tridentine notion of justification became
the driving force behind the Roman Catholic European missionary's preaching.

Luther maintained that human nature had become so corrupted as a result
of Adam and Eve's sin that man alone could do nothing but evil. Man's will
was so enslaved that he could play no active part in his own salvation. Mankind
was damned. Only a few had been chosen by God to be saved irrespective of
any merits they might possess. Man was the garbage in a garbage can, but
Christ's redemptive work (his blood shed on the cross) covered it. The Council
of Trent, on the other hand, maintained that justification (the process whereby
the sinner is restored to the favor of God, virtues developed, and salvation
achieved) came through Christ and was united with hope and charity and
linked to morality. Baptism, while universal in its effects, was completely effective in removing the guilt of original sin, and therefore absolutely necessary
for salvation.[12] Natural virtue, that is, a state apart from grace, could not alone
achieve the supernatural life, but the human spirit was dignified to the degree
that it was perfectible. Later, Jesuit speculative theologians would carry this
idea further. Luis de Molina stated that there existed a hypothetical "state of
pure nature" in which man, even though exempt from original sin, was still
deprived of the supernatural life and subject to death and all other miseries of
life.[13] In much of Jesuit thinking at the end of the sixteenth century there
existed a "good pagan," one who was not damned simply because of his or her
separation from the church. Although removed from divine favor, man retained
a nature, which made him a creature of dignity, worth, and potential virtue.[14]

The Council of Trent's opposition to Luther's pessimistic view of human
nature was carried by the Jesuits to America. This was not a wholly optimistic
view that believed in the natural perfectibility of man, but one that instead

believed that divine grace could intrinsically affect man's nature. The Council of Trent also reemphasized the sacramental system of Catholicism. The sacraments were seven visible signs or symbols believed to have been instituted by Christ as vehicles for obtaining divine assistance or grace. Luther denied the need for the sacraments of baptism as necessary for salvation, auricular confession of sins as the traditional method for the forgiveness of sin, and the Eucharist as the actual body and blood of Christ. Trent, on the other hand, insisted on baptism's essential role and on confession and the Eucharist as vehicles for God's grace. These three elements of the sacramental system, baptism, confession and penance, and the Eucharist, became the kernel of Jesuit teaching in America, the sine qua non of Indian reception into and participation in the active life of the church.

Baptism was the standard rite of initiation into the Christian community. In the sixteenth century, the rite, usually performed soon after birth, invoked the power of God to cleanse the soul of sin, making the individual a member of the church. The rite left an indelible mark on the soul of the person receiving the sacrament whereby the individual was expected to worship as a Christian. Since popular Roman Catholic belief denied salvation to those outside the church, "*extra ecclesiam nulla salus*," the sacrament of baptism was considered a required rite or ceremony.

Marriage was a sacrament that had to take place in a church, with prescribed words and rites.[15] The council considered each of the sacraments to be unique and divinely created opportunities to acquire a remedy against the power of Satan.[16]

For the sixteenth-century European Jesuit, religion was not just concepts or even ethics, but a collection of rites and symbols as well. For a European still possessing an understanding of the meaning of symbols, rites were a Christian shorthand that explained the substance of his or her belief system. Baptism spoke to the American Indians in shorthand about their entrance into another life. What in actuality the viewer understood was another matter. The Roman Catholic Mass with its movements, gestures, and words, reenacted the master idea of Roman Christianity, the redemptive death of Christ. The bread and wine symbolized the body and blood of Christ. These two elements were raised heavenward during the rite, changed into the actual body and blood of Christ at the part called the Consecration, and the host (the Eucharistic bread) was broken in half to symbolize Christ's death. Then the water and wine were consumed.[17]

The council's decrees did not equivocate or leave room for interpretation. "If anyone shall say that baptism is a matter of choice, that is, not necessary for salvation, *Anathema Sit*," stated the Canon on baptism. Or, "If anyone shall say that a real and proper sacrifice is not offered to God in the Mass and that to be offered means no more than Christ is given to us to be eaten: Let Him Be Anathema."[18] Those two Latin words, *Anathema Sit*, meaning let him be anathema, driven out, cast away, express the aggressive and exclusive spirit of the Council of Trent.

Religion of the late medieval period had wandered far from official traditional practice. Antipapalism, the rift between popular belief and official teachings, the power of brotherhoods, and the crisis of authority were all part of the dynamic that created the aggressiveness of Trent in the sixteenth century.[19] This truculence became part of the missionary endeavor in America. The Council of Trent created a new and different version of Catholicism unlike medieval Christianity and unlike the Christianity suggested by Luther and Calvin. It ushered in a period of Spanish-led reforms (over 218 of the 270 bishops at Trent were either Italian or Spanish). The new Catholicism was didactic and disciplinary. The Roman Inquisition came into being as well as a prohibition against books considered dangerous reading called an Index of Forbidden Books. Corrective pastoral discipline became the spearhead for order and deference to civil and ecclesiastical rulers.[20] Religious unity was equated with uniformity. These were the ingredients for a successful authoritarian state.

The textbooks used by Jesuit theology students in the sixteenth and. seventeenth centuries reflected and reinforced the vitriolic tone of the Council of Trent.[21] What was called Fundamental Theology, *Theologia Fundamentalis*, defended prescribed theses that either supported the Tridentine view of Christianity or denied the principles of reformation theology. The church, the sacraments, grace, the nature of God, and predestination were explained through revelation or through the magisterium of the church, the depository of all revealed truth. It was clear, intelligible, and needed little interpretation. Whatever was questionable was studied in Speculative Theology, which began with a declaration of faith and created the boundaries outside of which the speculator was not to proceed. *Fides quaerens intellectum*, faith seeking understanding, was the phrase used to govern the inquisitive mind.

Despite the movement toward conformity of religious doctrine that the Council of Trent advocated, the Jesuits managed to defend theological and philosophical positions that made the American Indian fundamentally humane and naturally theistic.[22] This led to an ambiguity in their writings about America and its inhabitants. Descriptions of Indian cruelty—lust, gluttony, thievery, polygamy, sodomy, filth, superstition, lying, and blasphemy—abounded. But in these descriptions the Indian's intrinsically valuable humanity was never denied. The Council of Trent provided doctrinal and ritual parameters for the Jesuit agent of change. It also provided a generous view of

human nature that encouraged European agents of religious change to under-
take the task of conversion.

The European missionary brought with him to America a complex configuration of values and ideas about what the world was and what it should be.
These values and ideas had been shaped and refined by his family, society, and
the religious order to which he belonged. What he absorbed in his seminary
training and Jesuit life was more often than not surrounded by the values that
were operative in the Western world around him. Before the final acceptance
of a Jesuit value core, many values had been rejected, some replaced, and others
revised by the prospective missionary to accompany the new order of values
that the Society of Jesus expected to operate in the individual. In addition, the
Jesuit's other ideas about religion that he carried in his intellectual knapsack
are keys to understanding both sides of the cultural fence in the European-
Amerindian encounter.

The Christianity that the European brought with him to America had been
a negotiated form of Christianity that had animistic or pagan roots. However,
by a twist of logic, the Christian's rites became a pure form of religion, and
the Indian's were a sign of demonic intervention. At no time did the Jesuit
missionary offer to the Native American a solely rationalistic, post-Tridentine
version of Catholicism. The presentation was always mixed with elements of
rituals and imagery that were part and parcel of popular European Catholicism.[23]

The goal of the Jesuit in early America was to create a community of
believers who one day would ascend to heaven and the beatific vision. Creating
a Christian community was the intermediate goal, heaven the ultimate. The
missionary believed that Indians possessed the spiritual and attitudinal qualities whereby they could achieve these goals. The means to achieve the ultimate
goal had to be conveyed to the Indian through instruction. On their part the
Indians had to be willing to listen to, accept, and carry out what they heard.
These three elements, goal, givens, and methods to achieve the goal, were
encased in cultural assumptions and attitudes that the Jesuit had learned over
his own lifetime from his culture. Indians, on the other hand, were caught
between competing and rival rituals, one that they had practiced from child-
hood, the other brought by the invaders.[24] The European believed that the
major obstacle to attaining the goals was not the inability of Indians to accept
or practice what they heard, but the tireless activity of the devil who thwarted
and deceived all Indians. Demonology, black magic, and pacts with the devil
were an obsessive concern in sixteenth-century Europe.[25] Demons had to be
confronted and it was believed that Christian angels were more than a match
for Satan's army of winged devils. The rosary could undo curses and spells.

Relics of the saints protected against bad luck. Opening the Bible to a random passage replaced casting lots. A saint's medal guaranteed protection in danger.[26] This mix of Christianity and magic was not seen so much as a blending of the pagan with the Christian but as an authentic expression of true Christian belief. The European did not see his religion as a pagan-Christian blend. His methods of opposing the devil by substituting images, shrines, rites, and an omnipresent cult of the saints, were time-honored ways of Christianizing the European frontier, a popular theology that had little foundation in the Council of Trent. In fact, the liturgy and modes of piety that the missionaries brought to America were those of the rural world of the European peasant.[27]

Mass, considered the most powerful form of intercession with God, could only be performed by a priest. Baptism, marriage, and penance were also more appropriately performed by the priest. These rites formed the core of Christian ritual and they were enunciated as such. But almost on equal footing was the cult of the saints. In Europe saints in the countryside were venerated within specific regions as protectors, intermediaries, and granters of favors.[28] The Virgin Mary occupied the most important position in regional shrines and this preeminence was transferred to America. The missionary would have argued that the shrine, the medal, and the rite were metaphors, symbols, hints of what God is like, not an attempt or a magical instrument to force God to do what we want. It is questionable whether the Indian or the Jesuit saw the statues and rites in those terms. The Spaniard and Mediterranean European preferred the concrete to the abstract. The virgins clothed, decorated, and pampered in Seville during Holy Week or in Lima, Peru on June 21, occupy an important place in the popular spectrum of theological values. Layers of devotions focusing on relics, local saints, the Virgin Mary, and on Jesus rivaled the official Catholic liturgy for preeminence.

Although most Jesuits came from sophisticated cities or as young men had been sent from their villages to city colleges, they nevertheless carried with them to America these popular religious practices that in fact helped the Native American ease the transition from pre-Hispanic to post-Tridentine belief systems. Just as early European Christianity almost winked at homosexuality[29] so the European missionary freely substituted his rites for the Indian's, his medals for the Indian's talisman's, his prayers for the Indian's incantations. The European's tolerance ceased only when he met the *hechicero*, or native priest, because only he threatened and implicitly (and sometimes explicitly) challenged the authority and social status of the missionary.[30]

The religious imagery and popular rituals of late medieval and sixteenth-century Spain reflected the kind of religious world in which the Jesuit was situated and the kind of a world he wanted to re-create in America.

Why They Went

Soldiers, bureaucrats, farmers, merchants, and artisans sailed to America seeking very personalized goals. Only missionaries had as their primary aim to change the religion of the Native American. These were the individuals who became the front-line representatives of Western culture. In the villages, the cities, and on the frontier, they encountered, influenced, and reacted to the attitudes, values, and behavior of the New World inhabitants. Their first contacts with the Native American had been through letters sent from the Indies and America to Europe. They in turn volunteered for the overseas missions.

Letters from Jesuits asking to be sent to American missions in the sixteenth century were filled with references to Francis Xavier and desires to imitate him.[31] Xavier had been chosen by Ignatius Loyola to begin the work of converting Portuguese India. His reputation as a Holy Man and saintly proselytizer grew enormously in the sixteenth century due in no small part to the many letters he sent to Rome and his Jesuit brethren.[32] These letters were copied and read in Jesuit houses throughout Europe, striking a resonant cord among the hundreds of Jesuits who wished to be sent to the missions of Asia and America.

By elevating Francis Xavier as the model missionary, the Jesuit administration endorsed the methods he used in India, his ascetic and personal life as a Jesuit, and the practice and procedures he used as a missionary. From 1542 to 1552 Francis Xavier catechized the inhabitants of the Cape Comorin coast. He organized the mission, instructed, and traveled through southern India attempting to establish other missions. His neophytes were among the poorest of Indians living under the jurisdiction of Portuguese colonial rule. However, his experience among the Cape Comorin fisherfolk bore little resemblance to what future missionaries would encounter in America. Xavier's converts were used to Holy Men seeking alms, preaching an austere way of life, promising freedom from affliction and pain. They were part of the cultural context of India. Xavier and the missionaries who worked with him had the protection of the Portuguese colonial government. Future missionaries in New France, Maryland, and China would have to work under far different circumstances with people who neither sympathized with nor appreciated the way of the European Holy Man. Francis Xavier's letters, however, painted a picture of physical discomfort, psychological isolation, and adventure. The reward for enduring would be the realization that souls were going to heaven instead of to hell. His letters became the chief recruitment tool for Jesuit missionaries

and a keen public relations vehicle. Only in the late seventeenth century would
Jesuit letters from America replace Xavier's accounts of India in Jesuit pulpits.

Who were the European messengers of Christianity in America? The European in Florida and Mexico came out of a harsh form of Catholicism at war
with the nonbeliever, whomever that may have been. The seventeenth-century
French missionary may have been less truculent but he was no less unbending
when it came to issues of orthodoxy. Did different national origins affect what
the Jesuit said and how he said it? Or was the European Jesuit poured from
one mold, making him speak and act in a uniform way?

Going a step further, can some sort of an evolutionary process be detected
between the Renaissance Jesuit of the sixteenth century and the Baroque Jesuit
of the eighteenth? Did the intervening two centuries create a change in thought
patterns or behavior among the Jesuit missionaries? In response, one can say
that there was no change about core beliefs. The Mass, the sacraments, the
Trinity, the role of the Catholic Church vis-à-vis individual salvation, remained
the same. These beliefs were projected back into New Testament texts. The
concept of the "development of doctrine" had not yet been broached. However,
there were shifts on the periphery. The New Science was gaining adherents.
Bacon, Descartes, and even Hume found their way into Jesuit college libraries,
albeit under lock and key. But how many of their ideas filtered into the lecture
hall and classroom is unknown. Nevertheless, the eighteenth century was a
century that fully accepted as morally right the buying and selling of human
beings. It would only be a twentieth-century pope who would classify the act
as "intrinsically evil." The absolute indissolubility of marriage, the "error has
no rights" position, and of lending money for interest, were essential beliefs
of eighteenth-century Jesuits. These core beliefs were unaltered, and it would
be another two centuries before significant peripheral beliefs began to
change.[33]

Aside from some individuals who became well known because of their
ethnographic studies or geographical discoveries, we know few faces and only
a few scattered statistics about the missionaries who came to America. We
know some of the essential characteristics, the ages, the status in the Jesuit
group, and geographical origins of many Jesuit missionaries. More difficult to
learn are the internal forces that drove them from Europe to America.

The Jesuits who worked on the frontiers of America were volunteers. Hundreds of letters from Spanish, French, and other European Jesuits volunteering
for the missions of Asia, Africa, and America are still preserved in the Jesuit
Archives in Rome. Between 1651 and 1700 Jesuits from the Province of France
(the administrative unit responsible for staffing New France) sent over 268

requests to serve on the missions. A handful were allowed to go. Between 1583 and 1604 Spanish Jesuits wrote at least 412 letters requesting a mission post. This number represents 15 percent of Spanish Jesuits in the Society. In 1616 the missions of Mexico, Peru, Paraguay, and the Philippines had 929 Jesuits, most of them Spanish, about 34 percent of the total number of Spaniards in the provinces of Castile, Toledo, and Andalusia.[34]

Why did they volunteer for Maryland, New Spain, Peru, or New France? What mix of impulses and motives prompted the seventeenth-century Jesuit to leave the relative security of Europe for the uncertainties of an overseas post?

The letters requesting a mission post provide clues about individual motivation but they do not explain why certain Jesuits were chosen and others not. Criteria used by those doing the choosing remain mostly unknown. Jesuit spirituality placed volunteering for the missions on the highest rung of service. This meant that Jesuit missionary work in the sixteenth century was international in scope. Young Jesuits were reminded in their early novitiate days of the apostolic activity that was a major characteristic of the post-reformation church and a hallmark of the Society of Jesus. This cast of mind coincided with the opening of new fields for evangelical labor in America. During the lifetime of Ignatius Loyola, Jesuits were in missions of Portuguese India, Africa, and Brazil. Loyola's immediate successors added Florida, Mexico, Peru and New France.

Some clues about the criteria that Jesuit superiors used in sending men to America are revealed in the secret personnel reports on prospective missionaries, called *Informaciones*, that were sent to Rome. The provincial of Aragon, Pedro de Villar, wrote in 1597 that Rafael Ferrer, who was going to Peru, was of good health, a good religious man, was firm in his vocation, mortified, devout, prayerful, and was persistent in his desire for the missions. Villar added that Ferrer had no talent for governing, "*para regir no descubre talento.*"[35] This comment possibly reveals a major piece of information about the individuals who were selected as front-line representatives of European Christianity in America. Provincials were reluctant to send to America potential theology professors, orators, or those showing outstanding intellectual gifts. The result was what José de Acosta complained of in Peru: the Jesuit houses, he wrote, were filled with pious nitwits who roamed the Andes seeking neophytes.[36] Villar's letter reaffirms that the stolid, plodding long-distance runner was preferred over the sprinter.

Another major motive that moved Jesuits to volunteer for America was adventure. In the sixteenth and seventeenth centuries this meshed with the more apostolic motives of helping to Christianize the nonbeliever. If it could be done in an exotic spot where the risk of danger was present, it became all the more alluring.

Letters from Jesuits volunteering for the missions underplay the idea of what the missions did for the individual Jesuit. No one ever wrote that leaving a certain college or province in Europe would improve his mental health. Emphasized instead was what the individual could do for a particular mission. Francisco de Lugo joined the Jesuits, he said, precisely because he wanted to go to the missions, for the *conversión de los infieles*.[37] When Serafín Cazar wrote in 1583 from the Jesuit College of Valencia asking to be sent to Japan, he said that "he always wanted to go to Japan." For Cazar, the missions were a means of perfection, *caminar a la perfección,* he wrote.[38] Francisco Serrano volunteered for the missions of America in 1602. Diego de Torres from Mexico had spoken in the Jesuit house of Toledo during a recruiting trip and he emphasized "how greatly the Indians suffered from lack of priests."[39] Jacques Gerard's request for the missions of New France was couched in similar terms. He wanted "to work for the salvation of the souls of the barbarian Iroquois since I hear daily that the laborers in that vineyard are few."[40] His entire argument focused on how he was the appropriate person for the missions. Etienne de Carheil (9 July 1662) wrote no less than four letters, one rather morbidly signed with his own blood, concluding that "to pass my whole life in Canada would make me the happiest of persons!"[41] He was sent to New France and arrived in Quebec in 1666.[42]

There was no age limit or status preference for America. But in the bundles of letters from the province of France, from which volunteers for Canada were drawn, only twenty of 268 requests between 1651 and 1700 asked explicitly for New France. The requests from the Spanish provinces were even less specific. "Working with the Indians" was the general request. This may have been due to the desire to appear indifferent, an Ignatian virtue much emphasized by Jesuit spiritual directors. Indifference allowed the superior to use the subject without reference to personal wishes. Abnegation of the will was the ideal sought. So letters such as Antoine Corbon's in 1658, state that the writer is willing to go to "China, Tunquin, Japan, Africa, Canada, or anyplace else [*vel alia quaecumque*]."[43] One is tempted to think that Antoine just wanted out from wherever he was! However, a good number of requests were couched in similar terms emphasizing the indifference of the writer to his destination.

Jean de Brebeuf thought that the qualities needed for New France were those that would please the Indians.[44] He ranked genuine affection for the Indian first. Patience, promptness, cheerfulness, silence, and the capacity to endure physical hardships were next. Nowhere in Brebeuf's hierarchy was philosophy or theology listed, thus underlining the general Jesuit perception that the missions were for the less intellectually endowed. The brighter were kept at home. In fact, the volunteers' letters did not consciously describe their writers' intellectual accomplishments. Most Jesuits who went to America had completed the prescribed theology and philosophy courses. What weighed with superiors in Rome was striking a balance between the stated manpower needs of a province and the individual desire to go to America or Asia. Persistence sometimes won out and counted someplace in the equation, along with solid motivation and good physical health.

Jacques Thurin's letter is typical of letters sent to Rome from the Province of France in the seventeenth century requesting a mission assignment. Thurin had requested several times to be sent to the missions of Canada. He declared that he had felt a strong calling by God to serve in Canada since his novitiate (the first two years as a Jesuit). The feeling had increased and Thurin was certain that God wanted him to go: *"que Dieu me vent."*[45] Thurin claimed to be in good health and at twenty-eight years of age he felt he could be of great assistance to the fathers already working in Canada.

Thurin was not selected to go, perhaps because he was certain that "God called him" and such certitude is difficult to come by, or because his superiors thought that other voices might have been calling him. Whatever the reason, Thurin remained in Lyon.

Jacques Gerard, a successful volunteer, took another tack. He had not yet finished his theological studies, but he had completed his classical studies in Rhetoric and Humanities, so he asked to be "put on the list" when the time came for selection. What especially moved him, he wrote, were the "barbaric customs of the Iroquois." Daily, Gerard wrote, he heard of the scarcity of laborers in the vineyard and how the fields were being watered with the blood of martyrs.[46]

Gerard does not mention the Jesuit Relations explicitly but the detailed descriptions of his brethren's adventures and deaths published in the latter seventeenth century must have had some effect on his desires to go to New France. His reference to the *"tot martyrum sanguis irrigavit"* indicates an acquaintance with Paul Ragueneau's vivid description of the destruction of the Huron mission and the deaths of Brebeuf and Lalemant in 1648.[47]

Gerard's letter reflects the general tenor of requests that Jesuit superiors in Rome received from French Jesuits. They were encouraged to apply for the missions as an act of generosity although no more than 15 percent of the volunteers would ever see New France or the Orient. A selected volunteer would be less likely to complain about his lot and he would bring with him a great deal more enthusiasm than one sent against his will. Although other missions received "troublemakers," New France was not a place where the disgruntled from the home province could easily be hidden. The physical demands were heavy and a uniform community life rare. The mission provided an outlet for those who desired a different kind of apostolate, not the colleges and residences that the European Jesuits were gradually accepting as appropriately Jesuit. The missions attracted those of average intelligence. It was believed that keen enthusiasm and a willingness to endure physical hardships were a fair substitute for philosophical and theological expertise. This might have been one of the reasons why in 1670 Fr. François de Mercier complained that there was no Jesuit in New France capable of assuming the post of provincial or general superior of the mission. "No one here," he wrote, "is fit to govern the Jesuits. Experience and talent is lacking."[48] On the other hand, the Jesuit who went to New France was not seeking administrative positions in an urban college and could well have shied away from anything that smacked of a sedentary or decision-making position. Volunteers were acutely aware of the difference in environment and cultures they would face. They knew that they would have to live like the Indians or even dress like the Chinese if they had to. This they accepted while they were far from their possible missions. The harsh reality was sometimes much different. The Indian languages proved insurmountable for some. Other Jesuits in New France were described as *non affectus* toward the missions, which could mean that they were unable to live the life of the itinerant missionary.

Understanding the basic characteristics of the Europeans whose major task was to present Western religious ideas to Native Americans should assist in comprehending the Native American reaction. The mind-set of the sixteenth-century missionary was formed by the Renaissance and Reformation. Another layer was added by the visions he formed from reading books, seeing drawings, and listening to talks about the Indians by Europeans returned from America. These latter tended to enhance their experiences, overstate their accomplishments, and embellish the opportunities awaiting the Jesuit in the American missions. The initial waves of European Jesuits that came to America shared an exaggerated set of expectations that were modified only with experience.

A clear psychological profile of the missionaries who worked in America has not yet been drawn. The diversity of personalities, ranging from the ascetic and scholarly José de Acosta of Peru and the circuit riders of Maryland, to the overpowering and rather cold characters of Brebeuf and Jogues in New France belie generalization. But they all shared a decidedly American institutional culture in the seventeenth century, which did not equate unity with uniformity.

Church and State

No matter how independent the individual might be, he worked within the parameters set by sixteenth-century church-state relations. The missionary in Maryland was forced to deal with an inimical state that at times hindered his primary aim. New France theoretically assisted its missions since the government was keenly aware of how its North American possessions depended on the missionary-explorer. New Spain and South America manifested a unique integration of church-empire building that was only duplicated in the nineteenth century by France and England in Southeast Asia and Africa.

The image of the New World shaped the attitudes that evangelized it. Christopher Columbus, the prototypical discoverer, had described the Indians as gentle people who were without covetousness. Columbus was convinced on his second voyage (1498–1500) that the mouth of the Orinoco River was indeed the Terrestrial Paradise, the Garden of Eden. For Columbus and thinking men of the sixteenth century, the discovery and conquest of America was an event of massive proportions. For the more ascetical and mystical, it meant that the medieval myth of a messianic-emperor-world ruler, a *dux populi* of Christian universalism who would convert all to Christianity was about to be realized. The idea spread that the doors of the Western sea were opening and through them would rush multitudes of missionaries to convert the gentiles, to bring on the millennium, to hasten the building of the Kingdom of God just prior to the second coming of Christ. There would be one pastor, one flock, under the universal monarchy of the Spanish Crown.

This could only occur if church and state joined forces.

The peculiar blend of church and state unity that developed during the centuries of the reconquest of Spain from the Muslims (1200–1492) served as a model for America. For medieval Spain, and for the rest of the Western world, the ideal society was informed by Christian principles, one that saw no contradiction in civil and religious cooperation toward a common goal, the common good, and the salvation of souls. This ideal had been formalized in Spain in the fifteenth century under an agreement between the church and state called the Royal Patronage. As the Iberian powers moved into the Atlantic in search of new land and peoples, papal intervention through decrees and statements gave a framework of legitimacy to Portuguese and Spanish conquests. In 1508 a separate, more radical version of Royal Patronage was applied to America. The pope granted the Spanish Crown jurisdiction in essence over the Catholic Church in America. The enterprise of building churches and establishing clerics and the infrastructure of the church in the vast domains of America required large sums of money. Church construction and transportation of missionaries and their maintenance in America was a financial burden that Rome could not easily afford. So a bargain was struck between the King of Spain and the pope. The Spanish Crown assumed the obligation of paying all expenses incidental to the maintenance and propagation of the Catholic faith in America and in return the Spanish crown could appoint bishops, approve which clerics went to America, oversee their movement in America and their return to Spain. The king thus became the legal patron of the church in America, enjoying a sweeping control even greater than that enjoyed in Spain. The crown controlled the clergy, the clergy controlled the faithful, and so Catholicism was indissolubly linked with Royal Authority.[49]

The missionary thus played a key role in the Spanish plan of conquest and colonization. Exploration and conquest was the task of the conquistador. Evangelization was considered a joint effort that obligated civil as well as religious authority. Both stood to gain. The crown could count on new resources in the form of gold and silver, mined by or collected from the inhabitants of its new kingdoms, and the church could satisfy its zeal to enroll new members. Just when Satan, it was argued, was tricking thousands of the faithful in Europe into following Luther and Calvin, untold numbers of souls were made available in America for the waters of baptism and entrance into the one true church. God, gold, and glory was the sacred triad. But which came first in the hierarchy of values? Future decades drew a very wobbly line dividing gold from God and glory. After the first fervor of extraordinary zeal in spreading the faith among the Indians of Mexico, the clergy, it is generally believed, grew somewhat complacent in their task, the edges were dulled and what had begun as genuine fervor soon changed to a self-serving institutionalization of religious structures. The bureaucratic church became more interested in preserving itself in its archaic forms than in adapting itself to the needs of new flocks.

Sixteenth-century Europe and indigenous America collided and interacted on a broad stage. The European was predisposed to change the way Indian America believed. A microcosm of this encounter occurred in Brazil in 1549 when Jesuits began to change the belief system of the Tupinambá. However, initial success came to a grinding halt. Manioc beer, tribal wars, multiple marriage, and white slave raids proved to be the European Jesuits' nemesis.[50]

Over a decade later Florida was the scene of another European attempt to bring indigenous America into the European pale, this by the Spanish. The lessons learned in Florida served future agents of religious change in America.

2

La Florida

On November 10, 1568, the Jesuit missionary Juan Rogel, reported optimistically to his superiors in Rome about the future of evangelization in Florida. "The Indians," he wrote, "are good farmers, they don't have too many idols, and they sow and harvest abundant corn." All of Florida, he thought, "was ready for a spiritual harvest."[1] Two years later Antonio Sedeño, another a Jesuit missionary in Florida, also wrote to the Jesuit General in Rome, Francisco Borja. He described Florida as one long pile of sand, infertile, full of swamps and rivers, "the most miserable land ever discovered by man." The native Americans did not fare much better in Sedeño's view, "sensual, savage beasts who preferred going to hell with the devil than to heaven with Christians."[2] Sedeño thought that the best thing the Jesuits could do there would be to leave as quickly as possible.

Much had occurred in the years between Rogel and Sedeño's reports. The Spanish garrisons that were strung along the Florida coast had been burned, the soldiers killed, the settlements gone. A major reorganization was underway. The Jesuits wanted no part of it.

The beginnings of the evangelization of Florida had been much more hopeful. Pedro Martínez, Juan Rogel, and Francisco Villareal were the three Jesuit missionaries chosen to go to Florida. All had professional backgrounds before becoming Jesuits but were dissimilar in temperament and personality. They got along reasonably well. The novelty, adventure, and shared goals of the enterprise bonded them.

Martínez had been a chaplain to Spanish troops in Oran, Africa, was a decent theologian, and "kept a portfolio of notes on all subjects including extracts from cook books with many recipes for dishes for the sick and for the well. . . ."[3] Martínez preached and catechized and described himself as having great powers of endurance "for toil, hunger, thirst, sleeping on the ground, etc. . . . I don't see why God has given me so much robustness," he wrote, "unless it is to offer it to him by my service, and if he grant it, with my life." But he cautioned his general superior in Rome about leaving his selection for the Indies to the will of his superiors in Spain, "for none of them will let go of a subject who is in good health and ready for anything."[4]

Juan Rogel was Martínez's companion priest. Rogel had studied medicine at the University of Alcalá before joining the Jesuits and had continually petitioned for service in the missions. He was a parish priest in Toledo until his appointment to the mission of *La Florida*.

Francisco Villareal accompanied the priests as the humble lay brother, whose future tasks in America would not require priestly duties. He had been a clerk in a law court and Martínez described him as "a most likeable Brother and one after my own heart."[5]

None had any special preparation for America. It was assumed their classical background, their training in philosophy and theology, and their grounding in ascetecism was preparation enough. Spain's Catholicism was aggressive, its culture considered superior to whatever would be encountered in the New World. What was out there would have to adjust to them, not the other way around.

On July 7, 1566, the fleet in which the three sailed landed in the Canary Islands. A month later it was in the Caribbean. Between Puerto Rico and the Virgin Islands the missionaries transferred to a sloop for the trip to San Agustín, Florida. With them went a crew of twelve, but with no chart, no pilot, and only a vague idea of San Agustín's location.

They soon were lost sailing up and down the Florida coast. Martínez, two Spanish soldiers, and six seamen went ashore in the ship's boat "to ask directions."[6] A sudden squall drove the sloop out to sea and Martínez and his companions were stranded. Twelve days passed before Martínez and his companions moved inland. They saw only isolated huts from which they foraged food. But disaster struck suddenly. On September 28, 1566, Martínez and five of his companions were killed on the beach by Indians probably near what is today Fort Georgia, Florida.

The Indians who watched Martínez and his associates land were part of the southeastern Indian groups that occupied almost all of *La Florida* from the Atlantic to west of the Mississippi River.[7] They had arrived in southeastern

America when the massive mastodon and saber-toothed tiger still stalked the American continent. When the barbarians were invading Spain during the collapse of the Roman Empire, the Indians' ancestors were trading with the Maya across the Gulf of Mexico and exchanging their beads for copper from inhabitants of the Lake Superior region. They believed that the sun was the source of all life and sustenance. By the time the Spaniards arrived in 1565, the Atlantic coast from the Carolinas to the tip of Florida, around the Gulf of Mexico up to Tampa and all the way over to the mouth of the Mississippi was occupied by peoples who lived off the sea and the land. Sedentary agriculture and the reliance on fish and seafood enabled the Indians to enjoy a rich social and ceremonial life. Their material culture was similarly abundant thanks to the semitropical climate that provided the staples they consumed, which defined their way of life. Some grew maize inland, collected it in giant storage bins and planted and harvested with elaborate ceremonies. The fish of the sea were plentiful. Houses were functional and adapted to the climate. The *chicaskee*, a dwelling consisting of a roof of palmetto palms resting on poles with raised platforms for living and sleeping areas, was easily rebuilt after a violent summer storm blew it down. Houses could be stretched along a trail or clustered in a village sometimes surrounded by a palisade. The village was the focal point for social gatherings. The bark canoe was an essential vehicle for a coastal people. Little clothing was needed in the tropical climate but cloth was woven, pottery fashioned, and foods prepared.

Society was regulated by a rank order. A ruler governed a cluster of towns, each of which had its own chief. The village leader presided over a group of elders. Male and female roles were fixed. The hunters who trapped the deer, racoons, and reptiles; the fishermen who netted the tuna, crawfish, turtles, and snails; the women who took care of the children; and the cooks and builders, all had their social rank.

Cementing the sociopolitical structure was religion. Priests whom the Spaniards called shamans regulated the rites of worship that were usually focused on planting, harvest, birth, and death. Three deities ruled over nature, political matters, and warfare.[8] The sun was the most honored deity and fire was its symbol. Religion, agriculture, and social relationships were integrated to a high degree.

But not all was work. An elaborate array of games, exercises, and play filled the Indian's world. Versions of lacrosse, ball playing, and archery were carefully recorded by amazed Europeans in sixteenth-century *La Florida*.[9]

The reality of "savage" life jolted the first Jesuits only because they saw its most somber side. They were not allowed to lift the veil on the world they had invaded.

The first Indians that the Spaniards met in significant numbers were the Calusa of southwest Florida. They numbered about ten thousand souls and were clustered around the main Calusa town of thirty-six thatch and wood houses just south of Charlotte Harbor.[10] Calusa territory bordered the Mayaimi on the east and the Tequesta on the southeast. North of the Calusa were the villages of the Tocobaga around Tampa Bay, no friends of the Calusa. The Calusa did not practice agriculture, subsisting mainly on fish and seafood. They lacked hard stone to make implements but their artistically carved painted wood was notable.

Menéndez de Aviles first came upon the Calusa in 1566 while searching along the Gulf Coast for his shipwrecked son. He realized immediately that the region was ideal for a fortress to guard the shipping lanes of the treasure fleets sailing through the Gulf of Mexico. The Indian leader of the area, Carlos (corruption of Calus), agreed to receive missionaries and eventually accepted a Spanish garrison. To solidify the arrangement Menéndez agreed to marry Carlos's sister, Antonia, and they went through a ceremony. Menéndez must have known that the Indians did not consider marriage a permanent bond but even so the Jesuits with him looked askance at the procedure. Carlos welcomed his new brother-in-law because he expected the Spaniards to help him defeat the Tocobaga to the north who were Calus's rivals and enemies. Carlos even became the vassal of the Spaniards.

In March 1567 the Jesuits began missionary work in Calus and a fortress for Spanish soldiers was erected. Juan Rogel was the missionary and Bro. Villareal began working with the Tequesta on the eastern coast. At this time Menéndez's Florida enterprise consisted of six forts along the Atlantic and Gulf coasts. The Jesuit missionaries's task was to use these forts as focal points from which to evangelize the surrounding Indian groups.

Assigned to each fort were thirty or forty Spanish soldiers. Because they were not farmers, they said, they refused to sow and few if any food supplies arrived from Havana. The local Indians were forced to share their meager stores, thus putting an enormous burden on an already pitifully poor subsistence economy.[11]

The arrival of the Jesuits added further stress to the food crisis. For the entire span of Jesuit activity in Florida, the characteristic feature of the Europeans' plight was their total economic dependence on either the Indians or the Spanish military. The Jesuits moved from fort to fort attempting to preach Christianity to the Indians on forays into the surrounding villages and hinterland. On occasion they returned to Havana.

Message and Response

The arrival of the European missionaries was marked by scenes that the Spaniards described as controlled chaos. From the first hastily constructed settlement of San Agustín, Menéndez de Aviles led processions of soldiers and priests to nearby Indian villages. The soldiers were followed by trumpeters blaring martial music and three or four soldiers carrying a cross. Outside a village the cross bearers would erect the cross and all would gather round it chanting the litanies. By this time the *cacique* of the village would approach and Menéndez would explain that a representative of God was there to speak with him. The priest among the Spaniards would briefly explain Christian doctrine to the cacique and ask if he wanted to become a Christian. If the answer was yes, then the cross would be left standing and the Spaniards would promise to send a priest. Menéndez said that "there were many who are asking with great insistence that missionaries be sent to them."[12]

For the Spaniards these were appropriate acts that had their origins in the belief that the papacy had dominion over the universe, all peoples had the obligation to listen to the preachers of the Christian gospel, and if they did not, they would be justly punished. Bringing Christianity to America was part of the agreement between the papacy and Spain that gave Spain the right to conquer America.

Apparently, what Menéndez de Aviles was doing in Florida was a modified *requirimiento*. A half-century before, the reading of the unintelligible document was invariably followed by the roar of canon and the screams of Spanish soldiers. But times had changed, somewhat. The intervening years witnessed bitter debates in Spain over the legitimacy of the conquest, the way it was carried out, and the obligations to the Indians.[13] By 1565, Spaniards were not so sure of the righteousness of their cause. So Menéndez asked the Indians if they wanted to become Christian and did nothing if they refused.

To the Spaniards who were dragging a wooden cross through the Florida sands or the trumpeters blowing in the wind, the scene of hundreds of painted Indians mulling around shouting incomprehensible words was alarming. They felt isolated, overwhelmed numerically, with limited ability to communicate directly with the Indians and ignorant of the geography and physical conditions of the land. Such conditions made the Spaniards oversensitive to perceived threats to their lives.

The Spanish soldiers could not understand what they saw. They reported in horror the human sacrifices of a cacique's servants, the "enchanters" who wore horns on their heads and howled like wolves, the idols that made noises like mountain animals, and the deboning of a chief at his death.[14] The macabre reports from Florida about the customs of the Indians had a deliberately sensationalist intent. The Spaniards, however, could only explain the wild dancing, shouting, drinking out of the enemy's skull, and lack of clothing as features of a society under the devil's control. The only criterion they had for judging such behavior was from their Western culture. "Bestiality," was the characteristic description of the Indian's customs.[15]

Juan Rogel and his Jesuit associates brought with them the same cultural prejudices as the Spanish soldiery. The only difference was that the Jesuits believed that the Indian was capable of modifying his behavior. One might be tempted to say that the European missionaries were content to modify the religious beliefs of the Indians while tolerating the rest of their behavior. Such was not the case. Having long hair, dressing in short loincloths, and speaking the native language were elevated to almost equal rank as unbelief in the Christian God.[16] The Spanish missionaries at first seemed to view short hair and Western clothing as essential to Christian belief. Long hair, after all, was for women. However, Rogel stated early on that he found "no impediment to planting the faith among these people, if God enlightens their understanding and moves their wills."[17] Rogel felt that the Indians' custom of polygamy was no obstacle to conversion. The paradox was apparent and frequently expressed. On the one hand, the Jesuits witnessed acts of tender love between Indian children and parents; they observed the Indian laboring at farming, hunting, and building construction; they noticed the reverence the Indian had toward elders.[18] In the Jesuit mind these qualities and behavior could only have originated in a natural theology that disposed the Indian to goodness. "Thoughtful, reasonable people," were the words used by Rogel to describe the Indians.[19] On the other hand, the incestuous unions of chiefs, widespread polygamy, and almost continual interaction with evil spirits convinced the Jesuits that the hand of Satan was at work although not in complete control.

The apparently contradictory qualities that the Spanish Jesuits observed in the Florida Indians were explicable only in their own moral and ethical terms. Whether the Indians were categorized as Juan Rogel saw them, "of good disposition,"[20] as "thoughtful, reasonable men,"[21] who presented no serious impediment to evangelization,[22] or whether they were viewed as "beasts who walk around nude, sensual, blind to their vices and sins,"[23] "with little or no desire to hear the word of God,"[24] the European could not see the Indian in his own terms.[25] Indians practiced infanticide because they were blind to the evil of murder. When the Indians retorted that they (the Spaniards) killed Frenchmen, the Spaniards answered that their deaths were justified because the Frenchmen were bad Christians.[26] In the eyes of the European missionaries, the Indians worshiped idols because the devil convinced them that he was supreme; sodomy was widespread because vice was equated with goodness; Indians moved frequently, planting crops anew because they were shiftless; their houses were flimsy because they were too lazy to build solid structures. In Berkhofer's words, the Indian was being judged not by what he had but by what he did not have.[27]

The Jesuits responded to the paradox by filling what they perceived to be the deficiency. The first step was to teach the Indian about the Christian God. Menéndez de Avilés had already begun the indoctrination. In moving around San Agustín with his soldiers he encountered Indian villagers. He reported the interchange.

SPANIARDS "There is only one God which Christians adore, to whom they go when they die if they are good and where they are happy and content. Those who are not Christian descend after death to the eternal fires of hell where they continually cry.[29]

The Indian response to this statement simply circumvented the Spanish assertion about God and an afterlife. What lived after death? For the Spaniards the answer was the soul. For the Indian the Aristotelian concept of a spiritual *anima* contained within a material body was incomprehensible. In fact, when Rogel later attempted to explain how the souls of all deceased Christians were awaiting a final resurrection when they would be united with their bodies and how the souls of those condemned to hell were suffering and how the souls of the unbaptized were waiting in a place called limbo, the Indians laughed. "They laugh at me," wrote Rogel, "when I tell them that all souls are either in heaven or hell and they cannot die."[30] So instead of asking about God or the afterlife, the Indians replied:

INDIANS Why have you come here?

SPANIARDS The Christians have a captain on earth, called the Pope, and one who is in Spain called King Felipe, and both of these sent us to tell you that there is one God and if you want to be obedient to these captains, they may rule you as Christians.

INDIANS You killed fellow Christians, the French.

SPANIARDS They were bad Christians.[30]

Although we cannot be positive about the sequence of the interchange, the content of the response is clear. In these early contacts the Spaniards tried to legitimize their presence. By a twist of logic, in accepting Christianity the Indian had to accept Spanish dominion. Accept the Christian God, Jesus Christ, the pope as earthly representative of God, and the king of Spain as legitimate receiver of the pope's domain, and the conclusion is clear. Submission to God means submission to the king of Spain. Interpreters were used to convey the message, Spaniards who knew a smattering of the Indian language or Indians who knew some Castilian. In this first interchange the Indians chose to judge the message by the messengers. If heaven is for the good, they seemed to say, and you say killing is evil, why did you kill the French? The Indians confronted Spanish behavior rather than fuzzy notions about deities and souls.

The Europeans began their proselytization by trying to explain the concept of God. This was the cornerstone of their catechesis. The Indian did not object to the concept of a divine being or beings who controlled the world. Their own belief system explained how the world came into being, why they were there, and how they were to achieve a measure of happiness in it.[31] They believed sincerely in a broad range of divine beings. When Rogel asked a cacique about his belief in God, the Jesuit was not surprised at the Indian's answer.

ROGEL   Do you believe in the unity of God, the creator of the universe?
CACIQUE   Yes.[32]

When Rogel used the word "God," the interpreter probably translated it with the Indian word "Ate." To the Indian the Ate was the sun, a superpower, one who was responsible for the light, the brightness, one for whom each February the choicest stag was skinned and filled with roots and vegetables and carried with music and song "to a very large splendid space where they set it up on a very high tree with the head and breast towards the sunrise. They then offer prayers to the sun that he would cause to grow on their lands good things."[33] The divine was an integral part of the Indian world, only the Indian conceived his role in it in a manner totally different from the Christian Westerner. For the Indian, three deities governed the world hierarchically: one controlled nature, the movement of the stars, the weather; another ruled political matters; and a third governed warfare.[34] For the Jesuit, God was personal and took a personal interest in the daily lives of his creatures, in fact so personal was the interest that he punished those who refused to obey him and rewarded those who did. The Christian missionaries knew what God demanded, and they wished to share that knowledge with the Indian. When the Jesuits said that they *knew* what God wanted, the Indian asked how they found out.

CACIQUE   Where did you learn all of these things about God?
ROGEL   We have them written from many years ago. The message has not changed over time.
CACIQUE   You cannot see your God. Our ancestors told us that *they* saw God at the time of burials. They had to fast many days to see him.

ROGEL   God does not have a body. Your ancestors saw the devil. The devil tricked them by turning into different shapes.[35]

Not only was the Indian cacique bewildered at this interchange, but the
Jesuit Rogel wrote that he himself was troubled, in *"gran duda y perplexidad."*[36]
He knew the cacique to be a good man, one whose intentions were apparently
honest. Rogel saw him kneel in front of the cross he had erected in front of
the village and offer sacrifices to the cross like those he offered to his idols.
Rogel did not object to this. Why then did he not accept baptism? Rogel noted
that when Menéndez returned, he would ask the cacique to "burn his idols,
dress like a Spaniard, and be instructed in the faith."[37]

For the European Christian there was one God. All other claimants were
creatures of the devil. "They don't understand about the devil," Rogel protested.[38] In order to give Satan his due, Rogel described in detail the seven days
of creation from the book of Genesis, the angel's rebellion, and how Satan and
his angels became the powers of darkness aligned forever against the powers
of light. Each side was engaged in a war for the souls of the just. The cacique
and his people could not understand this because they believed that each individual had not one but three souls. The small pupil of the eye was one, the
shadow cast by the body another, and the reflection seen from a shiny surface
was the third.[39] At death the second and third departed, the first stayed with
the body and spoke with the living. "It is here," wrote Rogel, "that the devil
speaks to them."[40] The other two souls entered an animal, and when the animal
died, they entered a smaller animal. The Indians were so convinced of this,
wrote Rogel, that "only a special act of God could persuade them of the immortality of the soul, the resurrection of the dead, and a reward in another
life."[41]

That the Indians laughed at the Jesuit's explanation of what happened to
a soul at death indicates that they understood something of what he was saying.
And they rejected it. Rogel through the interpreter first had to disabuse the
Indians of their accepted notions of the nature of the soul, then convince them
to accept the Aristotelian version of the Western anima. It did not work. Rogel
was disappointed and disheartened. If they did not accept the Western notion
of the immortality of the soul, then God had no sanctions with which to
threaten the Indian, and the whole Christian construct would collapse.

On one occasion Rogel said Mass outside the village of Carlos, the chief
of the Calusa. The ritual itself, with its movements to the left and right, turning
away from and then toward the audience, its genuflections, audible prayers,
and general solemnity was not totally alien to the Indians. They too had their
rites and processions accompanied by prayers, dances, and incantations. Their
own priests led rites and prayed on certain occasions for the community. The

shaman was a key figure in the Indian social and religious world.[42] So when the Christian shamans performed *their* rites, the Indians were respectful and sat in silence. They knew something important was happening. Rogel recited the Confession of Faith, the Introit, the Gloria, the Prayer and, after reading the Epistle and Gospel lessons, he preached. Rogel spoke through an interpreter, explaining again how God was the creator of the world, how all men owe vassalage to him, the immortality of the soul, the resurrection of the dead, the reward that awaits those who live a good life, the punishments of hell prepared for those who do not. Adoring idols, he concluded, was a trick of the devil, an *engaño*. Then Rogel dismissed Chief Carlos and all of his staff. As nonbelievers they were not permitted to witness the most solemn parts of the Mass, the Offertory, Consecration, and Holy Communion.[43]

The Indian leaders were ambivalent about Christianity. On the one hand, embracing the religion of the Spaniards insured military aid against a non-Christian enemy. On the other, they saw Christianity as destructive of their own religious and social fabric. "These people are here to destroy our Gods. I will jump into the fire with my wife and children and my Gods rather than submit," they said.[44] This absolute and determined rejection discouraged Rogel and the Jesuits. "This shows how far the Indians are from receiving the law of God. *Nondum venit hora ejus* [Their hour has not yet come]."[45] However, there were occasions when individuals told the Europeans that they would have accepted the new religion were it not for the caciques. The caciques must first accept Christianity, then the others would follow.[46]

The caciques hesitated. The missionary's demand that they keep only one wife was a major stumbling block. Rogel thought he had convinced Carlos to become a Christian. Every day he taught the catechism to him, his wives, vassals, and children. He taught him the Our Father and Hail Mary prayers in Spanish, which was the language, Rogel explained, that is for speaking with God.[47] The cacique learned the prayers and because he seemed to accept the notions that went with them, Rogel believed that the chief would become a Christian and all his people would soon follow. But to the surprise of Rogel, Carlos one day married his sister in an elaborate ceremony. Rogel protested but to no avail. The Jesuit recounted the interchange between himself and Carlos. "I felt obliged to declare the law of God to him [Carlos]," wrote Rogel.

ROGEL　God gave Adam, the first man, only *one* companion, Eve.

CACIQUE　It is difficult for those of us raised in this custom to forsake it. You want old men, adults, to abandon their way of life and become perfect Christians and that they cannot do.

ROGEL　It is the law of God for a man to have one wife.

CACIQUE   You should be content that the young people learn Christian Doctrine, the old folk burn their idols, reject sodomy, not kill babies, avoid painting their faces, and even cut their hair. But give up their wives? This they cannot do.[48]

One cannot help suspect that the cacique's argument was in fact Rogel's, written for his brethren in Europe in an attempt to remind them that modifying long-standing customs was a tedious if not impossible task. He had heard the cacique's response from others. After one particularly long session with a group of Indians, Rogel pointed out how God hated sins, so much so that he died for men's sins, but the Indians continued committing these sins such as infanticide and idolatry. The Indians then stopped going to instructions. They said that "their ancestors had lived according to those customs for generations and they wished to continue doing so and that I should leave them alone and they didn't want to listen to me."[49] In fact they did not return. Only when Rogel began giving a ration of corn to those who came to catechism did they return. "As long as I gave them something to eat, they came to listen. If not, not."[50]

Did in fact the Indians even listen to the Jesuits because they received food? Possibly. By the end of 1569, 327 Spaniards lived in Santa Elena alone, enough to dislocate the existing native economy.[51] Rogel and his companions frequently returned to Havana for food supplies, some of which they distributed to the Indians. The severe strains on an already meager food supply resulted in Spanish soldiers raiding Indian villages looking for food. The Indians retaliated in kind.[52] The Spaniards in Florida were unable to exploit the land nor were sufficient supplies available in Havana. Therefore, the colonists and soldiers were left with one option: exploit the Indians even more. In retaliation, starvation became a weapon that the Indian used adroitly.[53]

The Jesuits tried to use it, too. Francisco de Villareal, the Jesuit brother who worked in Tequesta, sought advice from Rogel about how much and to whom he should give his extra food. Rogel had advised Villareal to act in such a way that the Indians would grow to love him. Should he demonstrate his love by giving his food to the Indians?[54]

Villareal taught catechism in the local cacique's house, giving instructions every morning and night for the children, the shamans, and adults not taking part. He taught the four prayers, the commandments, and the creed in the Indian language. But he also used Spanish words and tried to explain their meaning.[55] He organized processions with a cross. And what must have been a historical first, Villareal put on two plays (*comedias* he called them), one on June 21, 1567, "portraying the conflict between the flesh, the world, and the devil and how they make war on mankind, and all the soldiers loved it."[56] Thus,

Villareal has the distinction of staging the first theatrical performance on North American soil.[57]

Villareal was also the first to report on what became frighteningly repetitive: death by epidemic disease. There is little accuracy in the mortality figures between 1565 and 1570, the years that the Jesuits speak of a widespread plague. However, repeated references to children's deaths in 1568 point to the beginnings of epidemics that began on the coast and spread inland.[58] This affected Indian village size and settlement patterns. Disease also affected Indian attitudes toward the Jesuits. When a cacique brought his four- or five-month-old daughter to Bro. Villareal for a cure, the Jesuit read some lines of scripture over her and she recovered. Others brought their children to Villareal hoping he would cure them as well. One died and the *hechiceros* who prayed over the child after Villareal said that if the Jesuit had not intervened, she would have lived.[59] Villareal asked Rogel what to do in similar cases. If he baptized children and they died he would be blamed for killing them. "Should I visit the sick only when they are dying?" the Jesuit brother asked.[60] Villareal put his finger on a major problem, one which was to torment the Jesuits throughout America. Following the Council of Trent, the Jesuits firmly believed that baptism was essential for salvation. But by baptizing the dying, their deaths became inextricably linked with both the Jesuits and the sacrament they administered. In Florida they were accused of being witch doctors and child killers. Those receiving baptism almost always died—not adults who uniformly refused baptism but children. When a killer epidemic (smallpox?) raged in Guale in 1570, Antonio Sedeño reported that the Indians there accused the Jesuits of deliberately sending their children to heaven. "They saw that the children died *after* Baptism because we baptized only *in articulo mortis*. The survivors are bitter against us."[61] Unfortunately, none of the Florida Jesuits associated disease with the presence of Europeans. Seventy years later the French Jesuits in New France would when faced with the same accusation. On the northern Mexican frontier the Jesuits turned the accusation around and used the presence of disease to argue that Christians were protected by their God. *They* didn't die. Only pagans did.

Europeans and Indians

Rogel was puzzled at the features of Calusa society that were obviously "civilized." The ability to organize massive construction, to plan, to apply labor to complicated tasks were traits that he did not expect to find among the Indians of *La Florida*. These traits were evident from the large, intricately constructed temple mounds on which the Indians performed their religious rituals and to which they sometimes carried victims for sacrifice. In Calusa the Spanish fortress was on a height, which was probably sacred ground. Rogel described an incident that illustrates the inability of either Indian or European to understand what the other was about.

> And they even tried to come up to our fort to walk around with their masks, coming from the hills where their houses were to the height on which our fort stood. Between these there was a small valley through which they used to walk with the aforementioned display and affrontery to be seen by the people. And the women worshiped them and sang praises to them. They tried to carry out devotions before these idols while I was at the door of the fort. I screamed at them commanding them not to ascend the height but they paid no attention to me. I called Capt. Francisco de Reinoso to stop them and he came out with a lance and he struck with the handle one of the Indians who was leading the procession. He sprawled on the ground with the fallen idol. The Indians became angry and came out of their huts with hatchets and boat poles. However, they did not climb up to the fort, for our soldiers were already armed and waiting for them. After this they stopped bringing their idols up to the height where our fortress was.[62]

Modern archaeology has confirmed what Rogel described as background for his story. Unique circular mounds, 130 of them in the Calusa area alone, rows of conical mounds, ridges, and canals associated with the mounds dot the seacoast.[63] Their size indicates planning, execution, worker-appointed tasks, and the necessity of large food supplies. Similar ceremonial mounds are found inland as well.[64] Confrontation with such visible manifestations of an advanced civilization confused Rogel and the other Jesuits in *La Florida* but did not reduce their feelings of cultural superiority.

By judging the native American on the basis of what he did not have rather than by what he had tells us what the European thought an ideal society should be.[65] There is no solid evidence that the Jesuits thought that the Indian first had to be "civilized" (Hispanicized) before becoming a Christian, but acceptance of European dress and behavior seemed to help. However, Rogel went so far as to say that "their way of living is so ordered and regular that even if they become Christians, there will be absolutely no need to change anything in their lives."[66]

The missionaries expected the Indian to reject certain cultural practices and they were surprised, even indignant, when the Indians persisted in observing time-honored customs that the Jesuits thought contrary to God's law. This disappointment reveals a certain naïveté of the Europeans who imagined that the sheer weight of reason and logic would overwhelm the "superstitions" of the Indians. It did not. The Jesuit's theology taught that divine assistance or grace could not operate for an unbaptized Indian but reason could. So the Jesuits felt it their obligation to prepare the Indian's rational capacity to accept God's free gift of faith.

When Juan Rogel first wrote about the Indians to his superiors in Rome in 1568, he praised their natural qualities and abilities. "In that Province of Guale," he wrote, "the soldiers go two by two without a hand being laid on them by the Indians. They even feed them all the time. . . . and I do not doubt that of the Indians' natural inclination and disposition, a missionary could reap great fruit if placed among them."[67] Rogel insisted that the Indians were not cannibals. "Do not believe that there is any place in all of Florida that up to now has been explored where the Indians eat human flesh."[68]

Most Jesuits were convinced that man's nature was capable of seeking out and finding the perceived good. Luther and Calvin instead posited that man was disposed to and inclined toward evil. Jesuit theology of the sixteenth and seventeenth centuries rejected this view of the human personality, convinced that humans could attain virtue and good through their own natural efforts. In this they were greatly influenced by the writings of Luis de Molina.[69] In Molina's purely hypothetical state, man was born exempt from original sin, deprived of the supernatural life, and subject to death and all other miseries of life. When applied to the Indian of North America, it meant that he always retained as part of his nature virtues that made him a creature of dignity, worth, and moral rectitude. This contrasted sharply with what Calvin and the reformers thought about the nature of man. It aided the Jesuits in their struggle to find virtue in the indigenous American. Jesuit humanistic training with its emphasis on classical tradition and learning inclined the Jesuit to treat differences as shades of variation that were not necessarily a sign of inferiority. Thus, the Jesuits by their own educational philosophy sought in men of whatever belief or degree of civilization they possessed the goodness of which they were presumed capable.[70] This was easy for Rogel to do at the beginning of his work in Florida. After two years, it was much more difficult.

In 1568, Rogel characterized one of the Indian leaders as a man "who listens and considers carefully the arguments proposed to him."[71] He was a "reasonable" man. But it was difficult for Rogel to put aside the external differences that separated European and Indian. "If only he wouldn't decorate his face and body with markings, and if he would only cut his hair, he would be on his way to becoming a Christian," he wrote.[72] The Jesuit equated external differences with the polygamy, idolatry, infanticide, and homosexuality that the Indians permitted, much to the missionaries' horror.

The Indians of the east coast of Florida were more affable.
In the middle of August I was ordered to live in Orista in an Indian village five leagues from St. Helen's where the Indians constructed for me a house and church. I resided there with three young Indians who taught me the language, alone with the Indians, with no Spaniards around. Up to now all is going well and if I remain, there will be many conversions.[73]

Rogel did not observe any of the "abominations" he had witnessed elsewhere. On the contrary, he was pleased to observe monogamous unions. Everyone worked. The Indians even had a "municipal hall" where elders gathered to set laws and govern the village.

And they live with great order and respect among themselves. When I lived among them, I saw nothing reprehensible, except perhaps a tendency to gamble. They're great traders and merchants and they know how to buy and sell with the other people inland. I never saw the vice of theft and if they do anything bad it's because the Spaniards taught them such. They do no evil to those who do good to them. I feel very secure among them.[74]

Rogel stated what became repeated missionary complaints about the Spaniards's behavior and dissatisfaction over the poor example given to the Indians. The missionary drew a somewhat exaggerated portrait of the Indian as a pristine human being untouched by vice. Whatever vice was present had been acquired by contact with Europeans. Eventually, the solution adapted in both North and South America was to segregate the Indian from the white man.

Although Rogel and the Jesuits with him imagined the Indians capable of perfection, there was the lurking suspicion that the Indian was intellectually and morally inferior. The Jesuit superior general, Francisco Borja, put it clearly in 1571 in instructions to the missionaries of Florida. "Always consider carefully the softness of those souls and the primitive states of those minds. They will not be able to shoulder the load that can be borne here in Europe by perfectly rational people who have greater knowledge of God Our Lord."[75]

Did Borja mean that the Indians were incapable of rational thought or logical reasoning? Or that they were at some preliminary stage of understanding the complicated belief system called Christianity? The core of the system, belief in one God, the redemptive death of God's son, and the establishment of a universal community of believers that adhered to laws established by the hierarchy of the community, were not potentially troublesome. However, the corollaries were. Monogamy and personal salvation were antithetical to traditional Indian beliefs. The missionary's Western logic saw sin in behavior that the Indian viewed as natural. And while the Indian at first listened to what the Jesuits had to say about God and eternal life, he really saw no compelling need to adopt a new belief system.

The detail with which the Jesuits related the accounts of Indian religious beliefs indicates a degree of fascination that bordered on admiration. The missionary had come face to face not with primitive animism but with a complex of beliefs that were integrated with the daily life of the Indian. There was the glimmer of a recognition that something greater than Satan was at work, but the Jesuit did not come out and say precisely that. European society of the sixteenth century, however, was convinced that the devil was behind all forms of non-Christian religion.

Rogel declared: "Great have been the efforts of the devil in the past and each day he continues to keep the Indians apart from our preaching of the truths of God. He instills in them great fears and distrust that we are going to drag them off as captives and so frequently they decide to leave us and go inland to live near the lakes . . ."[76] The Jesuits believed that the devil was actively working through the native priests they called witch doctors. Europe, and especially Spain and France, of the sixteenth and seventeenth centuries witnessed an obsession with witchcraft and satanism.[77]

The witches (brujas in Spanish) were obviously working in league with the devil to cloud the minds of the Indians and prevent the Jesuits from preaching Christianity. The devil spoke through the dead and through the smoke and fire of Indian rituals. The Jesuits saw the native priests as the witches and wizards, and the common people as misled devil worshippers.

In sixteenth-century Spain, prominent theologians accepted the reality of metamorphosis, nocturnal flight, and magic. Despite the years of philosophy and reasoned learning, these were ideas that sixteenth-century Europeans brought to La Florida and were palpable reasons why their doctrine was not accepted. On the other hand, Jesuit theologians of the seventeenth-century caused a stir by accusing the Inquisition of forcing confessions of witchcraft through deception and malice, and pointing out that Inquisition lawyers were remunerated according to the number of convictions they obtained.[78] This might have had some resonance in America where Jesuit missionaries in the seventeenth and eighteenth centuries were less likely to describe Indian religions as devil worship and witchcraft. The Europeans had come to Florida thinking that the internal dynamism that they experienced from their own culture would compel the Indian to listen and accept Western ways. But the Florida

Indians resented the white men who demanded a share of their corn and suggested that they change their belief system and some of their most cherished social habits while threatening them with eternal punishment if they did not.

A second group of missionaries arrived from Spain in 1568, but their reports to superiors in Rome grew more discouraging. Their superior, Juan Baptista de Segura, wrote that the Indians were intransigent, the health of the Jesuit personnel failing, and the missionaries were continually being assigned to act as chaplains in the forts. But Segura did not entirely give up on the North American coast. He thought that the land and Indians near the Chesapeake Bay might bear more fruit.

Subsequent Jesuit letters to Rome from Havana unanimously condemned the Florida mission as a fruitless waste of time. "Florida," wrote the new superior in May 1570, "or the 300 leagues that I have seen of it is one long pile of sand. That's why there are so few Indians living here. Everyone goes nude unless they have a little piece of deerskin to cover themselves. The great variety of languages take a lifetime to learn. . . . For nine months of the year the Indians are hunting or scavenging for roots which makes it impossible to preach the gospel to them. They live like beasts and are given to the most heinous sins among themselves. Florida," he concluded, "is not for the Society of Jesus."[79]

Borja agreed. He wrote to Menéndez de Aviles in 1571 that he was withdrawing the Jesuits from Florida "because one can count on the fingers of the hand the number of converts made." The initial shock of meeting the American Indian dispelled the myth among the Jesuits of the ennobled savage. Most Jesuit writers were hard put to discover anything noble about people who were scantily attired, skillful with a bow, and inclined to war.[80] Florida to them was the precinct of the devil. Most of the Jesuits who tried to convert the Indians of Florida between 1566 and 1571 portrayed them as little above the beast. The last Jesuit superior of Florida, Antonio Sedeño, described them precisely that way. "They are like beasts wallowing in sin," were his words.[81] By the time Sedeño wrote, he already had one foot on the ship to Mexico. His parting blast only served to reconfirm the decision to abandon the inhospitable land that proved to be a mirage: from a distance attractive and full of promise but up close, insubstantial.

The Europeans were disappointed with Florida. They had been filled in Europe with the images of an America of towering mountains, golden treasures, and noble savages. Instead they found desolate beaches and a people who lived by a subsistence economy. The Indian languages were incomprehensible and their customs and religion reprehensible. Conversion was difficult and immediate success unattainable. In 1572 they abandoned Florida for the richer pastures of Mexico.

The Indians could not adjust so easily to the demands of Christian missionaries. The Europeans were there to stay. The indigenous people had listened to what the Jesuits had to say. They could understand the concepts of a creator, a world shared with spiritual beings, a spiritual leader, priests, and even a ruler who was allied with the representative of God. But a place where spirit-souls existed (heaven), a redeemer, strange notions of good and bad, new ways of dressing, eating, and clothing themselves, these ideas were unacceptable. Accepting what the Europeans suggested would destroy the social fabric of their world. They were drawn to the white men as potential allies in their intervillage squabbles, not as models of behavior. The Spaniards could not control the Indians so they let them alone, for the time being. The Jesuits thought that their message was universal, that anyone of good will would understand who God, his son, and the church were. Equally logical to the missionaries were the saints, Mass, matrimony, and the sacraments and peripherals of Western civilization. What they didn't realize was that not only was their message hidden by layers of cultural assumptions but also that the nature of the message was irrelevant to the Indian. The Jesuits were not able to vilify and destroy the native symbols of culture in order to replace them with their own. The Native American cultural system presented a bulwark against the assaults of the new and it did not even comprehend the symbols of the westerners. Because Indian society retained its political structure and economic base as unthreatened, it was able to reject the European cultural and spiritual message with impunity.

After the Europeans left, other Christian missionaries took their place. In 1572 the principal Spanish colony in Florida was at Santa Elena. Later San Agustín became the major settlement. By 1700 the Calusa and Tocobaga Indians had been wiped out by smallpox. The Native American successfully resisted the religious assault but lost the confrontation with European pathogens.

3

The Four Rivers of Sinaloa

The Florida mission was a failure. The evangelization of Mexico's northern frontier was a success. Why the difference? What was present in Mexico that was absent in Florida? Was the message changed? The methods of proselytization? What dynamic permitted the hearers of the message to consent to its acceptance? When discussing evangelization, one can legitimately ask: what is success? or failure? How can success be measured? Several years ago James Axtell spoke about the legitimacy of North American Indian conversions to Christianity. Were they sincere, or in good faith? How long did they last? Axtell came to the conclusion that in most cases their conversion actually was sincere. The North American Indian saw the new religion as offering solutions to long-standing problems. The Western missionary, according to Axtell, was not merely a tool of Western imperialism and the Indian not a naïve victim of clerical oppression.[1] Latin America was much the same. But it had a peculiar Spanish spin to it.

Sinaloa and Sonora

The conversion of the Indians on the northern frontier of New Spain was the key to advancing Spanish economic interests. At least this is what Viceroy Luis de Velasco thought. "[The Jesuits] are proceeding to convert and indoctrinate the Chichimeca Indians and this is the most important thing. To make sure their work is lasting, they've begun to select sites for churches and religious houses around which the Indians can form towns and villages, something they have not wanted to do in the past. With such organization and the stability that the religious establishments bring, I hope that the Indians will be persuaded to accept Spanish rule and they will be less a threat."[2]

A few years later Philip II asked the Jesuits to begin working in the northern mission, the fringe of New Spain, where "great success" could be expected.[3] What Philip Wayne Powell called "North America's First Frontier"[4] was a complex of settlements and thrusts into northern Mexico motivated by the discovery of rich silver mines in Zacatecas and beyond. The Indians there were determined to keep the Spaniards in check so a bloody, drawn-out conflict called the Chichimeca War lasted from 1550 to 1590.

Several factors coincided to bring the Jesuits north at just this time. First was the Jesuits' own desire to serve on missions. Second was the unstable northern frontier. The Indians were uncontrollable. They had no fixed residences, no fixed fields for cultivation, nor did they even live in houses. Even though the Franciscans were in the area, the governor of Nueva Viscaya asked the Jesuit provincial to send missionaries. "To remedy this," wrote the Viceroy, "Our Lord has moved the fathers of the Society of Jesus to send four of their men, *lenguas*, experienced men to aid in this undertaking."

However, the Governor of Nueva Viscaya did not send the Jesuits who arrived, Gonzalo de Tapia and Martín Pérez, to the Chichimecas but west to Sinaloa and Sonora. There the Jesuits began a complex and controversial mission that eventually reached across the Gulf of California to Baja California and north into the present state of Arizona. The mission's first two decades (1594–1615) are a microcosm of the Indian-European interaction that lasted for almost two centuries. These were the key years during which attitudes and antagonisms formed and developed, when Christianity was presented, accepted, or rejected.

The site of the Jesuit mission was in the highlands of and on the western slope of the Sierra Madre Occidental Mountains, traversed by the Mocorito, Fuerte, Sinaloa, and Mayo rivers that flowed down the western escarpment into the Gulf of California.[5] The region was called Sinaloa. As the Jesuit missions pushed northward into Sonora, the Yaqui River came within their scope. Numerous settlements and villages dotted the banks of these rivers and the missionaries would later describe their missions with reference to the rivers. Estimates put the population along the Mayo River at forty thousand and thirty thousand along the Yaqui River at the time of first contact with the Spanish. Roughly the same estimates hold for the population along the other riverbanks.

A few years after the Jesuits arrived, they estimated the entire population of Sinaloa to be one hundred thousand people. However, European killer epidemics had penetrated the native populations before actual physical contact with the Spaniards, so these estimates are questionable.⁶ Much of the region is broad coastal plain but the river valleys have rich alluvial deposits that sometimes were swept into the coastal plain by floodwaters. The average mountain rainfall is seven- to nine-hundred millimeters. Flood season, from February to June, would sometimes ruin the crops and caused widespread famine. The peaks of the Sierra Madre reach 2,000–2,500 meters in places through which rivers have carved deep canyons. These were the favorite hiding places of the Indians fleeing Spanish soldiers and the demands of Spanish rule. The forests of the uplands were thick with thorny vegetation. Oak and pine stands dotted the upper parts of the mountains.

When Governor Rodrigo de Río de Losa wrote to Philip II in 1591, he painted a dismal picture of Sinaloa. The Indians had killed three Franciscan missionaries, and there were only thirty Spaniards and two Jesuits present. The province was "abandoned."⁷ However, a year later the Jesuit Visitor, Diego de Avellaneda, described Sinaloa as the *"gran provincia,"* with a potential *"copiossísima"* harvest of seventy thousand Indians.⁸ Enthusiasm had increased among the Jesuit administrators in Mexico City perhaps because, in the words of Avellaneda, Sinaloa was *"preciosíssima"* in the eyes of the Spanish viceroy, Luis de Velasco, suggesting that the political gains to be achieved by evangelizing the northern frontier were not lost on the viceroy.

In 1591 the Jesuits Gonzalo de Tapia and Martín Pérez began evangelizing the Indians of Sinaloa. They first resided in the settlement called the Villa de San Felipe on the Sinaloa River. Spaniards were not totally unfamiliar with Sinaloa. Francisco Vásquez de Coronado had tramped along the coast in 1545 while searching for the Seven Cities of Cíbola. A settlement of forty Spaniards had sprung up on the Sinaloa River a few years later but the leader of the settlement, Diego de Alcaraz, treated the Indians heavy-handedly, so the Indians wiped out the Spanish settlement and thus discouraged any future attempt to live along the riverbank. Only the lure of silver could bring the Spaniards back. Francisco de Ibarra led an expedition through Sinaloa in 1563 looking for signs of gold or silver. He found them: the Indians decorated themselves with what looked like precious metals.⁹ That was enough for Ibarra to plant a settlement of sixty families at Carapoa along the Fuerte River. Indeed, the settlers did find rich mines, but the hostility of the Indians drove them away. Twenty years later the Spaniards again tried to find the mines of Sinaloa. In 1583 Pedro de Montoya received authorization to found a town. He enlisted thirty Spaniards from the settlement of Culiacan and went looking for silver mines. The Zuaque Indians wiped out the band of future miners. It was then that the governor of Nueva Vizcaya, whose jurisdiction included Sinaloa, petitioned for Jesuits to evangelize the Indians. In June of 1591 Tapia and Pérez were in San Miguel de Culiacán, one river and one hundred miles south of the Mocorito River on the southern edge of Sinaloa.

The Mission: Organization and Methods

Gonzalo de Tapia and Martín Pérez apportioned villages for evangelizing, preached in the native hamlets with the help of interpreters, and wrote a catechism in the local Indian language.[10] With interpreters at their side they insisted that they were not like the other Spaniards who preceded them. "We have not come for gold or the silver that's buried in your land. We have not come to make slaves of you and take your wives and children. You see only two of us, alone, unarmed. We have come only to tell you about the creator of heaven and earth. Without knowledge of him you will be unhappy forever."[11]

The Indians were suspicious of the missionaries. The past encounters with the Europeans were hostile. In the beginning the Indians thought that they were like the other Spaniards but they soon realized that they were not. "The Jesuits learned the language, carried no arquebus, demanded no corn or food but spoke only of *Virigeva*, the Eternal God. That first year 2,000 people were baptized."[12] The two missionaries were optimistic. They portrayed the mountain valleys of Sinaloa as the gateway to an infinity of other barbarous peoples and even to New Mexico "about which so much has been written."

The Jesuits described the people of the towns of Barboria, Lopocho, Matapan, and Ocoroni as great farmers. There was no poverty and no beggars. They raised corn in two harvests a year as well as beans, cotton, and squash. Fish were abundant. They hunted wild cattle, deer, and rabbits. They made a drink of fermented corn and used it to get drunk. "These people do not have a king or a lord. However, in time of war they gather around a strong leader as their captain and they all obey him. In peacetime, they do what pleases them. Each nation respects the other although there is much fighting."[13]

The Jesuits were especially curious about the belief system of the Indians. At first they did not uncover any idols or even personal gods. The Indians did not believe in the existence of heaven. Instead, the dead passed under the earth to some dark region whose ruler was named Yori. There was no distinction between good and bad. What gave pleasure was licit. The dead were cremated although sometimes a corpse was buried alongside a tree with all of the deceased's belongings including blankets, headdresses, bow and arrows, food, and a large gourd with water for the long trip into the kingdom of the dead. The deceased's dogs and cattle were slaughtered and his friends got drunk over the grave site. Nothing belonging to the dead remained behind. Everything went with them.

> They have no idols. But they do not understand that there is a Provi-
> dence in Sinaloa, nor do they hope for happiness in another life.
> They simply believe that the dead go to a place under the earth
> called Darkness, whose prince they call Yoris. There, they say, those
> who live righteously or wickedly on earth will all be equally cared
> for, and whatever they will wish to do will be allowed . . . Both men
> and women cultivate a great head of hair. The women always have it
> hanging down. The men braid and arrange it, making it up in a va-
> riety of fashions and adorning it with much plumage. For this they
> raise in their homes different birds with beautiful feathers . . . When
> someone dies, in their heathen way they cremate the body. Some-
> times, however, they bury a branch of a tree with all his blankets,
> plumes, beads, bow, quiver of arrows, and much food, and a gourd
> full of water. They intend these to be of some assistance for the long
> journey he has to take. On that occasion they customarily solemnize
> their drinking bouts, and they likewise put a great quantity of wine
> on the sepulchral fire. They kill the dogs and other animals of the
> dead man, so that nothing of his possessions remains alive.[14]

The earliest reports from the Jesuits in Sinaloa were notable for the absence of criticism about Indian beliefs and customs. They were straightforward
descriptions with a touch of admiration and probably a bit of embellishment
about how the Indians lived. The Indians were basically honest, the Jesuits
wrote. "No doors are ever locked and the corn remains untouched." Even the
implications inherent in the Jesuit descriptions of interpersonal relations—
courtship, marriage, homosexuality, and polygamy—were passed over lightly.
Having many wives, as many as one could support, eliminated adultery, the
Jesuit report of 1593 stated. This acceptance changed later as the novelty of
initial evangelization wore off. However, there was one exception: drunkenness. Drinking to excess was never condoned or rationalized. This response
by the missionaries was partly culturally conditioned since the Spanish considered drunkenness a form of induced insanity and thereby contrary to the
natural order of things. It also led to "orgies" that had some sort of religious
connotation but that remained mysterious and unresolved by the missionaries.

The Jesuits in Sinaloa evangelized their way north river by river. Their
central base was on the Sinaloa River in the Spanish town of San Felipe y

Santiago, later called Nuestra Señora de Sinaloa or simply Sinaloa. From here the first two Jesuits, Gonzalo de Tapia and Martín Pérez, began to visit neighboring Indian settlements referring to their visits as an *entrada*. The person of prime importance in the Indian settlement was the cacique and the Jesuits targeted him as the first potential convert. If the cacique received them well and accepted baptism, the villagers usually followed suit. A small church made of brushwood and reeds set on poles with a layer of earth as a roof would be erected, and here the missionary would begin to teach the fundamentals of Christianity. In the settlement of Guasabe on the Sinaloa River the Jesuits started teaching the catechism in Latin. This extraordinary occurrence took place in 1593 so the missionary must have been either Tapia or Pérez. The Annual Letter notes that the missionary quickly switched to an interpreter, "a woman who knew Mexican [Nahuatl?] because she was a slave for several years in the Spanish town of Culiacán."[15] Twice daily the villagers would come to the church and recite what they had learned. They sang what was called the *doctrina* "in the evening hours which in the past were spent in superstitious dances."[16]

These native dances were a favorite target of the missionaries. They associated them with religious orgies and drunkenness and so attempted to replace them with simpler dance movements they introduced from the central valley of Mexico. Some of the villages had "wine" and their orgies reportedly lasted for three months! The dancing at these native celebrations lasted so long that it was explicable only if the devil was inciting the Indian to perform beyond the level of human endurance.[17] Before the Jesuits had established themselves in the community and considered it safe to forbid native drinking and dancing altogether, they simply absented themselves when the dancing and drinking started. The organ, flute, violin, and trumpet classes that were held at the Jesuit College in Sinaloa for Indian youth had at their root the desire to replace the native celebration with the Spanish-like music and dance becoming common in colonial New Spain.

One of the earliest multivillage fiestas organized by the Jesuits occurred in 1595 after a drunken Huacabe Indian killed a Christian woman. Panic ensued. The Indians expected massive Spanish retaliation so almost everyone fled in fear to the mountains. Adding to the panic were the speeches of a local *hechicero* (native priest) who encouraged the people to flee. According to the Jesuit report, the *hechicero* was always accompanied by "a personal devil." So his followers "scampered up into the mountains like a herd of deer." The Jesuits were disheartened. Even though by 1595 almost eight thousand Indians had been baptized in the entire mission of Sinaloa, a wholesale bolt by entire villages could have major effects on the enterprise. The Jesuits hid their disappointment from the Christian Indians who remained "so as not to dishearten them," and proceeded to counter the abandonment and fear by gathering twenty-three towns in Sinaloa for a massive fiesta, "even though the people spoke different languages."[18] The fiesta was held at Christmastime. On the first day the *Danza de Pastores* was featured and a series of dances by "Mexican" Indians followed. A long procession was held the next day with each town represented led by a cross decorated with multicolored feathers. Mexican singers entertained, the *juego de caña* and mock battles took place. Children dressed as angels put on a pageant singing newly learned *villancicos* alternating between Nauatl and Ocoroni. An orchestra of flutes, trumpets, and oboes (*chirimías*) played constantly. On the last day the missionaries, now six in number, preached and Capt. Hurdaide blasted his artillery from the fortress walls.

Such gatherings, although not as large as this, were held several times a year on the occasion of major Christian feasts, e.g., Holy Week and Christmas. Repentance and confession of sins were major events of Holy Week and some missionaries encouraged flagellants to beat themselves in public as a sign of repentance. The Annual Letters reported the flagellation *a sangre* with a certain pride saying in a sense that our Christians were doing the same thing that real European Christians do! Most missionaries interpreted these external manifestations of Spanish Catholicism as visible signs of authentic Christianity.

By 1610 a fortress called Ft. Montesclaros had been constructed on the Fuerte River. Situated on a hillock, one side of the fort faced the river and the other a flat grassland where cattle were pastured. The fort's four towers looking out over the settlement were the visible symbol of Spanish presence and power in the area. The missionaries considered the fortress and its contingent of Spanish soldiers an essential ingredient for the spiritual conquest of Sinaloa. The first missionaries in the area prided themselves on having carried no weapons, on being different from the Spaniards who came searching for silver. Within a decade they changed their tune. Revolts, killings, raids, and general tension between those who accepted the new religion and those who did not convinced the Jesuits that the lascasian strategy of appearing before the Native American with no visible link to Spanish military power (i.e, a gun) was not wise. Instead, the Jesuits thought that "a great deal of help in the conversion of these peoples has been given by the Fort of Montesclaros . . . with this check on the Indians the Fathers can go about their ministries more easily."[19]

In the early days of the Sinaloa mission the Jesuit spent a month visiting Indian villages at the end of which he would spend two weeks back in the central residence of Sinaloa. By 1614 this schedule shifted a bit. The missionary spent two two-week periods a year in the central residence of Sinaloa *reforzándose*, regaining physical, spiritual, and psychological strength. He made the Spiritual Exercises of St. Ignatius (a retreat) and in general reintegrated himself into Jesuit common life. The reintegration did not always work. By 1597 all the missionaries knew the local languages and the periodic sweeps that the missionaries conducted through areas not yet visited sometimes lasted more than a month. In one mission sweep in 1601 through the Valley of Culiacán the missionary visited over twenty villages "where the *cocoliztli* raged furiously."[20]

By 1597 the Jesuits had established a solid base for mission activity in Sinaloa. Their residence in Sinaloa had eight rooms and a few offices. An adobe church had been constructed for 1200 pesos and "not another like it is around for 100 miles." Spaniards, Mexicans, and Tarascan Indians worshiped in it. The total number of Indians baptized by the Jesuits since their arrival was over eight thousand. But the Indians, reported the Annual Letter for 1597, were still fierce and rebellious. Even though forty more Spanish colonists had moved into Sinaloa in 1596, the land was described as sterile and undeveloped. The Jesuits agreed that one major difficulty was the inaccessibility of the Indian villages, hidden in the hills, in remote pockets into which there were no trails. If these villages could be relocated or integrated into other villages, the task of the missionaries would be greatly facilitated. In 1599 Fr. Juan Baptista Velasco reported that three remote villages in the area had been moved to a more accessible location.[21] As a result, instead of hiding when summoned to doctrina class as they had been accustomed to doing, the Indians now attended Christian doctrine classes regularly. "The place where they were resettled doesn't

TABLE 3.1. Missions in Sinaloa, 1662

Missionary	Towns	Population	Stipend
Gabriel Carrero	Mucurilo	180	300
Domingo de Urbino	Tamasula, Vasauve	1,100	300
Pedro de Maya	Bamoa, Cubiri, Nio	562	300
Pedro Villanuño	Ocoroni, Sinaloa	160	300
Antonio de Urquza	Oqueri	350	300
Prudencio de Meca	Cicorato, Bababurito	700	360
Gonzalo Navarro	Urea, Huytes	1,100	360
Alonso Flores	Toro, Soes, Baimena	1,050	360
Jacinto Cortés	Chara, Sibirioa, Maeori, El Fuerte	1,360	300
Francisco Medrano	Aome, San Miguel, Mocficague	1,800	300
Juan de Cuera	Santa Cruz, Etzohoa, Quirimpo	1,100	300
Luis Sandoval	Naboa, Jesia, Cayaman	1,000	360
Tomás Hidalgo	Raum, Potain	3,500	350
Francisco Diserino	Conicari, Comayaqui, Tepaqui	1,300	350
Diego de Molina	Torim, Vicam	2,800	350
Antonio Tello	Bacum, Cocorim	900	350

Source: ARSI, Mex. 5, fol. 104–5.

even have a tree to hide behind. The place even looks like a town, with a church and streets. People have an imperfect understanding of the faith, but they will grow with continual watering from the words of the gospel."²² The move to reorganize villages grew. In 1600 a major resettlement program was started.

Baptism and Epidemics

In the plague year of 1623, Fr. Miguel Godines baptized eighty children, seventy of whom died. Juan Castini baptized almost the same number and 33 percent fell to a killer epidemic. The writer of the Annual Letter for that year spoke of the deaths as a "premature harvest from an uncultivated field," *una cosecha temprana que se ha echo en aquel erial.*²³ A curious juxtaposition of baptism and death caused an equally curious mixture of emotions in the missionaries. Christian tradition associated baptism with joy because the initiated entered the community of believers. The death of the old self was symbolized by washing with water and the ritual displayed a new life in Christ as flamboyantly as circumstances allowed. However, in the New World baptism was associated with death. The missionaries in New Spain faced the same dilemma that their confreres encountered in New France. Contemporary theology taught that baptism was essential for entry into heaven and if the sacrament occurred immediately before dying then the soul was guaranteed eternal life. But death on the northern frontier of New Spain was the result of epidemics that the Europeans vaguely suspected had come from themselves. "The illnesses that the Indians suffer came after we arrived. They were in good health before never having experienced pestilence," confessed the Annual Letter of 1593.²⁴ And the worst part of it, continued the letter, was that when the priest began to baptize, the people died suddenly, and many continued dying. The writer expressed the dilemma clearly: "On the one hand it is a great shame to see so many dying yet it is a consolation to see so many going to heaven."²⁵ During periods of pestilence the missionaries went about their task of baptizing dying children not with the joy normally associated with the ritual but nevertheless believing that the baptized soul was on its way directly to eternal happiness. There would be no chance of commiting a mortal sin that could jeopardize eternal salvation with this early baptism. The language the Jesuits used to describe the events of baptism reflected the ambiguity of sadness over death and joy over entrance to heaven and eternal life. Tempered by the sorrow of death, the Jesuits described the epidemics as violent and evil, not as welcome producers of eternal life. The symptoms of the killer epidemic were described in minute detail.

This epidemic [1593] was so violent that the burning fever took away one's ability to reason. The victims jumped into the river to cool themselves or fled to the mountains where they became food for wolves.[26]

Pus covering the victim from head to foot had a terrible smell and it took only a few days for the victim to die. It was horrible to see the maggots feeding on the wounds. People fled to the mountains to escape. The villages were filled with weeping and sorrow for their dead children.[27]

The epidemic of 1601 was devastating.

This year there was a cocoliztli during which many died. Some took fourteen hours to die, others two days. The old people, the women, and the young were the quickest to go. Babies had swellings on the throat and they could not speak. Others seemed to lose their minds. The epidemic lasted three or four months. Just when we thought it ended, it rose again and in less than 48 hours carried off people from the villages. The victims hardly knew what hit them and they were dead. We grieved because it came so swiftly when we were outside the villages that we could be of no assistance.[28]

Epidemic diseases that occurred at five- to eight-year intervals throughout the seventeenth century in Sinaloa were described by several names. Garrotillo (mumps), sarampión (measles), viruelas (smallpox), and tabardillo (typhus) were recognized by the Europeans. Many of the missionaries were native born so they applied local as well as European remedies. This meant frequent swathings with wet cloths (sometimes the cloth was dipped in wine), purges, bloodletting, application of hot towels, blessings with Holy Water, and sometimes confession and baptism.[29] Reff points out that although this kind of care did little medically for the victim, nevertheless, statistics showed that those receiving such kinds of personal care were more likely to survive an epidemic disease.[30] When recovery occurred in Sinaloa, it was another proof of the effectiveness of the Christian God and another persuasive argument against the hechicero who, during epidemics, not only fled and refused to assist the dying but discouraged the reception of baptism. The European stayed with the sick and for the most part because the missionary remained unscathed, he was thus able to confirm the power of his God.

Although the missionaries grieved at the sight of so many deaths during killer epidemics, they reasoned or rationalized its presence. ". . . many babies die with the grace of baptism so that putting together the chosen grains from this place and that Our Lord is filling his granary. This is what greatly consoles us and encourages the missionaries who with so much sweat cultivate his fields."[31] By a twist of logic, the epidemics were made into an act of love. Our Lord, went the explanation, actually demonstrated his love of the Indian by permitting his death so soon after baptism. "Our Lord so loves them that he takes them while they are in the state of baptismal innocence."[32] Their deaths were a true sign of their predestination. *"Y que les daba Nuestro Señor la salud corporal pretendiéndoles dar la espiritual con el baptismo y la eterna llevándolos baptizados de esta vida."*[33]

One wonders what Luis de Molina, the Spanish Jesuit who wrote so vigorously against Calvin's notion of predestination, would have thought about this "sign of predestination." However, what made the Jesuits pause was the death of adult Christians. They could explain the child's death as the permissive will of an ultimately caring God, but the need for model Christians should have prevented the deaths of the already baptized. The death of so many Christians in the 1601 epidemic was described as a "blow."[34] It was not explained.

Only a fraction of the baptisms performed in Sinaloa occurred during epidemics. In 1623 the Annual Letter from Sinaloa reported 11,290 baptisms performed the previous year, and over the past thirty-three years, 101,300.[35] Twenty-nine couples were married by the missionaries. The average yearly number of baptisms occurring in Sinaloa was around three thousand. The mission there with its twenty-seven Jesuits scattered on the northern frontier became a major factor in the Jesuit presence in Mexico. The yearly statistics sent from Mexico City to Rome showing the number of adults and children baptized in Sinaloa, the number of couples married in the church, and the number of confessions heard were palpable signs of pastoral care and souls saved. But why the Indians of Sinaloa and later Sonora converted to Christianity almost en masse is more complex.

Fair with Occasional Showers

Soon after Frs. Cornelio Godinez and Santiago Basilio were killed by Indians in the Tarahumara uprising of 1654, an inquiry began about the motives behind the slayings.[36] The investigators were biased. They wanted to prove that the Indians burned churches, destroyed the priests' vestments, and murdered the European missionaries out of hatred of the faith, *in odium fidei* was the phrase used. They could not. The contradiction even appeared in the words used by the investigators to describe the uprising, *rebelión* and *alzamiento*, implying political motives. Godinez had been in Tarahumara country only a year. He did not intend to stay. He was going farther inland, *tierra adentro.* He was on the move, looking for virgin territory to evangelize.

By the time Godinez arrived in Sinaloa, a half a century of missionaries had come and many had gone. From the original two, missionary numbers had grown steadily from sixty in 1654 to ninety-four by 1708.[37] River names no longer defined areas of proselytization. Sinaloa and Sonora were divided into *partidos* and *rectorados* with missionaries assigned to specific towns. Each missionary received a stipend from the crown.

As more missionaries were needed to instruct and convert more Indians, more money and supplies were needed by the missions. Famine relief was a major expenditure that attracted good will and potential converts. The king's stipend was insufficient to cover this expense so the Jesuits introduced cattle by 1620, organized farms, and engaged in commercial transactions to ensure an adequate supply for themselves of clothing, chocolate, flour, tobacco, and wine. However, commercial transactions meant trouble. Local Spanish farmers accused the Jesuits of keeping Indian labor for themselves and engaging in buying and selling that was forbidden to religious institutions. Eventually, the courts decided in favor of the Jesuits. However, when the provincial of Mexico dispatched a visitor to Sinaloa in 1664, he was not only interested in learning whether the Jesuits there actually played cards, wore their cassocks, or carried arquebuses, but whether they were making loans at 5 percent interest and not *whether* Jesuits had silver in their possession but *how much* each had, and whether they were supplying the mining district of Parral with cattle.[38]

The superior general in Rome wrote several warnings about avoiding anything that smacked of business transactions. However, the Jesuits in the mission field argued for greater latitude in the acquisition of food and clothing and commerce. They were much worse off than their brethren in the colleges and they did not hesitate to say so. Guillermo de Figueroa thought "the missionaries live in far worse condition than those in colleges because the latter do not have to provide for themselves. The superior is there to provide everything."[39]

The proportionately large number of Mexican-born Jesuits on the northern frontier might have had something to do with the controversy about commerce and the friction between European colleges and missions. Through the seventeenth century the mix of Mexican-born Jesuits, foreign and Spanish missionaries shifted considerably.

Mexican-born Jesuits were posted to the northern frontier because they were familiar with the Indian languages and they adapted more readily to regional food, clothing, and housing. In addition, they might have been more eager to care for the indigenous Mexican. They were also more conversant with

TABLE 3.2. National Origin of Sinaloa-Sonora Missionaries

Year	Total	Mexican	Foreign	Spanish
1604	8	3	1	4
1620	48	17	10	21
1638	63	32	8	23
1659	43	23	8	12
1690	75	39	17	19
1708	94	66	15	13
1740	86	48	22	16

Source: ARSI, Cat. Trienn., Mex. 4, 6, 7.

Mexican customs and mores and presumably more tolerant of the way things were done. There is no record of how European Jesuits in New Spain were chosen for the frontier missions. Presumably, they were volunteers. A major criteria was facility with the Indian languages. From the late sixteenth century, learning languages had been a bone of contention with the Jesuits in New Spain. Few Spaniards attempted to learn the languages of indigenous peoples because it meant that they would be destined for the missions instead of the more prestigious posts in colleges. In 1600 the catalogue of Jesuits in New Spain listed 55 Jesuits out of a total of 314 (17 percent) who knew Indian languages. In 1669 the superior general in Rome ordered all Jesuits in Mexico to spend two years on the missions "with no exceptions"[40] in order to learn the languages, but nothing came of the order. This gave rise to the general feeling that the missions were for the less talented. A quick survey of the *Talenta*, or Talents, category applied to the Jesuits on the missions bear this out. Few were placed in the higher categories of *apta ad gobernandum* or *optimo ingenio*. Almost all were listed under average or mediocre intelligence.

Who went to the northern missions and the circumstances of his assignment affected the missionary's attitude toward the Indian.

Attitudes: Indian and European

Decades before the Jesuits arrived in Mexico, controversy raged over the character of the American Indian. Who was he? Was he man or beast? Was he a rational being? Could his lands be expropriated? Could he be made to work and pay taxes? If he were a beast, why should he not be enslaved? Could the Indian be obliged by force to become a Christian? What type of religious instruction should he be given? Once converted, did he have a right to all the sacraments, including the priesthood? Should he be taught only grammar or Latin? Could he be left to govern himself?[41] These questions were never fully resolved and each European missionary group proceeded to evangelize according to the style and spirit that they brought with them to America.

The style and spirit of the Jesuits helped to mold their peculiar mission methodology. Between and sometimes within religious groups contradictory and conflicting ideologies rose. Sometimes the opinions held in Spain about the Indians were tempered and nuanced once the missionary arrived in America and came face to face with Indian customs and beliefs.

The European Jesuits brought with them to America a high opinion of the Mexican Indian. This must have been at least partly a result of the debates in the immediate post-conquest years between Dominicans and the Spanish home government about the basic ability of the Indian.[42] The Jesuits began indirectly to form their own views of the Indian when their theologians began responding to Calvin and his followers' beliefs about depraved human nature. Taking a positive view of man's nature, the influential Jesuit theologian Luis de Molina portrayed human nature as basically sound and perfectible. The first Jesuit missionary in Sinaloa, Martín Pérez, the companion of Gonzalo de Tapia, echoed Molina's view. In 1592 he spoke of the excellent nature of the Indians, their gentleness, docility, and kindness.[43] This view was tempered by Tapia's death in 1594. After the killing, Jesuits relied heavily on the military might of Diego de Hurdaide to provide an iron fist of justice, retribution, and intimidation—the Spaniards called it pacification. After 1596 Jesuit missionaries were often accompanied by Indian bodyguards.

The various words used in the Annual Letters to describe the Indian demonstrate that the Jesuits perceived differences among Indian groups. The Indians of Sauceda, stated the Annual Letter of 1597, clothed themselves with a type of grass that resembled wool, "like savages do" ("*a manera de salvajes.*")[44] The fact that the writer did not call the Indians savages (*salvajes*) of course does not prove that he did not think they were. Even though it was politically correct at the time to refer to the Indian as a savage, he did not do so. However, in the same account, the writer described the missionaries going from settlement to settlement and then he corrected himself, "or rather from one wild beast's lair to another."[45] The writer, wishing to underline the difficulty and danger of the mission, tried to elicit sympathy or simply exaggerate the missionary's difficulty hoping to increase the glory he thought they deserved. While the word *salvaje* (savage) is not frequent in the Jesuit letters, *bárbaro* (barbarian) is. But the Spanish frequently used *bárbaro* as a synonym for heathen with lesser connotations of rudeness and cruelty. The words, whether *bárbaro, salvaje,* or *naturales,* indicate a superiority the European believed was inherent in the relationship between himself and the Indian. In Western Europe and Spain the cleric saw himself superior to the layperson. In America this superiority was compounded by conquest and a perceived cultural superiority.

"Our principal task in Sinaloa," stated the Annual Letter of 1615, "is to force the Indians to live within a fixed political structure because they are so wild and barbarous."[46] Once they were controlled, they could be evangelized. Because the Indian was sometimes enticed out of his new political world of towns and villages, taxes, labor, and churchgoing, monitored by Spanish-approved *alcaldes, fiscales,* and *alguaciles,* and forced to conform by soldiers and priests, he was judged weak (*pusillánimo* was the word the Spanish used). The Indian was considered deficient because he could not long maintain a way of life imposed by the Spanish and considered by the Spanish to be the only way civilized persons should live.[47]

The Spanish Jesuits were fixated on external conformity perhaps because the persistent presence of the Spanish Inquisition in their own lives had created a pattern of ritualistic observance of rules. So they demanded behavior and symbols that they felt were essential to civilized man: hair cut to the nape of the neck for men, clothes (going about naked was *"de animales"*)[48], no drunkenness, no adoring idols, but living in villages with stable authority figures, singing and dancing according to the European model, playing European musical instruments, monogamous relationships, abjuring the old religion, and living in stable agricultural communities were some of the missionaries' demands. No cultural relativists they! The college run by the Jesuits in the town of Sinaloa had as its main goal the Hispanicization and Christianization of Indians who would return to their villages and act as agents of change. Among Indian groups it was common to exchange "hostages" who were reared or kept for a period of time by another group. So the Indian village of Comosipa left eleven young men in the Jesuit college as "peace hostages" (*rejenes de la paz*) where they would learn to read, write, and sing.[49] As long as the young men remained in the college, the Indian group was friendly to and supportive of the missionaries. Not to be outshone, other villages did the same. The cacique of Ziribotari conferred with all the other caciques and asked Capt. Hurdaide to send them the fathers, "just like the Navas and Nures peoples have."[50]

It delighted the Jesuits to see the Indians behave like Spaniards. It affirmed their work and encouraged them to continue. "[In confession] they go into great detail about their sin just like Spaniards do."[51] And in the report of 1600: "It is wonderful to see the Indians in procession on Sunday and holydays with flower-decked crosses, chanting prayers as they enter the church."[52]

To the Jesuits the more the Indian appeared to be European, the more civilized they became. They distinguished two kinds of Indians. Those who were under twenty-five years of age were docile "like a ball of wax" and could be shaped and made into a good Christian. The other kind was composed of older Indians who were used to their drunkenness, women, freedom, wars, and murders. These, wrote Alonso de Santiago, "will never be good Christians, although many have been baptized. In general they are a treacherous and cruel people, having grown up in sin."[53] Fleeing the reorganized village life for the mountains, sometimes being pursued by Spanish soldiers and missionaries and sometimes not, full-scale armed revolt—such as what took place among the Tarahumaras in 1626 and the Yaquis in 1740, and outbursts that spanned almost the entire period of the Jesuit presence in Sinaloa and Sonora—were obviously signals of dissatisfaction. The lingering power of the indigenous religious leaders who often took advantage of the dissatisfaction by channeling it into active revolt was even more alarming to the Christian missionaries. The Jesuits saw the devil and his agents, the *hechiceros*, behind the opposition and revolts. The comments on the revolt of 1596 are typical.

> The Indians have been reduced to towns where they live in communities and are taught Christian Doctrine. They grew restless. They did not want to serve the Spaniards any more and they wished to throw off the mild yoke of the gospel. They wanted their old liberty with which they lived before as beasts with no leader neither in heaven or on earth. . . . The devil incited them to revolt and they fled to the mountains and abandoned their towns and burned the churches and destroyed the statues. They even burned down their own dwellings to tell the Spaniards that they rejected this life and preferred the life of beasts in the mountains.[54]

During the first decade of Jesuit proselytizing, the "old folk" were targeted as major obstacles to the spread of Christianity. They "steadfastly refuse to accept baptism, certain that death would follow." Nevertheless, in the Annual Letter (1616) that complained about the elders's opposition, the writer noted that 1,800 babies and 3,332 adults had been baptized.[55] Apparently, the younger Indian population was more convinced of the efficacy of baptism than the older. The younger won out. As the total native population decreased, ravaged by disease, famine, war, and economic dislocations, the younger segment became Hispanicized (*ladinos*). In 1626 the Annual Letter reported that the Indians no longer called the *hechiceros* when they were sick. The priests had replaced them. This might have been true of one area but certainly not all.

And so the Hispanicization and Christianization processes continued. Fr. Juan Castini wrote in 1626:

My Huites mission goes well. The road is now open and the church built of adobes and most of my *convento* is completed. The people of the surrounding *rancherías* have settled around the church. Good news for me is that all the surrounding peoples, the Coripas, the Achaques, the Hoisuaves and another three whose names I forget all helped to make adobes for the church. . . . I am learning the language and hopefully I can preach for a good half hour in their language.[56]

Castini, an Italian, would spend many hours of his twenty-four years in Sinaloa preaching not only to the Huites but also to the Guazapares, the Temoris, the Varohios, and the Hios. When he died in 1663, he joined a select band of Jesuits including Gonzalo de Tapia and Martín Pérez that became the models for Jesuit missionaries who would come to Sinaloa and Sonora in the seventeenth and eighteenth centuries. Like Jogues and Brebeuf in New France, the missionary Jesuits of Mexico were able to develop an esprit de corps and a quasi cult around their martyrs and esteemed colleagues.[57]

At the risk of oversimplifying the attitudes of the hundreds of European Jesuit missionaries in Sinaloa in the early years, the image that the Europeans drew of the non-Christian Indian was one of nakedness, passion, cruelty, and incivility, a person locked in the chains of Satan's wiles. On the other hand, the Christian Indian, they thought, had emerged from paganism but only by a few steps. He was ever poised on the brink of retrogression and required constant monitoring to remain an authentic Christian. The Jesuits spoke warmly of the bonds that tied families together, whether Christian or non-Christian. Many nonbaptized Indians were considered "rational" and could hold their own in discussions. However, all Indians whether Christian or pagan were distinguished from the *"gente de razón,"* the "people of reason," the Spaniard. Once baptized, the Indian might have been the spiritual equal of the Spaniard, but never his social equal.

The Formality of Religion

In 1623 the Jesuit report from Sinaloa proudly stated that over 101,300 souls had been baptized since they arrived. "And 70,000 more could be baptized if we had more missionaries," the writer added.[58] No doubt a great part of the success of the Christian missionaries was due to military conquest. The white men had even conquered the powerful Aztecs. And their priests were fearless in destroying the old gods. In Sinaloa the missionaries threw the Indian gods to the ground breaking them into pieces. The gods were silent and the white men went unpunished. The old gods were dead and powerless.[59]

Daniel T. Reff recently developed one of the most solid propositions about the relative success of the Jesuit missions in Sinaloa.[60] According to Reff, the Europeans came on the scene just after Indian social and economic society had been destroyed by European diseases carried north on trade routes. The Jesuits proclaimed a god who would not allow his own to suffer the consequences of disease. Baptism could cleanse the soul and provide a protection against disease. The local shaman was powerless against the ravages of the cocoliztli; he abandoned the sick and allowed his people to be punished by the Christian god who wanted their adoration. The Jesuit filled a void in Indian life by replacing the shaman as the intermediary between god and man. These were the major factors that allowed the Jesuits to convert and control in Sinaloa and Sonora.

Reff's carefully documented account of disease and the missionaries in Sinaloa and Sonora must be taken into account whenever the Jesuits on the Mexican frontier are discussed. But the social and economic motivations for conversion were not the only factors at work. As pointed out above, James Axtell felt that Indian conversions in North America included a significant number moved by the attractiveness of Christianity.[61] For many in New Spain the new religion responded to inner needs in a way that the old did not. The struggle between the adherents of the old and the new was skewed in favor of the new. The Spanish soldiers who manned the frontier garrisons guaranteed that.

Had Spanish weapons alone conquered? The psychological element was also present since the Christian missionary preached a religion that insured continued domination. The Ten Commandments, the laws of the church, and the four prayers formed the *doctrina* that was repeated in the morning and evening in every Indian village. Respect for and obedience to authority was an essential element in the new order. Authority fused church and state into an alliance that made a revolt against the state a revolt against God. The Spanish corporate view of society made church and state one entity although each retained separate goals.

Allowing for the psychological impact of military conquest and the decimation of Indian society by disease, other powerful factors contributed to a smooth transition to or fusion of the old and new religions. When the Christian missionary preached about a structured religious hierarchy that dictated religious truths to its members, the Indian recalled his not-too-remote past when a structured hierarchy of shaman, spirit world, and divine being ruled *his* universe. They recognized the Christian angels, saints, and even devils as the lower-region helpers that were active in their own religious world. Omens and witches were familiar to them. Catholic priests were intermediaries just as their shaman had been and continued to be. Christian and Indian worshiped one major God. The Indian pantheon was similar to the Christian cult of the saints. Recitation by rote of the *doctrina* was strikingly similar to the shaman's incantations. The Jesuits in Sinaloa were surprised at how quickly the Indians took to confessing their sins, unaware of a similar Indian ritual.[62] All of these similarities eased the transition to a new religion, allowing the Indian to reach back into his past and link the new with the old.

The Jesuits added other features to Indian religious life. Singing and playing musical instruments added festive notes to religious services. Processions honoring the saints were always accompanied by song and sometimes dance. The centerpiece of the fiesta was a religious rite performed within the framework of gaiety and celebration.

Resettlement was a feature of evangelization that had major psychological and social consequences for the Indian. Forcible transfer was not simply moving from one site to another but the passage from the familiar to the unfamiliar. Whole villages were moved in order to facilitate instruction. Isolation from the familiar permitted easier indoctrination. The result was insecurity and increased vulnerability.

The Jesuits directed major efforts at the caciques who, under overall Spanish rule, held political control the villages. When the cacique became a Christian, the members of the village soon followed. Inducements to the cacique were many. Preferential treatment by Spanish authorities, food supplies in time of want, a steady labor supply were some of the rewards for embracing Christianity.

However, the new religion was accompanied by violence not only on the part of Spanish soldiery but also on the part of native resisters. Indian revolts in Sonora spanned the entire Spanish colonial period.[63] One can infer from the accounts of revolts and uprisings the true cause of the dissatisfaction. Violence was directed not only at the religious agents of Christianity but also at the Spanish community at large. Cattle were killed, farms burned, wagon trains attacked in outbursts of violence. The revolt of the Tarahumaras, for example, was caused, according to the missionary, Joseph Neumann, by heavy Spanish demands, hostility to the missionaries, and the resentment of the native priests.[64] The Indians attacked the entire spectrum of Spanish cultural life.

Conversions: Sincere or Fake?

One way of measuring the sincerity of conversion to Christianity was the post-conversion behavior of the Indian. Was the proselytized genuinely a "new person," still imperfect, but transformed? Or was the individual simply brainwashed into believing that the new religion was the wave-of-the-future belief system?

The Jesuit missionaries in Sinaloa were not the same as those in Florida. That is to say, they had learned that the Native American was not rushing to settle under the banner of Christ. The days of mass baptisms of great numbers of Native Americans as reported by the first evangelizers of Mexico were events of the past. Much more care was needed. The individual missionary in Sinaloa knew and understood the language—or languages. This directly impacted the quality of conversion. The Indian had to understand the basic tenets of Christianity, which could only be assured by the evangelizer understanding the words or concepts that were translated from European languages to the native tongue. Only those in danger of death were baptized without instruction. And this caused its own problems, since Native Americans drew a cause-and-effect relationship between baptism and the death of children.

But the European missionary did not rely solely on the word to convert to Christianity. The senses were brought into play as well. Music, elaborate rites and rituals, rich altar decor, rosaries, medals, all of the panoply of medieval European Christianity served not only as a spiritual bridge from the old to the new belief system but also a foundation for the new that the Native American could recognize as familiar. And the Native American needed all the help he could get because the demands of the new religion were extensive and intensive. That the shaman could be replaced by a hierarchical order of authority, descending from God, through the pope, and concluding with the priest was alien to a people with no hierarchical structure in their social lives. Marriage to one woman forever bordered on the absurd, as did the denial of the legitimacy of premarital sex. Choosing one, all-powerful God who had a son but not a father or mother over the traditional pantheon of Native American gods defied all reason. That more Native Americans did not backslide from their original acceptance of these tenets is more surprising.[65] But backslide they did. Apostates in Sinaloa leading the series of revolts in the seventeenth century used the rallying cry of a return to traditional religion and to old forms of social behavior.[66] However, by this time the economic elements of mine work and forced agricultural labor were thrown into the mix. The construction of churches, chapels, and regular visits from European missionaries gave the neophytes palpable evidence of continuity. Christianity was not a fly-by-night belief system but was in Sinaloa to stay.

Nevertheless, behind the evangelization process were the interests of the Spanish crown. It was in the Spanish government's interest that its New World subjects be docile and obedient. A corporate view of society required that they be Christian as well. The Indian was not oblivious to the benefits of siding with the conquerors. They were in Sinaloa to stay. And their religion went with them. The fact that the band of Spaniards, who in 1600–1601 roamed through the mountains of Sinaloa convincing the natives to cluster in larger villages and hand over their traditional gods, used economic inducements to achieve their ends does not negate the Native American sincerity. But the economic as well as psychological inducements were there.

It is difficult if not impossible to enter the minds of sixteenth-century Native Americans to try to discern motivation or sincerity in converting to Christianity. However, the quantity, quality, and continuity of institutional Christianity that persisted in Mexico indicate a lasting sincerity.

4

Conquest, Pacification, and Conversion

During the early years of the evangelization of Sinaloa, Europeans used two major tools to force the Native Americans to change religions. One was to demonstrate in as forceful a manner as possible the extinction of the old religion by physically destroying their traditional stone gods. The other was to move the Indian from a remote area to a nuclear settlement or larger village in order to facilitate administration or religious indoctrination.[1] The former was called the *extirpación de idolotría* and the latter, the *congregación de Indios*.

Andean Peru has become most associated with the *extirpación de idolotría* mainly because Pablo Joseph de Arriaga's widely known account is the major source for our understanding of the subject.[2] As well it should be. He explains in detail the role that the visitor should play in the *extirpación*, the methods he should use, their importance, and he makes no bones about the political as well as religious significance of the *extirpación*. But, in all likelihood, Arriaga's handbook, published in Lima in 1621, closely followed the methods that his Jesuit brethren used in Sinaloa in 1600. There, the methodology was much the same as that used in Peru decades later.

Robert Ricard pointed out the importance of the *congregaciones de Indios* in his classic study of the evangelization of Mexico.[3] In more recent times, Hanns Prem showed the importance of the *congregaciones* in his meticulous study of land transfers in colonial Puebla.[4] Both agreed that it was physically impossible for the evangelizers to post a friar in each remote village; better if hamlets united and formed one larger entity, making the process of indoctrination to the essentials of Christianity all that easier. As the scope of evangelization widened, from the core of Mexico City northward, the need for *congregaciones* became even more critical. Also at play, but to what degree is difficult if not impossible to measure, was the Western/Spanish attitude that considered the remote, rural hamlet as less civilized, less amenable to the civilizing effects of Christian evangelization. The Europeans who evangelized Sinaloa were for the most part urban bred and urban educated. They held a firm bias in favor of the city as the cultural, artistic, political, and religious center. For them, the agglomeration of villages was natural.

The importance of the *congregaciones* in the Hispanicization of the frontier is increased even further when they were linked to the attempt to root out all vestiges of the pre-Hispanic belief system. This was true of the mountainous region of Sinaloa where Jesuit missionaries began their own evangelization process at the turn of the sixteenth century.[5]

Fr. Alonso Santarén as the representative of the bishop, Capt. Diego de Avila, the *capitán pacificador*, Hernando de Silva, the chief bailiff (*alguacil*), and several soldiers spent February to December of 1600 visiting remote settlements principally of the Acaxe group and ordering them to resettle in predetermined villages.[6] The local Spanish *encomendero* of the Indians and the Indian caciques were made to cooperate in the enterprise that was called a *"Jornada, pacificación, y conversión."* Avila's orders that came directly from the viceroy of New Spain stated that he was to resettle and pacify. The Jesuits were to preach the gospel.

> In the valley of Minas Viejas de la Próspera at the foot of the mountain about a league from the Real de Minas of San Andrés on February 27, 1600, Diego de Avila, citizen and encomendero of this jurisdiction, said that with the Jesuits who have come to take the Indians from the mountains for their conversion, he has received a commission from the Viceroy of New Spain specifying that as Captain and Pacificador, he is to see to it that he lead them down to the regions where the Fathers can teach them about Christianity and that he settle them, pacify, and protect them. . . . And in fulfillment of what the Viceroy ordered the said Captain Pacificador and Fr. Hernando de Santarén, Rector of this mission, have begun by visiting the towns of the more Europeanized Indians and have instructed them in how important is was to be gathered on the level parts of the country so that Fr. Santarén and the others who are involved in the conversion

of the Indians can visit them in order to instruct them. As they are now, they live in the most rugged of terrains.[7]

Upon entering a village, Fr. Santarén and the Spaniards would first prostrate themselves before a cross they brought with them and then the priest would announce: "By virtue of the commission I have from the Bishop and the Superior of the Company of Jesus I take possession in the name of Holy Mother Church and of the Bishop of this Kingdom and I found here a Church for teaching Doctrine to the Indians who will live here and in the future dwell here."

The Indians were then summoned from the surrounding hamlets called *rancherías* and instructed about the move. First, they were to move their houses to the new site, each family choosing its own house site and farm land; second, they were to construct a church out of wood and palm within four weeks; and third, they were told of the advantages of the move: fish in the streams, proximity to the church for learning Christian doctrine, and for some, proximity to a place of employment (either large estates or mines) where they could work and earn a salary. "The said captain told the fathers of the Company of Jesus that it was very suitable to the service of Our Lord Jesus Christ and to the service of the king that the complete conversion of the people of this valley would be furthered if the many settlements they now live in could be merged into three large villages since now their settlements are outside of the usual routes and trails. This encourages their idolatry and drunkenness."[8]

After a few days a sacristan, called a *temestián*, was put in charge of the church, a bell and a statue were symbolically placed in the church if one had already been built, and after the missionary instructed the townspeople, the group of Spaniards moved on to the next site, repeating the process. "Fr. Santarén said mass and afterwards he baptized several children. He then asked for my testimony. He appointed a fiscal and a *temestián* for the Church then using the authority given him by the bishop, he named the church San Joan de Naspezes."[9]

Although we are led to believe that the process went smoothly and the Indians consented to their relocation, indications of active and passive opposition to the process suggest otherwise. Some Indian groups protested that they had no hatchets for cutting wood, so they could not construct churches. Others said that they really were not from that place but fell under the jurisdiction of another encomendero, so they could not move. Others simply agreed to the move but did nothing. The inhabitants of Coapa all came down to resettle but within two days scattered back into the mountains. Others said that "they did not want to attend doctrina classes nor to serve the Spaniards."[10]

Rewards were offered to encourage the hesitant and entice the indifferent. Knives, fish, cloth, salt, and hats were distributed to the Indians who resettled. Fear of punishment was also a motivator.

> And so the captain told them other things relating to good govern-
> ment, and he offered them gifts of woolens, knives, fish, salt, and
> other things like the Spaniards gave to Indians in other parts of the
> country because they had done well, and to those that did not, he
> would have to punish. The Indians said that they would comply.
> Also the said Captain and the fathers ordered the Indians to cut
> their hair because long hair was ugly and actually the said captain
> with his own hands cut their hair with scissors especially the *algua-*
> *ciles* and *alcaldes* because their example could influence others.[11]

If no church had been built or people resettled within six weeks, the te-mestián and the cacique were publicly lashed. This occurred in several places. In the town of Don Pedro, about twenty-four miles from San Martín, no church had been built, no Indians resettled, so Juanillo and Andrés each received five lashes with the warning that more would be administered if the church were not built and the people moved in thirty days.[12] The Indians argued that other Indians would attack them and destroy their crops if they acceded to the re-settlement program, as actually sometimes happened.[13]

Alternatively, many groups moved their houses without incident. Villagers chose land for *milpas* and were confirmed in them by Diego de Avila. In the town of Nazpeces, Santarén gathered two hundred fifty villagers and an-nounced that good firewood, good land, and plenty of water were available in the new site, so all the neighboring *rancherías* should gather to form a town. The *principales* and townsfolk agreed. Santarén and Avila gave the Indians who had gathered gifts of salt, knives, and cloth not only for themselves but also for those who had not come and needed convincing. *Alguaciles* and *alcaldes* were appointed by Avila.

Long hair remained a bone of contention between Spaniard and Indian. Because the Spaniards considered it inappropriate that an official should have long hair, Avila himself cut off the long locks of the new officials. The Euro-peans conducted a major campaign to have the men cut their hair. Long hair, they argued, "was only for women." In one town the Spaniards took it upon themselves to cut the Indians's hair, but no sooner had they done so than the Indians demanded hats to cover their shorn heads.[14]

Some Indian groups joined in the resettlement program voluntarily. On one occasion twenty Indians from the mountains appeared and asked to be part of a newly organized town.[15] The newly organized Indian towns were legally distinct from Spanish villages. Only baptized Christians could live in them. Spaniards were forbidden from entering the towns to impress Indian laborers. Nor could caciques from other villages enter these towns and command the Indians to do what they ordered. A fine of one hundred pesos for Spaniards and two hundred lashes for Indians were the penalties for contravention of these local regulations.

The relatively minor opposition that the Spaniards encountered in the *jornada* of resettlement is explicable for a number of reasons. Placing themselves on the side of the new conquerors meant that the Indians would receive food during times of famine, which almost always followed the epidemics that had become frequent with the arrival of the Europeans. During the epidemic itself the European priests cared for the ill and sometimes that care resulted in cure.[16] Therefore, it was advantageous to choose the Christian priest as the more powerful shaman. Joining the Europeans also meant protection from traditional enemies. The Spaniards were quick to retaliate against attacks on Christian converts.

Santarén and his band resettled at least four thousand Indians in 1600. Some of the hamlets were so large that two or three new villages were formed out of one hamlet. To each new settlement were attached lands "granted" by the Spaniards to each family or individual. The grant was called a *merced*, but there is no record of individual titles going along with the land distribution. This increased the possibility of future land litigation but also may have been based on traditional landholding rights and usage.

The Uprooting of Idolotry

During their march through the Acaxe country, Santarén and Avila uncovered what for them was a surprising number of Indians practicing the old religion. The Jesuit and the captain felt it their duty to root out the practices that they believed allowed Satan to maintain a hold on the Indian mind. Friendly persuasion was not in their bag of motivational tricks. Physical punishment and in at least one case, execution, was the order of the day. The Spaniards offered no apology for their actions. They answered to a higher order of being. The operation of this mini-inquisition and the sustained terror it spread through a relatively minor region of New Spain's frontier is an excellent example of how church-state worked hand in glove during the post-conquest years. It was Capt. Avila's purpose to intimidate so as to control the native population. Fr. Santarén's goal was to Christianize the Indians. Avila's intimidation persuaded the Indians to accept Santarén's new belief system—two sides of the same coin, the Spaniards felt. Jesuit records refer to this aspect of the resettlement as the "*Extirpación de Idolatría*," the uprooting of idolatry, a first step before beginning the study of Christian doctrine.

The Spaniards discovered stone sculptures of human heads, horned figures, anthropomorphic figures that might have represented gods or petitions of prayer.

> In the town of Naspezes on December 7 of the said year Captain Diego de Avila and Fr. Hernando de Santarén of the Company of Jesus made all the appropriate due diligence inquiring with care and ingenuity among the Indians where, how, and who possessed idols and bones and who encouraged idolatry so that they could demolish the cult and adoration of the devil and exault that of Christ Our God and Lord. One settlement had a huge number of bones which the Captain and fathers ordered to be carried down to them. They were. Three Indians carried them down on their backs. The bones were from heads of human beings, many shinbones, bones from hands and fingers, ribs, and shoulders. There was a problem when they asked for more bones and idols because an old man steeped in his idolatry received four stripes before handing over the bones he had, namely heads, shinbones, hands and human fingers.[17]

The stone figures may not even have been gods but representations of friends or ancestors.[18] Santarén and Avila, however, were certain that they represented the cult of the devil that had to be replaced by the cult of Christ.[19]

On December 7, 1600, both Santarén and Avila questioned the inhabitants of Nazpeces about who owned and where either idols or piles of bones that were adored by the townsfolk were hidden. With the help of three Indians, Santarén dragged skulls and bones of fingers, arms, and legs out of houses into a pile in the center of the village. One elderly Indian had a pile of ancestral bones in his house that he refused to part with. Then and there Santarén ordered a Spanish soldier to give the man four lashes. The idols, the Jesuits reported, were like dolls carved out of stone. The Indians offered these idols corn, beans, and other foods. The pile in the village center grew and when the Spaniards thought they had collected everything, they broke the bones and idols into pieces, dumped them onto a raging fire, and made the Indians watch their gods become dust.[20] The purpose was to demonstrate how helpless the Indian gods were in the face of the Christian deity. On occasion, Santarén would preach while the fire raged and the gods were being destroyed.

Some stone figures were wrapped in cloth. Once unwrapped they had the appearance of a human figure, but without eyes. One god the Indians called

Tecajuatl. The Spaniards also learned that there were gods of the air, of the water, the fields, "and other superstitious beliefs." One god had the head of a lion (jaguar), another of an eagle. The god of the fields (*milpas*) was given the first fruits of the harvest, and the Indians would dance around the statue and touch it.[21] The Spaniards learned that the Indian gods embodied nature and all its manifestations.

The Spanish attempt to root out the old religion created internal divisions within Indian communities, thus weakening the resolve and fabric of native society. An informant from San Jerónimo, named Gaspar, made the Spaniards promise not to reveal his name "because the people would hate him and want to kill him."[22] To counter such fears, the caciques of each village were offered rewards if they revealed where the idols were hidden. Christian Indians whether out of zeal or a desire to curry favor with the Spaniards were quick to lead Santarén and Avila to the hiding places of the gods. In the town of San Martín one Indian named Pedro Hernández came before Santarén and Avila and said that in compliance with the decree he and another Indian named Turbano along with two others who were *"gentiles bárbaros"* found idols in the remote hiding places of the *ranchería*. They were made of stone but had no distinctive features. The idols were adored like gods.[23] The Spaniards must have made a public announcement upon their arrival at this site of idol storage, which resulted in Indians scurrying to either settle old scores or publicly demonstrate their new loyalty to the Spaniards. This Mexican equivalent of a Salem witchhunt must have deepened the chasm between Christian and pagan. The adherents of the old gods and religion must have seen that the only option left to them was flight. The mumblings of an old lady struck no sympathetic cord in Santarén. "For all the idols that you and the Captain destroyed and burned, you have angered God and you have angered our enemies the Xiximes and the Guapixuxe. They will swoop down on us and destroy us."[24]

The native religious leaders, called *hechiceros* by the Spaniards, countered the Christian attack by saying that as soon as the Christians would find out where the gods were kept and remove them, all the people would die.[25] According to the Jesuit account, the *hechicero* as loyal servant of the devil was responsible for all the revolts and obstacles put into the missionaries's path. The *hechiceros* were in league against the missionaries and guarded their secrets so carefully that not even the Catholic priests or Captain Avila understood what they were about. They spread the rumor that death would surely follow for anyone who accepted baptism. Only infrequently were they confronted successfully. In one town the villagers paid a *hechicero* to make it rain. Instead, a Jesuit reported with satisfaction that Our Lord caused a dry spell to envelop the land. Only when a Christian procession was held did the rains come.[26]

The missionaries realized that the presence of the *hechicero* was a major obstacle to spreading Christianity. But they also realized that the minds and hearts of the Indian were not going to be won by a wholesale roundup and elimination of the *hechicero*. He had to be discredited and he was, mainly during the times of disease and famine when only the new "shamans" of Christianity displayed any power over sickness and the ability to supply food. One *hechicero* was executed by the Spaniards. According to records, this was a middle-aged man called Taxicora who was venerated by the Indians. He rode a horse with spear in hand and announced to the Indians that they should not fear the captain or his soldiers. He had the reputation of speaking with the devil. He was a threat to the Christian missionaries, so in 1601 "he was hung and he was kept on the gibbet to convince others he was mortal."[27]

The assault on the native religion and way of life during the jornada of 1600 illustrates the European intention not only of replacing native religion with Christianity but also of recasting the Indian mind. Resettlement, indoctrination, and appointing village officials based on the new religious and cultural criteria, which included cutting hair, wearing European clothes, organizing fiestas, holding Mass and confession, and working for a salary were elements of the new way that combined the essentials of Christianity with the accidental, but in the minds of the European were integral to what a civilized person should believe and how he should behave.

The importance of the *congregaciones* and *the extirpación de idolatría* goes beyond conversion to Christianity. They represent the attempt to change not only a belief system but fixed, traditional ways of behaving. The attempt was based on a Renaissance-like certainty: The European was certain that his way was the right way, that he was God's instrument in acting thusly, that his civilization had arrived at the pinnacle of cognition, that wisdom, knowledge, and proficiency were his. And now the supreme authority, God, had placed in European hands the power to change the world, or at the least, change Sinaloa.

5

Julí: Utopia or Theocracy

The European missionary carried with him to Peru in 1568 fixed notions about religion, God, and how a belief system linked ordinary
people to the divine. In attempting to characterize Andean religion,
early chroniclers tried to identify which Andean gods had been confused with the Christian hierarchy and which with the Hebrew one.[1]
By the time the Jesuits arrived, this early attempt at syncretism had
been replaced by a more truculent view. Andean gods were simply
manifestations of the devil, native priests were Satan's ministers,
and Huarochirí, the first Jesuit mission in the Andes, was labeled
the "Cathedral of Idolatry."[2]

Xulí of the Andes

The first contingent of eight Jesuits arrived in Callao, the port of
Lima, on March 28, 1568.[3] By then the conquest of Peru was history, the civil wars had subsided, and royal rule was very much in
evidence. The government bureaucracy was functioning, and the city
of Lima, grandiosely named by Francisco Pizarro the City of Kings,
was growing with each shipload of Spanish immigrants that docked
in Callao. When the Jesuits arrived, the city was in the throes of one
of its perennial food shortages. Lodgings were limited so the Jesuits
moved in with the Dominicans until quarters of their own were arranged, as they were within a few months.

In the immediate years after their arrival the Jesuits placed strong emphasis on catechetical work with Indians and blacks in Lima. Each day, a group of Jesuits would leave their house and walk through the streets of Lima with bell ringing and cross uplifted to attract a crowd. Nor was rural Peru neglected. In 1571 five priests and three brothers began evangelizing the village of Huarochirí, about seventy miles southeast of Lima, in the Andes Mountains. But the mission proved disastrous to the assigned personnel; two priests died and the health of two others was broken. Huarochirí was abandoned. The Jesuits changed the thrust of their work from rural missions and work with Indians to urban-centered education emanating from colleges.

Two reasons account for the change. For one, the Jesuits divided the viceroyalty of Peru into four zones: the New Kingdom of Granada and Quito was one zone, Charcas another, Chile a third, and Peru, the central part of the viceroyalty, was the fourth zone. The Jesuits of Peru were left with the area from Trujillo to Arequipa, a coastal zone with a heavy concentration of Spaniards. A second reason why they concentrated on colleges was that two extremely influential members of the order thought that they should not commit themselves so heavily to mission work. José de Acosta, the scholarly author of *De procuranda indorum salute* (1576), who was the Jesuit provincial superior in Peru from 1576 to 1581, bitterly criticized the Jesuit province as a whole for permitting so many of its men to tramp around as "holy vagabonds." Acosta wrote that if the Jesuits were going to make a lasting contribution to the church in Peru, it would be through scholarship and schools. Otherwise, he wrote, the Jesuit province would become a province of idiots. His colleague, Diego Alvarez de Paz, agreed. In a letter of 1601 to the Jesuit superior general in Rome, he wrote that Peru needed good administrators, learned men with academic degrees, and excellent preachers. Such men were not nurtured, he continued, by wandering through the mountains in search of Indians but in the silence of their studies.[4]

After 1600, colleges became the major Jesuit apostolate in Peru where students learned Latin, philosophy, theology, and literature. Missions to the Indians and parish work became a secondary activity of a relatively small group of Jesuits. Through the seventeenth and eighteenth centuries, the number of Jesuits and their colleges steadily increased from 282 Jesuits with eight colleges in 1601 to 542 Jesuits with fifteen colleges in 1754.

One notable exception to the emphasis on colleges was the mission of Julí, a village on the windswept Andean altiplano, the high plateau at 12,500 feet above sea level, 15 degrees latitude south of the equator, 180 miles southeast of Cuzco on the shores of Lake Titicaca. Here the Jesuits established what was to be their only exclusively Indian mission in the Andes. It began in 1576 and was relinquished only at their expulsion from Peru in 1767.[5]

The year the Jesuits arrived in Peru, Garci Diez de San Miguel, a government official, wrote to Philip II asking that Jesuits be sent to Julí on Lake Titicaca.[6] Julí had been a thriving village before the Spaniards arrived and it was still the most populous village in the province of Chucuito. The potato was its major crop although by the end of the sixteenth century their scarcity was being blamed on the coldness of the region rather than on the loss of the pre-Inca technology that enabled the Aymara to grow bumper potato crops. The Aymara had used raised fields called *suka kollus*, earth platforms about ten to twenty feet in width, three-hundred feet long. During the day the water-filled canals captured the sunlight and when the temperature dropped at night, the waters in the canals formed a mist over the fields like a warming blanket. The water was drawn up into the soil platform heating the roots of the tubers. This technology had been abandoned, possibly for lack of workers who had been resettled or taken away by the Incas who ruled the region from 1438 to 1532. According to Diez de San Miguel who wrote around 1567, the people of Julí were not being properly evangelized. The future Jesuit mission in Julí was far from Lima but it was a key crossroads town linking the flourishing silver mine of Potosí in modern Bolivia with Cuzco and the port city of Lima. Julí would be a key supplier of Indian laborers.

From June to September the hills surrounding Lake Titicaca turn a desiccated brown. No grass grows so llama and vicuña pastures are distant. Lake fish are not abundant. Firewood is scarce. In January steady rains begin to fall but die out by April. Nights are bitterly cold. Despite the harsh living conditions the Aymara Indians in 1576 numbered about fifteen thousand souls.[7] It was this large Indian population that attracted the Jesuits to the area.

In October 1576 the Jesuits of Peru gathered in Cuzco to hold their first Provincial Congregation. They decided to accept Julí as their first purely Indian ministry. Several reasons were behind the choice. First, the government pressured them to choose some form of Indian parish ministry. After leaving Huarochirí, the Jesuits returned to Lima and began to work with the Indians in Cercado. They even put up a mud wall around the place to keep Spaniards out; hence, the name Cercado, or walled-in area. Second, Cercado had ceased to be primarily a ministry to the Indians. Soon the Jesuits put a novitiate there; then a school for the sons of Indian *kurakas* called the Colegio del Príncipe; then the Casa de Santa Cruz, a prison for recalcitrant *hechiceros*, both priests and "idol worshipers"; and then the Jesuits located in Cercado the house of Final Formation for Jesuit priests called the Tertianship, all by 1576. Both the viceroy of Peru, Francisco de Toledo, supported by Philip II, insisted that the Jesuits take up a purely Indian ministry in the Andes. And both Jesuits and Viceroy Toledo chose Julí.[8]

The Spanish government considered the Indians of Julí as different. They were Crown Indians, which meant that no Spanish encomendero could collect taxes from them or recruit them for labor. Francisco de Toledo's regulations for the organization of towns, designed to make evangelization and tax collecting more efficient, ordered the resettlement of Indians from smaller, isolated villages into larger, more populated towns. Villages around Julí were grouped into settlements and Julí itself was to have a church, the priest's residence, municipality, and jail.[9]

The Jesuits added their own spin to Toledo's regulations. Julí was declared an Indian town, a *pueblo de los Indios*, which meant that no Spaniard other than a missionary could live there. The anonymous Jesuit chronicler who wrote about Julí in 1600 listed five reasons for keeping Spaniards, the *polilla de los indios* (the parasites of the Indians) he called them, away from the Indians: they take Indians away from their farms; steal their property; abscond with wives and daughters; cheat the Indians; and sell them bad wine, rotten coca, and putrid flour for drunken orgies. The Jesuits would also prevent Indian governors from drafting Indians for labor, and they would reduce the number of Indians taken for the mine of Potosí. The mine, said the chronicler, was the killer and graveyard of Peru.[10]

Allowing for the self-serving nature of the chronicler's statements, they have a ring of truth to them. But in preventing other Spaniards from living in Julí, the Jesuits were accused of exploiting the native population for their own benefit.[11] Were the white conquerors simply squabbling over the spoils of conquest?

In 1576 the Jesuits found in Julí a typical Andean village. During the reign of the Incas in the fourteenth century, all of the Aymara hilltop villages on the western lakeshore were resettled to form the six *cabecera* sites of which Julí was the largest. The nearby raised-field complexes were abandoned.[12] The houses in Julí were in an orthogonal grid pattern with thatched roofs and mud walls. The fields where the potatoes grew were within walking distance but the pasturage for the llamas and alpacas was farther away. Recently discovered ridged fields indicate that the Lake Titicaca basin had sustained a population much larger than what the Jesuits found in 1576.[13] But by the time they arrived, a massive population decline was occurring. In 1567 Garci Diez de San Miguel estimated the total Aymara population around Lake Titicaca to be 117,230 souls, down 59 percent from the population in pre-Spanish times. It would decline even further. By 1620 the population had fallen another 39 percent.[14] Old World pathogens, population displacement, death in the Potosí mine (what the anonymous chronicler called the graveyard of Peru), and fleeing mine work in Potosí, all contributed to the decline.[15] In an Andean society in disarray, the Jesuits set about establishing a new order of political and religious priorities.

Socioreligious Structures

The height, size, and decorative quality of the Jesuit structures in Julí stood out in a village landscape formed for the most part of one-story homes. The high Inca fortification walls and the Lupaqa burial towers had been dismantled and even the Inca buildings on the Island of the Moon were disassembled and their masonry blocks were used for the church construction in Julí.[16] The church design was simple but the interiors were filled with statues and paintings designed in part to astound and instruct the populace. In Latin America in general, one function of Jesuit rural churches, residences, and hacienda structures was that of a "power house," a showcase, an image-maker displaying concrete evidence of power, the church militant and triumphant. The structures may not have been seen as such by the Jesuits themselves, but they were so interpreted by Spanish settlers and Indians.[17]

In Julí the large church, the Jesuit residence, and a hospital conveyed the idea of both permanence and strength. The conquerors and their religion were there to stay. In Mexico the Spaniards constructed their cathedral on top of the old Aztec temple, and not by chance. The symbolism was not lost on the Indians. The physical edifice illustrated the replacement of the old religion by the new—*mutatis mutandis*, the same psychology was at work in the Andes.

The Jesuits occupied the old Dominican church in the center of Julí. The houses in Julí were small, with rectangular rooms, gabled roofs thatched with straw supported by wooden posts, with an opening for smoke and ventilation.[18] Close by the church was the hospital with two wards. In both were beds with mattresses and blankets for sick Indians. A separate room housed Spaniards. The Jesuit chronicler wrote in 1600 that hospitals in Peru were commonly called "Death Houses" and Indians never wanted to enter them. Julí, he wrote, was different. They actually asked to be admitted and they left cured![19]

Not so in 1604. A lethal epidemic called the *tabardillo*, probably spotted fever, swept through Julí.[20] The Jesuit report for that year said that not one Indian home was spared. The hospital was filled to capacity so the Jesuits visited the sick in their homes and buried the dead. The Indian must have wondered why the Europeans were not affected by the illness. The hospital had medicine, preserves, and what was considered necessary to care for the sick.[21] But neither Indian nor Jesuit knew that antibodies were present in the European immune system that had not yet developed in the Indian. Instead, the believed reason why the Jesuits did not succumb was the strength of their God and their religion, a powerful incentive to conversion used effectively in Mexico.[22]

The church and the hospital represented two traditional activities of the Jesuits in the New World. The church became a focal point for Indian socio-religious activity just as the *huaca* (religious shrine), the plaza, and the *kalanka* had been in pre-Colombian times. Modern archaeologists have identified the not-so-haphazard configuration of houses in pre-colonial Julí.[23] The plaza that was a center of commercial activity in Inca times remained so during the Spanish colonial period. The orthogonal grid pattern remained. The large main church erected before 1576 when the Dominicans were in Julí faced Lake Titicaca and in front of it was the large plaza where buying and selling vegetables, coca, llamas, and vicuñas took place. The town was heavily populated since Julí had the densest Indian population in the region during the Inca period. Why this was remains a mystery. Perhaps because Julí was on the main Inca road, or because it was one of the seven equidistant Lupaqa towns, called the *Lupaqa cabeseras*. The Indians were used to gathering in the plaza so on Sundays and holy days a Jesuit would preach there. José de Acosta said that at fiesta time nine thousand Indians would gather in the plaza to hear sermons, watch the dancing, and listen to the music. They also came for food.

The distribution of food as alms, called a *limosna*, became a standard practice outside of the Jesuit church in Julí. In 1597 food was distributed only on Sunday but by 1599 it was distributed daily. In 1599 a total of two thousand pesos was spent for food for the poor throughout the year. By 1603 this sum had risen to five thousand pesos a year.[24] Each week about one hundred fifty pounds. of meat was doled out and many llamas (which the reports call *carneros*) were distributed to the Indians going to work in the mine of Potosí.[25] Recipients of corn, potatoes, and meat were not only from Julí but those passing through, the *pasajeros*. In 1597 so many requested assistance from the Jesuits that one of the fathers was appointed to be the *limosnero*, the almsgiver, and a list of three hundred fifty Indians requesting food was compiled. The corn and potatoes was distributed in proportion to the size of the family.[26] A large storehouse was constructed sometime before 1600 in which corn, potatoes, and some vegetables were stocked to provide Indians with food in case of severe shortages or actual famine.

The reason for the inability of the Native Americans to support themselves was laid at the doorstep of the Indians themselves. "A great lack of food," and "Indian poverty" was never explained. The disruptions of the region's economic life, the shift to a partial wage-earning economy, loss of lands, and destruction of traditional economic structures were not mentioned in the Jesuit reports. Out of a total of around nine thousand Indians in Julí at least 12 percent could not feed themselves. The ridged fields that had supported a larger Indian population had disappeared before the arrival of the Spaniards, even before the Incas arrived on the scene in the 1400s. The Aymara population that the Incas had massed at Julí entered an economic wilderness when Inca domination ceased. The food shortage helped to enhance the reputation of the Jesuit missionaries who fed the hungry. "What shines in the eyes of all and what the Indians hold dear, is the frequent and massive alms that the fathers of Julí give to the Indians," wrote the anonymous chronicler in 1600.[27]

The church building was intended to replace the Indian shrine, the *huaca*, the key element in the socioreligious lives of the Aymara. Associated with the church were activities designed to demonstrate adherence to the new religion. In Julí the Jesuits ran four parishes, Santo Tomás, the largest; San Juan Bautista; San Pedro; and Nuestra Señora. On Sundays one of the priests would preach a sermon in the church. The church was also the scene of large gatherings of Indian children learning prayers and catechism. Singing lessons for the church choirs and instruction in musical instruments took place in the afternoon.[28] In 1579 upward of three hundred sons of kurakas and native nobles studied reading and writing in the church school.[29]

Just as the church structure was supposed to replace the *huaca*, so the hospital was designed to undercut the powers of the *yañca* or native priest. Illnesses were attended to in the hospital not by extricating the spirits within the body that caused them but by personal care, medicine, and special foods. The deadly epidemic of 1589–1590 was especially devastating. Smallpox (*viruelas*) and measles (*serampión*) swept through Quito, the Peruvian coastal valleys, and the highlands. The government in Lima urged encomenderos to give Indians sugar, raisins, oil, and barley to strengthen their bodies. The sick were to be isolated in churches and hospitals. The nonfeverish ill were to be fed lamb, chicken, goat, vegetables; the feverish were allowed only barley, sugar, raisins, and vegetables, but no meat. Bloodletting was to be performed three or four times daily. Those recovering could have meat, wine, cold water, and corn liquor. But they were to be kept out of drafts and away from the wind. Sores in the throat were to be swabbed with a mixture of vinegar, sugar, and barley. The clothes of the infected were burned or cleaned in boiling water.[30]

These weapons were in themselves useless against killer epidemic disease but when attached to personal care they were effective. Reff has shown that victims of epidemics in sixteenth-century Northern Mexico had significantly higher survival rates if given basic personal care.[31] The sight of the Jesuits in

Julí visiting the homes of the sick and caring for the ill in the hospital helped to solidify the Indian concept of the missionary as possessor of authority over sickness. He was a person of service as well as power.

The central rite of the Roman Catholic Church was the Mass during which the celebrant priest was clothed in colorful garments and accoutrements, moved left and right and around the altar almost as if performing a ritualized dance, and employed a mysterious, unintelligible language. The rite occurred within the church confines, within the sacred space dedicated to sacred activities. Devotions, prayers, and instruction also took place within this space. The Spanish missionaries attempted to transfer the focus of religious activity to a physical structure symbolizing the divine among humankind.

What resonated deeply among the Aymara of Julí was the formation of elite groups within the parish body. The Jesuits created in Julí *cofradías*, loosely translated as religious brotherhoods. They were sometimes called *congregaciones*. Just as the Indian could relate to a sacred space, a ritualized religious service, mystically endowed words, and an elite group of priests having close ties to the divine, so too the Aymara could resonate with the formation of groups made up of elite members of the new religion. Becoming a member of a *cofradía* was a way of separating oneself from the ordinary parishioner, a way to acquire prestige that may not have been available under the old social organization, and a means of acquiring social ranking in association with the conquerors. A great deal of rivalry existed over admission to and participation in *cofradía* activity.

The Jesuits in Julí established three *cofradías* by 1597. One was called the Nombre de Jesús, another the Santísimo, and a third Nuestra Señora. By 1604 the Nombre de Jesús group had six hundred members and was ordinarily referred to as the Cofradía de los Caciques. Each group had a distinct pious function. The Cofradía del Nombre de Jesús, considered the most pious, emphasized frequent Holy Communion, which meant receiving Communion at least once every two or three months. Each *cofradía* met monthly as a group, worshiped as a group on specific days, and walked together in religious processions with wax candle in hand.[32] A *cofradía* assisted in the distribution of food on Sundays and another visited the sick in hospitals. Being a member of a *cofradía* was a distinction that grew into a mark of honor. Indians who were not members of *cofradías*, stated the Annual Letter of 1610, were not considered reputable, nor were they thought highly of.[33] The *cofradía* was a European-inspired institution used by the Jesuits throughout Latin America to unify disparate groups within a parish. A secondary effect was to ease the transition from the Indian to the European religious system. They were mechanisms drawing the Indian into a colonial system possessing recognizable features that the Indian could relate to and accept.

The Jesuits also used the mission residence of Julí as a language school. It was here that the newly arrived priest or brother would spend several months mastering Quechua or Aymara before being permitted to minister to the Indians, whether in colleges along the coast or permanently in Julí. The grammar text used in Julí for learning Aymara was Luis Bertonio's *Vocabulario de la Lengua Aymara*.[34] By 1600 the Jesuit superiors in Lima realized that living in colleges and dealing only with Spaniards, whether Jesuit or lay, made learning the native languages difficult. In Julí those learning languages were focused solely on that task. The goal was to be able to preach, hear confessions, and converse in understandable Quechua or Aymara. The writer of the anonymous report of 1600 said that "with moderate application and no great talent for languages, one can acquire a speaking knowledge of Aymara or Quechua in a few months."[35]

The mission at Julí of the Andes functioned as Jesuit residence, language school, parish, and experimental mission station. The European missionaries applied a vertical approach to their activity. Social work, religious indoctrination, contact with Indians, as well as the Indians' political and economic lives were influenced wholly or in part by the missionary. However, the European agent of religious change faced a major obstacle when he tried to eradicate the traditional Andean religion from the lives of the Aymara. Try as they might, the missionaries could not make their gods go away.

Doctrina Christiana

The gauge by which the Jesuit missionaries in Julí measured whether the Indians were progressing toward the formation of a true Christian community was their knowledge, understanding, and application of the *Doctrina Christiana*. The *Doctrina* was a compendium of the Roman Catholic belief system. The tome, which contained these essential tenets of the Roman Catholic Church, became the most useful handbook of the European missionary. In 1539 a printing press in Mexico turned out the first printed copy of the *Doctrina*. In 1557 Goa produced one for the Portuguese missionaries in India, and in 1584 the printing house of the Hernandez Brothers in Lima, Peru, published a *Doctrina Christiana y Catecismo para Instrucción de los Indios*.[36] The *Doctrina* was a bilingual text, with Spanish and an indigenous language side by side. Aymara was the Indian language of the 1584 Lima edition.

When Fr. Pablo José de Arriaga wrote the Annual Letter from Lima in 1597, he emphasized that the *"doctrina y catechismo"* were explained every afternoon in Julí.[37] Arriaga could have been referring to the book *Doctrina y Catechismo*, or possibly he was making the distinction between the Prayers, Articles of Faith, Commandments, Sacraments, Sins, Works of Charity part of the book and that part containing Questions and Answers—similar to the old-fashioned Baltimore Catechism used for decades by American Catholics. Whichever he meant, one was not considered of less importance than the other. Each part was memorized and repeated again and again. Repetition was considered the key to learning. The anonymous chronicler of the Jesuits in Julí even wrote that the Indians of Julí knew more intricate theological points than many European theologians. "Rare is the Indian in Julí," continued the chronicler, "who does not know his prayers, catechism, and mysteries of the faith."[38] What were these prayers and mysteries that were considered essential? Did they resonate with the Indian of Julí, and if so, why?

The *Doctrina Christiana* was divided into prayers, articles of belief, and questions and answers. The first prayer learned by the Indian was the Our Father, the *Padre Nuestro*. According to the Christian priests, the Creator God was the source of all life on earth, and he possessed all the attributes of a father. He loved, cared for, and nourished what he brought into existence. Just as Tuñupa gave life to the dry earth by sending the rains, so the Creator God of the Europeans was the origin of all living things.[39] He dwelled where the Indian divinities lived, in the sky. From here came the commands when to plant, when to harvest, when to begin the rituals.[40] It was natural that the Creator God dwelled there. The Andean could understand and accept that honor and homage should be paid him. He ruled and his will was supreme. The Creator God sent the rains that provided the maize and papas, the "daily bread." Forgiveness for failure to do his will came only from him and only he could provide the strength to overcome evil. All of the major theological elements in the Our Father found a comfortable acceptance in the Andean mind.

The second and third prayers taught to the Indian honored the Virgin Mary, who had taken a prominent place in Spanish Catholicism from the time of the early Middle Ages. The Hail Mary and *Salve Regina* placed the Virgin Mary in the position of mediator between the Creator God and man. Andean anthropomorphism allowed their divinities to take human form so the function of an intermediary through whom God becomes human was not illogical. In these two popular prayers Mary is invoked as the advocate, the champion, the supporter. The Spanish translation of the Latin word *advocata* was *abogada*, lawyer. The Aymara word used was *taluma* or one who fights for another. In the popular mind, Mary became a goddess with power to influence the Creator God.

Following the Hail Mary was the Creed, a statement of belief epitomizing the wide range of Christian dogma. For the Indians of Julí, the notion of God taking a human form, as emphasized in the Creed, dying at the hands of other humans, then rising from the dead was a magnificent story that paralleled their own notions of a god become man. All the missionary added was the idea of the necessity in believing in the Holy Catholic Faith which the Creed proclaimed. The forgiveness of transgressions through confession was also part of the Indian's ancient belief system, as was the promise of another life in another world. The Christian Creed reinforced some very old ideas.

Next came the articles of faith, fourteen terse statements reiterating what were contained in the basic prayers and Creed. Seven belonged to the divinity of God, and seven to Christ's humanity.

1. There is only one All-powerful God.
2. The Father is God.
3. The Son is God.
4. The Holy Spirit is God.
5. God is the Creator.
6. He is the Savior.
7. He is the glorifier.

1. Christ was conceived by the work of the Holy Spirit.
2. Christ was born from the virginal womb of Mary, who was a virgin before, during, and after Christ's birth.
3. Christ suffered and died to save us sinners.
4. After dying, he descended into hell where he claimed the souls of the holy fathers who were awaiting his coming.
5. After three days Christ rose from the dead.
6. Christ rose into the heavens and sat at the right side of God the Father, All-powerful.
7. He will come again to judge the living and the dead; the good will enjoy his glory because they kept his commandments, the bad will suffer because they did not keep his commandments. Amen.

The articles of faith were alternate ways of expressing concepts about God's interaction with the human race that were already contained in the prayers that the Indian had learned.

The Ten Commandments were followed by the five commandments of the church, theoretically the logical consequence of the former. The church commandments enjoined the Indian to attend Mass on Sundays and on feast days, to go to confession once a year, to receive Communion during the Easter season, to fast at the appointed times, and to pay tithes.

The seven sacraments were part of the essential elements of Roman Catholic belief, essential because they were the ordinary vehicles through which God worked to sanctify the Indian. Matrimony caused the Jesuits the most problems. Polygamy among the ruling class of Indian society had been common, incest not uncommon, so the European missionaries saw inculcating the notion that Christ instituted marriage between two adults and relations outside of marriage were forbidden, as daunting tasks.[41] The ideas of confession and Communion were easily embraced because a type of confession was already practiced and the idea of consuming God in the form of bread was a step beyond offerings of *chicha* and *coca* in the *huacas*. The Christian sacrament of Holy Orders was perfectly acceptable to a people used to a ranked clergy caring for the major temples in Cuzco and who were also accustomed to lesser ranked priests who made divinations, presided over sacrifices, and cured the ill.

Following the seven sacraments in the *Doctrina Christiana* were the works of mercy, both corporal and spiritual. Visiting the sick, feeding the hungry, and giving drink to the thirsty made sense, but redeeming captives probably did not. Clothing the naked, housing the pilgrim, and burying the dead were recommendations that required explanations.[42]

The confession, *la confesión*, of having committed sin by thought, word, and deed before God, the Virgin, the saints, and all mankind was the last of the prayers required to be learned by the neophyte. In this prayer, an acknowledgment is made that sin has both spiritual and social consequences, that not only is God offended but in some way the Christian body is affected as well, so the Christian body is asked to intercede before God in behalf of the penitent.

Catechism questions and answers conclude the *Doctrina Christiana*. These summarize the beliefs contained in the *Doctrina*.

Q. Are you a Christian?   A. Yes, by the mercy of God.

Q. Who is a Christian?   A. A baptized person who believes what God and Holy Mother Church teaches.

Q. What is the sign of a Christian?   A. The Holy Cross.

Q. Whom do Christians adore?   A. Our Lord God.

Q. Who is God?   A. The first cause; the beginning of all things; He who made all things, and He who has neither beginning nor end.

Q. How many Gods are there?   A. Only one God.

Q. How many persons?

A. Three.

Q. Who is the First Person?

A. God the Father.

Q. Who is the Second?

A. God the Son.

Q. Who is the Third?

A. God the Holy Spirit.

Q. Are there three Gods?

A. There are not three Gods. The persons are three, and only one God.

Q. Which of the three became a man?

A. The Second person, the Son.

Q. How did he become a man?

A. Through the work of the Holy Spirit in the womb of Holy Mary, a virgin before and after the birth.

Q. Why did he become a man?

A. To free all men from their sins.

Q. What were the sins of men?

A. The sins of our first parents, Adam and Eve, and the sins we commit daily.

Q. How did he free mankind?

A. He died on the cross and took upon himself the sins of all mankind.

Q. After his death, what did the soul of Jesus Christ do?

A. The soul and the divinity descended to Hell and took up to heaven the souls of the Holy Fathers who were awaiting his coming.

Q. Was the body of Jesus Christ buried?

A. Yes.

Q. Did it rise?

A. Yes.

Q. When?

A. On the third day after his death.

Q. Did Our Lord Jesus Christ remain on earth?

A. No. After 40 days he rose up to heaven and is seated at the right hand of the father almighty.

Q. What role does he have in heaven?

A. The most advantageous of all.

Q. Will he one day judge the living and the dead?

A. Yes.

Q. When?

A. We do not know.

Q. Does man's soul perish with death?

A. The soul does not die with the body as takes place with other animals. Only the body dies and the soul lives forever.

Q. Do good and bad come to live again?

A. They do and the body is joined with the soul to be judged by Christ Our Lord.

Q. After the final resurrection of the body, will they die again?

A. No.

Q. What will God give to the good as their reward?

A. The glory of heaven to enjoy forever.

Q. What punishment will God give the bad?

A. He will condemn them to hell to suffer pains forever.

Q. What is the Holy Church?

A. The Church is made up of all Christians who believe in God, together with their head Jesus Christ who is in heaven, and his vicar on earth the Pope in Rome.

Q. In this Holy Church are there things that take away sins?

A. Yes.

Q. What are they?

A. Baptism and Confession if one is truly repentant and desires never to sin again.

Q. In this Holy Church is there the Communion of Saints?

A. Yes.

Q. What is the Communion of Saints?

A. The participation of good Christians in good works and the sacraments.

Q. Who is in the host that the priest raises up at Mass for adoration?

A. Jesus Christ Our Lord God and true man as he is in heaven.

Q. Who is in the chalice?

A. The true blood of Jesus Christ that he shed on the cross.

Q. What does the Christian have to do to be saved?

A. The Christian has to observe the Ten Commandments of God and those of Holy Mother Church.

The *Doctrina Christiana* was the most useful weapon in the quiver of the European missionary. Putting its contents to memory was an obligation that fell to each member of the Indian community. Its repetition proved to the Jesuits in Julí that the Christian was indeed serious about his or her new religion. Reciting Christian doctrine, however, was the first step. The number of communions taken, the number of confessions heard, the number of baptisms and marriages performed, as well as the activity of the *cofradías* in visiting the sick and burying the dead were meticulously recorded yearly as a measure of the increased religiosity of the parishes in Julí.

The Jesuit missionaries emphasized the elements of Christianity that resonated with the Aymara. Confession, the cult of the saints, the power of God the Father, Mary the Intercessor, the mysterious rites of the sacraments, the hierarchy of the Christian priesthood, God become Man through a virgin, were marvelous stories that the Indian in some form was already acquainted with. The missionary decorated the central sites of worship with statues and iconography that the Indian could relate to. The churches in Julí were complete with transepts while the ceilings and walls were splashed with color.[43] The Indian like the Spaniard preferred the concrete to the abstract. Not too much concern was given to explaining the nature of the Trinity. Instead, the Virgin Mary, the suffering Christ, and the all-powerful Father became central religious realities for the Indian. The prominent and highest position in each church was awarded to the guardian saint who watched over the parish and was honored at fiesta time. The music, dances, incense, incantations, prayers, petitions, and sacramental rites were what the missionaries selected from the *Doctrina Christiana* as religious essentials.

"The Devil Has Persuaded Them . . ."

A major theme of the Jesuit missionaries who staffed Julí through the late sixteenth and seventeenth centuries was the pervasiveness of the devil working through native priests and practitioners of traditional Andean religion. It was assumed that before they could plant the seed of Christianity, they had to eradicate the traditional religious system. But what the missionaries saw happening, and this was a cause of intense frustration, was an acceptance of Christian rites and rituals as coherent with the old beliefs. "They say that Jesus Christ is God, but Tuñupa is God also," reported the Jesuit provincial in 1603.[44] What the Indian saw as a tolerant acceptance of the white man's god was unacceptable to the European. The early missionaries viewed the systematic destruction of the old religion as an essential prerequisite in the process of Christianization.[45]

The Jesuit reports from Julí at this time distinguish among the practitioners, the priests, the fortunetellers, the herbalists, the held beliefs, the sacred places of worship, and the things worshiped of the Andean peoples around Julí. Each was assigned a proportionate share of blame for keeping the "poor Indian" in the realm of ignorance. The bits and pieces about Andean religion written by the Europeans in Julí coincide with the fuller analyses written by contemporaries.[46]

The Andean creation stories, divine and supernatural beings, and sacred objects, had a tantalizing affinity to the Christian pantheon of gods, saints, and what theologians called sacramentals. In Julí the Indians believed that initially a profound darkness existed. Out of this darkness emerged Pucica'ka[47] who created the heavens and the earth. He was the Creator God, the *Dios Creador*, all-powerful, making the light, the sun, the heavens, land, mankind, and all visible things. The sun envied the moon's beauty and threw ashes at her to disfigure her. Pucica'ka married Iqui and without sleeping with her, she conceived and bore a son from him whose name was Tuñapa. At his command the hills and mountains became level. He dried rivers. The animals and beasts obeyed him. When the Indians saw some great deed or achievement, they said: "It is the work of Tuñapa."[48]

The Creator God was associated with Lake Titicaca from which he emerged. He disappeared and reappeared only when humanity sinned against him. The Creator God destroyed humanity by turning human beings into stone. The forms of Tiawanaco were the models for a "New Humanity," which the Creator God drew from the soil.

The Creator God lived in the heavens, appeared in times of crisis as a hero, and even appeared on earth as a poor beggar. However, Pucica'ka left the governance of the world to the supernatural assistants he had created. The earth, the sun, the moon, the *huacas* were sacred. Periodic destruction renewed the universe and a cycle of creation assured the renewal of the earth.[49] Although variations of the Creator God's name and actions existed (the coastal people called him Pachacamac), no variation existed about his creative activity. He was the source of all creation. He had no beginning, no end, and would exist forever.[50]

The Jesuit missionaries in Julí attempted to impose their own concept of a Creator God. In Christian theology, he was part of a trinity, Father, Son, and Holy Spirit, but the creation of the universe was attributed to God the Father. This coincided with the Andean concept of God as creator. Further, the idea that Pucica'ka descended to earth fit neatly into the Christian belief system of the Second Person of the Trinity becoming a human being, born of a virgin. This apparently contradictory event mirrored the traditional Andean belief of Pucica'ka fathering Tuñapa without sleeping with Iqui, the woman who bore him. For this reason Bernabé Cobo, the Jesuit historian who lived in Julí for nine years, recognized that the Indians "understood that the true God and the First Cause was one and the same person whom the Indians adored, in an albeit confused manner, as the creator of all things."[51]

Because of the convergence between Andean Creator God and the Christian God the Father, less emphasis was put upon God the Son, Jesus Christ, and even less on the Holy Spirit. Christ was relegated to the rank of saint and placed alongside the Andean supernatural beings. Christ was represented in sculpture and drawings as a human being; he was described and portrayed within the context of his human experience. He was human. José de Acosta, another missionary with long experience in the Andes, remarked that "it has always seemed horrible to me that among the thousands of Indians who call themselves Christian, very few know Jesus Christ."[52]

The Creator God of the Andes produced supernatural assistants who ran the universe. Inti, the Sun, was the most powerful. According to G. Y. Pease, the worship of the sun was an Inca innovation that disappeared with their defeat by the Spaniards.[53] Nevertheless, because he was considered to have been made by the Creator God, Inti was likened to Jesus Christ, the Son who according to Christian belief, "proceeded from the Father." The parallel could not help but be drawn between the two.

Illapa, the god who governed the rain, was an essential element in an agriculturalist's existence. He was the third most important god in the Andean hierarchy.[54] Illapa was a man formed by the stars, carrying a mace in his left hand and a sling in his right, dressed in shining clothes. When he swung around to use his sling, the thunder sounded and the lightening flashed, all this before the rain fell. Illapa shared the celestial pantheon with Mama Killa, the moon.

Among the earth gods, Pachamama was supreme. She was the earth goddess, one who controlled the rites of sowing, watering, and harvesting. The Jesuit missionaries in the Andes were never able to replace Pachamama with Father God or even any of the many saints. No adequate alternative existed to the universal Earth Mother because Christian theology had created a dichotomy between God and creation. Although the redemption of Christ was supposed to have "divinized" the earth, the manichean view of material as evil and spiritual as good strongly influenced Christian views of the world. The Spanish Jesuit might have seen the Andean Indian as eminently perfectible and potentially a full Son of God but he saw little divine about the soil he tilled or the streams that watered his fields. What came to mind was a similarity to Greek or Roman pantheism, not a notion of God who is present in all things, a notion the Jesuits themselves studied in the Fourth Week of the Spiritual Exercises of their founder, Ignatius Loyola.

By extension, to the Indians, *huacas* were sacred as well as hills, springs, rivers, rocks, all of which Pucica'ka brought forth in the original creative act. Thus is explained the fierce native opposition to resettlement ordered by Viceroy Francisco de Toledo in 1571. Bureaucratic organization, tax collection, and Christian indoctrination were better served by Toledo's plan, but the indigenous population saw itself torn from the sacred objects and places that gave meaning to their lives. A wide variety of sacred images formed the Indian cult system in the Andes. Cobo refused to admit that Indian attitudes toward their images were similar to the Christian veneration of statues or relics. The Indian image possessed a sacred power in itself. "They are idols," wrote Cobo, "venerated in themselves. The simple Indian did not pass beyond the image to seek that which the image represented."[55]

The traditional Andean system also possessed its devil or *demonio*. The Zupay became the devil in the missionaries's lexicon.[56] He had his own habitat, the *casa de diablo*, but he acted on earth as well, tempting human beings so as to carry them with him to his world. Jesuit missionaries in Julí spoke of people having had pacts with the devil, the devil speaking to individuals, or the devil being kept in special places within the home, but there was no cult as such to Zupay. *Brujos* or *hechiceros* allied themselves with the devil only to use his power to harm others.

The Jesuit missionaries in Julí were as intolerant of the Andean divinities and *huacas* as the European Protestants were of Catholic images and statues, and for precisely the same reason: fear of idolatry. The Jesuit missionary considered the agricultural activity of the Andean farmer as a totally profane act that had little if anything to do with religious rites and symbols. The religious integration of the Andean was not understood. The result was an aggressive attempt to find and destroy all objects and ideas of the traditional religion, and to punish and isolate persistent practitioners and priests of the native religion.

So militant was the bishop of La Plata in his rage against traditional Andean beliefs, that he recommended to Fr. Diego de Torres in 1582 that *hechiceros* and their followers be executed, preferably by burning at the stake.[57] Instead of executing the Indians, the Jesuits used one of the buildings in Julí as a prison for recalcitrant *hechiceros* just as they did in Cercado in Lima. Isolation in prison was considered a proper remedy.[58]

Two years after the Jesuits arrived in Julí, they reported that they were rounding up some *hechiceros* whom they characterized as *dogmatizadores* and *maestros del error*.[59] These native priests were first kept near the large church in the center of town but later were moved into the *Casa Blanca*, the White House, where under strict surveillance they were daily instructed in the new religion. In 1599 the Jesuit most associated with the *Extirpación de Idolatría* movement in Peru, José de Arriaga, wrote, as the Jesuit superior in Julí, that only the vestiges of idolatry existed there. One of the major reasons why idolatry was being wiped out, thought Arriaga, was because in Sunday sermons priests asked their audiences to reveal the names of those who still practiced the old religion, adoring *huacas* and visiting old shrines. They guaranteed anonymity to the betrayer. A number of informants came forward with names. In 1599 more than forty *hechiceros* were discovered this way in Julí.[60] Each parish priest in Julí appointed assistants called *fiscales* one of whose major duties was to report to the priest any parish member suspected of practicing the old religion. The divisions and stress thus caused within the parish must have been extraordinary. Those who wished to associate themselves and be aligned with the Spaniards whether for temporal gain or out of sincere belief in the new religion aggressively confronted believers in the traditional faith. And the Jesuits encouraged their aggression. In 1604 the Annual Letter reported that "the bad seed of idolatry was present" in Julí.[61]

But the local Christians were battling against it. As an example of Christian opposition to the old religion the report described how one elderly woman from Julí met some *hechiceros* in another town who were practicing the old rites. Not only did she reprehend them but she made them kneel before an uplifted cross and ask pardon for their offences. The same woman encountered some drunken Indians dancing and singing "in the old fashion." Again she reprehended them and dragged them to the parish church.[62] Such examples abound in the Jesuit letters from Julí. They were recorded to underline the salutary effect of the new religion on the parishioners, but they also serve to indicate the social divisions in Julí created by the introduction of Christianity. *Curacas* in secret (out of fear and shame) brought their children to the Jesuit priests for instruction in the new religion.[63] Whom did they fear? And of what were they ashamed? Apparently they feared other *curacas* and many townsfolk. It was shameful to turn one's back on the old gods to adore the Spanish one. A particularly determined *cacique principal* threw out of his house several women when he was criticized for having more than one wife.[64]

The target of the early Christians in Julí was both *curaca* and *hechicero*. The missionaries were aware of the high degree of integration that traditional religion enjoyed in the government and society of Andean peoples. Cobo spoke about the sorcerers and diviners who always accompanied the Inca.[65] The linkage between them represented the major social connection between traditional Andean religion and the pre-Hispanic government. The connection between *curaca* and *hechicero* was clearly evident in the sixteenth century. Luis Millones has shown how the curaca's role changed in the seventeenth and eighteenth centuries.[66] However, between 1580 and 1600, when the Jesuits began evangelizing Julí, the *curaca-hechicero* link was still strong. "Each family or group has its priest," wrote Fr. Esteban Paez in 1604, "who was called *fala*. The principal duty of this priest is to instruct the *cacique principal* and the rest of the *ayllu* in the rites, rituals, and cult of the idols."[67] The fala, according to Paez, determined which animals were to be sacrificed for which purposes, and he chose the coca that was also offered to the gods. The coca, added the Jesuit, was "a variety of shrub that the Indians chewed. It increased their strength and they value it highly."[68]

For Esteban de Paez the *fala* was working in league with the devil. He was the devil's representative whom the Jesuit called the *ministro del diablo*. Paez made no attempt to see in the general confession that the Indians of Julí made to their priests, and which he described in detail, a reflection of Christianity as Cobo did. Instead, Paez portrayed the confession as solely for the benefit of a curaca who might have been missing some of his llamas or been ill and he wanted to learn whether one of the ayllu members had put a spell on him. In such a case, an Andean Trial by Combat decided the accused's fate. The curaca's *hechicero* put a mark on one side of a tortilla, threw the tortilla up in the air and if it landed with the mark up, then the accused lied and was stoned until he confessed his wrongdoing. The *hechicero* and the curaca ruled in tandem and Paez marvelled at the high esteem in which the *hechiceros* were held, "as if they had descended from heaven."[69]

The devil, according to Paez, worked directly with individual Indian *hechiceros*. Some kept shrines to the devil in their homes, or in their fields, speaking to him at will. Slowly the *hechiceros* were being weeded out, incarcerated, and "re-educated." The process was slow because the *hechiceros* were carefully protected by the villagers. The devil also worked directly with individual Indians principally through the stone and metal animals called *huacas* that most families possessed.

The *hechicero* was also a diviner or soothsayer.[70] He was a direct threat to the authority of the European missionary. By his very existence he served to remind the Andean of his past. Thus, he was the European's primary target.

Isolation and Indoctrination

The Jesuit missionaries in Julí benefited from a major advantage not possessed by other European agents of religious change. They were able to isolate the Aymara of Julí, keeping them away not only from other Spaniards considered a bad influence but also from those within their own community who continued to promote the old religion.[71] Thus set apart, the process of indoctrinating the Indian took place. A fixed weekly, monthly, and yearly schedule of instruction was set up because the missionaries could rely on a fixed Indian agrarian cycle of farm-related and pastoral activity.[72] The Indian agricultural year, whose activities were triggered by the position of the stars, as well as the altitudinal zone of the farmland, began with fertilizing, followed by turning the soil, planting, tilling, weeding, and finally harvesting. These activities required the entire Indian family's cooperative effort in fields sometimes far from Julí. Planting in upper altitudinal zones took place in August, harvesting in March–April. This fixed agrarian cycle allowed the missionaries to plan their religious activities to coincide with the agrarian cycle of the Indians, thus giving the Aymara farmer a continued sense of integrity to his works and days. Daily, weekend, and monthly religious instruction, punctuated by religious fiestas honoring the saint-protector of the town, were routinely attended, and the European missionary could count on a determined number of attendees.

However, the very nature and regularity of instruction and parochial ministry cut against the Jesuit grain. The Jesuit rector of Julí in 1578, Diego Martínez, thought that there were too many Indians in the area for the Jesuits to handle. Also, Julí was too far from Cuzco, a potential danger to the body and souls of the Jesuits there because if the Jesuits were to stay alone in a parish residence, temptations abounded and their isolation became a source of discontent. "Opportunities to punish the Indians physically were present and there was danger of becoming hateful to the Indians."[73] Martínez thought that the Jesuits should set up a thriving mission station in Julí and leave in four or five years, not remaining as parish priests.

Instead of four or five years, they stayed for over a century and a half, and in the time period constructed a model that served for other Jesuit missions in South America, especially for the reductions (missions, or *reducción*) of Paraguay.[74] And like the reductions of Paraguay, the notion of a Jesuit theocracy was attributed to Julí, where the missionaries controlled not only the religious life of the community but the political as well. The complaint of the *caciques* of Chucuito, later denied, asserted that the Jesuits controlled the *caciques* thus making Julí a theocracy.[75] It would be truly extraordinary if they had not. Given the fact that each of the local *caciques* were baptized Christians by 1595, had sworn fealty to the king of Spain, and viewed the Jesuits as the true Crown representatives, Jesuit influence with them must have been powerful. Although civil and religious authority was distinct, it was understood by the culture and society of the time that the religious authority was superior to the civil. Evident tension existed. The *caciques* did not want Potosí mine officials to interfere with their control of the native population. Nor did the Jesuits. The caciques did not want *alguaciles* from Potosí to come to Julí searching for escaped mine workers. "They burned our fields and put us in jail."[76] But the caciques might not have wanted the kind of control that the Jesuits exerted over them. It is clear that both missionaries and *caciques* needed each other to retain control in their distinct spheres. Cooperation between the new conquerors and the old local rulers was essential. The Spaniards needed the *caciques* to stabilize their conquests and to exact tribute and labor.[77] Without the pro-active cooperation of the *caciques*, the Jesuits in Julí would not have been able to retain the power they held for 189 years.

6

The Guaraní

Southeast of Julí was the River of Silver, the Río de la Plata, with its massively broad estuary that was first brought to Europe's attention in 1516. Asunción in present-day Paraguay was founded in 1537, near the region inhabited by Native Americans called the Guaraní. Religion played a major role in creating the bulwark against the Portuguese in Brazil for by the resettlement of the Guaraní into Christian mission towns called reductions, the rivals to the north were kept in check. The economic foundations of the reductions thus coincided with the political aims of the conquerors. Few places in the Americas witnessed such a tangle of the economic and the spiritual.

Beginnings

In 1656 Manuel Cabral de Alpoin, the military officer in Siete Corrientes, Northern Argentina, led three expeditions into the reductions of the Upper Paraná to uncover the gold mines he was certain the European Jesuits were hiding. Cabral relied on information provided by a Jesuit lay brother, named Pedro (he could not remember his last name) who had revealed to him the location of the mines. Cabral did not find any mines.[1]

The search for the elusive gold mines epitomizes the general attitude toward missionary activity in the Paraguay reductions: suspicion over their economic success and skepticism over the self-serving nature of the European relations with the Guaraní Indians. Few European evangelization efforts in America are better known than those of Paraguay. And the polemics and studies still abound.[2]

The Paraguay reductions attract historians for several reasons, not least of which is the copiousness of the documentation. The Jesuit Archives in Rome, the Archive of the Indies in Seville, the Argentine National Archives in Buenos Aires, besides scattered holdings in Europe and America, all have large sections on European economic, religious, social, and political activity in the Río de la Plata. All the more curious then, as Martín María Morales points out, that the same kinds of conclusions are reached in study after study, with relatively few attempts made to dig into the mass of documentary material available.[3]

Why have the reductions become the polemical trademark for critics and commentators of the Jesuits in Latin America? Even before Voltaire wrote of the reductions in *Candide* in 1759, characterizing them as opportunities for wealth and independence from the crown, the *Histoire de Nicolas I. Roy du Paraquari et Empereur des Mamelus* (Dresden, 1756), had made its mark. In the tale about Nicolas I, the Jesuits were accused of establishing an empire in Paraguay, amassing enormous riches, and defending their ill-gotten gain by force of arms. Although the historian of Brazil, Robert Southey, said that it "does not contain a syllable of truth," the book ran through four French editions, two Italian, and one in Dutch.

Could institutional success have been at the root of the criticism? We should discount, of course, the traditional enemies of the Jesuits who saw them as standing in the way of absolute Bourbon hegemony. The utopia which seemed so extravagant and almost fantastical had almost been accomplished and not in Thomas More's England, nor in the Sun King's France, but in America! The institutions of church and state, the economy, even a native army, had risen in the jungle, and they seemed to be long lived. Perhaps the "when my brother succeeds, a little bit of me dies," effect caused the reductions to become a lightning rod. Isolation and indoctrination bred suspicion, and for those who could not fathom economic success without specie, there had to be hidden gold and silver mines somewhere.

The documentary materials on the reductions also offer an excellent example of how one religion replaces another through isolation and indoctrination; how traditional political and social structures are changed through an indirect and sometimes direct use of military conquest. The impact of Spanish colonialism on an indigenous culture reveals not only what the aggressive westerner attempted through agents of religious change but also what coping mechanisms were employed by the targeted group. And finally, the reductions demonstrate how the Spanish government, the state, worked hand in hand with the church in order to achieve specific pragmatic, imperial ends, much as the "applied anthropologists" have worked hand in glove with governments to maintain effective colonial rule.[4]

Guillermo Furlong and Pablo Hernández have told us what the Europeans did in Paraguay.[5] Less well known and understood is the view from the other side of the cultural fence, how the Guaraní lost autonomy but retained their identity.

On June 22, 1625, the eve of the feast of St. Lawrence, the reduction of Nuestra Señora de la Encarnación was established in Guairá, the region just east of Asunción.[6] It was not a particularly large reduction, only five hundred families, but its beginnings contain the elements associated with the founding of other reductions. In other words, it is as close to typical as one can get.

Encarnación was geographically well situated. The nearby fertile land produced large quantities of what was to become famous throughout Latin America as yerba mate, also called Jesuit tea. It was close to the Paraná Pane River, a branch of the Paraná, and it was strategically located, a little southeast of the large reduction of Loreto, directly south of the recently founded reduction of San Francisco Xavier.[7] Unfortunately, it was also close to São Paulo and the Portuguese raiders who coveted the local Guaraní for their slave market.

Two years previously, Fr. Antonio Ruiz de Montoya, operating from the Francisco Xavier Reduction, had made contact with local people. They lived in an area that was called Taiati and were ruled by a chief named Zuruba, whom Ruiz described as a "stubborn and relentless enemy of Christianity." His rival was another *cacique* named Pindoviú who very much favored allowing the Europeans into their villages and establishing a reduction. Pindoviú eventually accomplished this by ambushing his rival, killing him, and celebrating a feast with Zuruba served up as the main course. Ruiz interpreted Zuruba's death as the intervention of God because Zuruba ended up "between the teeth of his enemies" and "once this monster was destroyed, the entire territory was opened to the word of the Lord."

Ruiz listed another advantage. He thought that once Zuruba was out of the way, his people could see how the people of Francisco Xavier had flourished under the new religion. They lived amiably with the Spanish and the other native groups. They enjoyed, in his words, peace and tranquility. Seeing this, Ruiz thought, the Taiatis would be attracted to the new religion. Ruiz did not immediately begin living with the Taiatis. He returned to Francisco Xavier because he thought that if he departed, a new cause for rivalry would be enkindled. However, he gave to the Taiatis the Spanish symbol of authority, a wooden staff, a *vara*, and this proved sufficient for the time being. Two years later, when he announced to the villagers of Francisco Xavier that he would take up residence with the Taiatis, they bitterly opposed him. Ostensibly, the inhabitants of Francisco Xavier did not want him to live with their traditional rivals. They said that Pindoviú was planning to kill him, they would eat him, and that even the *cavelludos*, the ones with long hair reaching down their backs, were plotting his death. Ruiz answered these objections by saying he would go anyway, "even if they eat him alive." Their souls were at stake.

Ruiz de Montoya also wrote that the people of Taiati asked him to live with them so that he would teach them "to live as human beings." "*Nos hagais vivir como hombres*," he wrote. Ruiz and Fr. Cristobal de Mendoza left Francisco Xavier and in four days were on the outskirts of Pindoviú's village. Instead of an ambush, like the *caciques* of Francisco Xavier foretold, the two Jesuits were met with drum rolls, horns sounding, and arches festooned with wildflowers. In a "little church" that Pindoviú had erected for the occasion, Ruiz preached to his neophytes, very briefly, he said. The chief offered them his own hut as their temporary living quarters.

On entering the village the Jesuits noticed that the Indians had built a large wooden palisade where their warriors were stationed. Another group was at war with Pindoviú. They had captured and eaten Pindoviú's mother, and he had retaliated by raiding and consuming several of them. Ruiz wrote:

> That very night Pindoviú's enemies had captured and killed three eight-year olds. They roasted them and put them in baskets to carry them off to their lands. Next day, Pindoviú gave chase, and when the enemy realized they were cornered, they shot one of the women captives with two arrows, one in each breast, and they split open another's neck with an axe. They escaped with the bodies of the three boys. We baptized the woman who had been shot with arrows and gave her the name María.

The Jesuits' original dwelling with Pindoviú was not to their liking. They preferred to stay outside the palisade so they found a place at the foot of a little hill where there were pine trees and a river. Ruiz constructed the symbol of the new civil and religious dispensation, a cross seven feet high, and he placed it in the center of what was to become the *plaza mayor* or main square. Blessings, prayers, and appropriate rites marked the placing of the cross in its site. On the feast day of St. Lawrence, the Jesuits said Mass outdoors because they had no church, and they drew lots, *echamos suertes*, to choose the patron for the new reduction. Three times the name Encarnación came out, and so Nuestra Señora de la Encarnación it became. The Jesuits appointed civil officials. Ruiz presented Pindoviú with the symbol of authority, the vara. Then they appointed the councillors (*regidores*), the bailiffs (*al-*

caldes), and their aides (*sargentos*). Both the religious and civil authorities were now in place.

The founding of the reduction of Nuestra Señora de la Encarnación is a micro-example of the different, competing, and divergent features present in the establishment of the string of mission stations along the Paraná and Uruguay rivers in Paraguay and present-day Argentina. Three vastly different motivational sets were functioning. The Guaraní wanted the European missionaries as protection from the slave raiding Portuguese in São Paulo and from the Spanish demands of Personal Service that came from the encomenderos of Asunción. Also they wanted access to the *armas mágicas*, the magic weapons, the thunder sticks, which made hunting both animals and enemy so much easier and efficient. The Guaraní also, one suspects, felt the need to associate themselves with the people who were in the process of changing their civilization. The proverbial handwriting was on the wall. In addition, there was present the attraction for a different approach to religion. How this entered the formula is far more difficult to ascertain. However, it must have existed. The thousands of baptisms and conversions were not performed on a self-serving and deceitful Guaraní population. There must have been true conversions to the new belief system just as there were true conversions among the Indians of North America. And for the Guaraní, just as for the Hurons, a change in belief system meant a radical change in the fabric of society. Their interpretation of how the world worked had to change. Interpersonal relationships would no longer be the same. What had been considered good was no longer to be considered good. And vice versa.

As far as the Jesuits were concerned, their set of motivations was equally as diverse. Overriding all was their belief in world evangelization. In this they followed closely the renaissance ideas of Antonio Possevino.[8] The biblical command to go and teach all nations, resounded in sixteenth-century Christian Europe. But for Possevino and the Jesuits, God had created a plan by which all regions of the entire world would be converted since saving a single soul was much more important than acquiring all the kingdoms of the earth. Possevino firmly believed that the evangelization of the world was at hand and that the Jesuits were major instruments in God's hand.

Besides world evangelization, two other motives were at play. One was the absolute certainty that the West and the missionaries who were its representatives had already achieved the highest rung of cultural superiority. Material and psychological culture, the view of how the world functioned, the spiritual and material world, were all understood and explicable in terms that the westerner employed. All other cultures, by definition, were inferior. Therefore, the Jesuits were participating in a *mision civilizatrice*, one that uplifted peoples and brought them to a higher cultural level. A second factor that acted as motive among the Europeans was the realization that they were engaged in a unique enterprise, an attempt to fulfill the Christian vision of the world, one that united God and man in a special way. The reductions were more than mission stations. They were an attempt to establish God's kingdom on earth.

Both sets of motivations operated to bring Jesuits and Guaraní together. Acting as the glue for these two sets of motivations was the Spanish colonial government. It as well had its own distinct motives for making sure that the Guaraní were Christianized and westernized. Spain was in the New World not only to assist worldwide evangelization but also to enhance the Spanish Empire. More souls meant greater revenues; more occupied land meant increased opportunities to find the sources of wealth, gold and silver. Empire building meant excluding rival powers by establishing fixed boundaries and nothing did this better than by establishing stable villages of Christian believers.

Thus, the confluence of three distinct factors produced the reductions of Paraguay. The object of the Spanish missions was the creation of a Christianized buffer that would keep rival powers away from newly acquired lands, to allow church and state to cooperate in constructing a power able to resist any rival onslaught. In doing this, the local people were caught in what was to become the classic bind, in what centuries later Chinua Achebe would describe as "a battlefield in which the children of light were locked in mortal combat with the sons of darkness."[9]

"Men of One Day"

When José de Cardiel wrote about the reductions in the middle of the eighteenth century, he characterized the Guaraní as being "men of one day."[10] They could not be counted on, he thought, for much foresight. Their horizons were limited, their goals restricted in spite of their exposure to over five generations of Jesuit Christianity and Western ways. Cardiel wondered why the persistence and even outright resistance to the best that the West had to offer.

The reasons for Cardiel's criticism were deeply imbedded in the Guaraní's view of the world. Their behavior, thoughts, and actions were derived from a culture to which Cardiel was not particularly sensitive. It had defined fundamental beliefs about how the world worked and from this flowed how the individual should act. Unlike the Incas of Peru, or the Aztecs and Mayas of Mexico, the Tupã-Guaraní had separated the social fabric of their society from their religion. The integration of religion and society was not as close as it was in other Native American groups. Consequently, the shaman, or religious leader did not play as powerful a role as elsewhere in the New World. To be sure, they were influential, but not to the degree that they were in New France. Early missionaries were hard put even to discover any religion flourishing among the Guaraní. One of the earliest Jesuits in Brazil, Manuel Nobrega, wrote in 1549 that the Indians had no knowledge of God, they worshiped nothing, and did not even have idols. Nobrega was concerned because without these basic ideas, even if wrong, he lacked a handle with which to teach "correct" religious concepts.[11]

Gradually, however, the missionaries learned that the Guaraní cosmology was peopled by a plethora of figures. Tupã was the god who caused thunder, lightning, and rain. Yurupari or Giropari was the evil spirit or the devil. The origin of the shaman was traced to the Maira-Monan, the transformer, the creator, the lawgiver, the culture-hero who taught the Guaraní how to plant crops and organize their communities.[12] Over time the shaman became almost godlike in both appearance and power. He provided a guarantee of supernatural protection.[13] Ruiz de Montoya accused a shaman named Taubici of killing people "by inflicting sickness."[14] Montoya wrote, almost approvingly, that the Guaraní killed the shaman, Taubici, out of revenge and fear.[15] With the arrival of Christianity, the power attributed to the shaman was readily transferred to the cross; hence, the importance of placing a wooden cross within the village compound.

Early seventeenth-century contacts with the indigenous population demonstrate, even if one even partially accepts the European version of the early encounter, that the Native American had a keen sense of religion, defining religion in its broad etymological sense of linkages between the divine and human.[16] The Native American was curious about things religious. He was intrigued by the idea that God became a man, that Mary, his mother, remained a virgin, that baptism washed away sins, that without baptism one could not enter the place where God lived.[17]

> He repeated this question two or three times. "How can Mary be the Mother of God? [Ko ai Tupan Marie?]"
> I answered that that's the way it was, because God chose her to be the mother of his son; that she was a princess among all women, and because of her purity she was chosen to be the mother of God, and after her death angels carried her to heaven where she is seated next to her son.[18]

Early encounters also indicate that confession of sins was not a major obstacle once it was realized that the priest was the representative of God.

Baptism, redemption, heaven, hell, punishment for sin, reward for leading a good life, all of these concepts, the Europeans thought, connected with the original belief systems of the Native Americans in Brazil.[19]

> There was no great difficulty in making them confess their sins, even women . . . nor was there the least hesitancy in their understanding the efficacy of baptism, or washing away their sins, or the Son of God become man, or attaining heaven, . . . they've always believed in hell, where Jeropary and the evil ones lived. They also believed that God was very happy in heaven, living among the good spirits, and that his children who lived a good life would join him in a place where nothing would be lacking to them.[20]

Besides the one God in heaven, the Jesuits discovered that families kept idols (*ídolos*) in their homes. They were human forms, some small, some large, but never exceeding two feet. They were made out of wood or wax, and on fixed days sacrifices of food, whether meat, fish, or vegetables, were offered to them.[21] The Europeans made the distinction between idols, which were of evil origin allowing the owner to communicate with evil spirits, and images that brought one to a closer understanding of the true nature of religion.[22] For the former, idols were clearly the handiwork of the devil. The latter came from the one, true God. Clearly, the forces of light were arranged against the forces of darkness. Which was which, as Garrett Mattingly said of the Spanish Armada battle, depended on where one stood.

The Guaraní, as relative newcomers to the eastern shores of the Atlantic, were in continual search for the "Land Without Evil." This was a place where crops grew by themselves, where people spent their days feasting and dancing, where no one ever died.[23] This was the place where the good, those who fasted, chanted and danced, were rewarded. Where was this Land Without Evil? Perhaps in the center of the earth. Perhaps across the wide expanse of the sea. Or where the sky met the earth. Only the most powerful shamans, the *carai* or *caraiba* could find this land. The *pajé* or ordinary shaman could not. The journey to the Land Without Evil almost always involved a series of hardships, whether epidemics, famine, or attacks by hostile groups. It was not too big a leap for the Indians to understand Moses leading the faithful to the Promised Land, the Garden of Eden, or the land of Jacob's Feast. However, the paradise that the Guaraní sought was an earthly one and not found in the kingdom of heaven.

It was upon these ideas that the European missionary constructed the foundations of a new religion. Its psychological benefits replaced those of the old. The unknown became explicable in equally understandable terms. Aspects of the old religion, its rituals, dances, offerings, were retained but some were declared to be false. Human conduct was aligned with the new notions of right and wrong. Just as the old religion made sense of the Guaraní world, so the new would offer the Guaraní a new pantheon with new spiritual intermediaries.

Why the European Came

In 1632 a Guaraní cacique named Ytapayu asked the Jesuits of the Navidad reduction to visit his village, "which was on the other side of the Igay [Paraguay River] where the river becomes navigable towards the sea," raise a cross, and baptize his sons.[24] Frs. Cristobal de Mendoza and Pedro Romero went, found the village of four hundred Guaraní, raised the cross, and dedicated the place to Santa Ana. For the writer of the *Carta Anua*, the village was a vein "in the rich mine of souls that Our Lord has allowed us to discover in this time."[25] For Ytapayu, the Spanish priests provided protection not only against the incursions of the Portuguese slavers from São Paulo, Brazil, but also against the demands of the Spanish encomenderos of Asunción.[26] Both of these factors weighed heavily in the Guaraní decision to invite the foreigners to their village. By this time the Native Americans were well aware of the European presence, both to the northeast in Brazil, and to the west. The Guaraní also saw the Spaniards as allies against their traditional enemies, the Guaycurus and the Agaces, just as the Spanish government would later view the Guaraní as military allies against the Portuguese and hostile Indian groups, even naming them the "Guardians of the Frontier."[27] This European-Guaraní military alliance was a major power block within the Río de la Plata, and combined with the Jesuit monopoly of the tea trade and Jesuit control of the labor force, led to the massive anti-Jesuit movement of the eighteenth century.[28]

The early governor of the Río de la Plata, Hernando Arias, had definitely mixed motives in his repeated insistence that the Jesuits create reductions in northern Paraguay. Royal Orders of 1591, 1605, and 1608, that had Hernandarias's hand all over them, ordered the Society of Jesus to build houses in the Indian towns "and wherever they wanted to teach the Divine law and preach the gospel," as well as "*reducir y convertir Indios naturales de aquellas provincias,*" after the governor had reported the scarcity of missionaries in his district.[29] Hernandarias wanted to create a buffer between the Portuguese in Brazil and Spanish holdings to the south. He underlined the importance of populating "the fertile lands that were ideal for raising cattle and for farms, lands that now held scores of Indians."[30] Hernandarias hoped to place the Jesuits in Guaira, a province just east of the Spanish settlement of Asunción, along the Paraná River, and in Tape, the easternmost region toward the coast. The Brazilians called the Indians there Tapes:

> but they were mistaken. They were Guaraní and they have their own language. The Guaraní were barbarians, bloodthirsty, ignorant, living in straw huts, with a leader called a cacique. They lived by hunting and fishing, almost totally nude, continually at war, and they ate their enemies. They were drunkards, lascivious, and given to soothsayers. In twenty years all of this changed. 50,000 people, 10,000 families, and thirteen towns had justice, culture, with judges, policemen, trades, farms, common land holdings, chapels with musicians. But the *mamelucos* of Brazil [in 1639] destroyed all of this.[31]

The writer of the *Breve Relación* quoted above was not at all as sympathetic to the Guaraní as was the missionary who sent the Jesuit provincial in Córdoba an account of the Guaraní in 1608. For him, whoever he was, the one hundred thousand Guaraní not counting women and children, were "people who harm no one, who were very valiant and kind to the Christian missionaries. They are first and foremost kind to strangers. They wear no clothes but they dress when they have to.[32] Fish and deer abound and they harvest corn and vegetables."[33]

When the Jesuits came on the scene in Paraguay, the Guaraní lived in isolated villages. They reluctantly provided labor service for the Spanish settlers in Asunción and Villarica but others had more freedom living on the outskirts of the Spanish controlled area. However, by living on the fringes, they were more exposed to Portuguese slavers from Brazil.[34]

Hernandarias wanted to consolidate Spanish holdings from Buenos Aires north through Asunción and set up a buffer between Spanish and Portuguese territory. He got his wish. By 1610 Diego de Torres dispatched six Jesuits to what was called the mission of *Guayra* and *Tinajiba*, about four hundred miles northeast of Asunción. Their task was to learn the Guaraní language. Eventually only two Jesuits, Joseph Cataldino and Simon Marseta, both Italians, received orders "to open a large scale reduction in the geographic center of Guaira in the most advantageous location they could find and stay there until they hear from me."[35] Marcial de Lorenzana and Francisco de San Martín were posted to the Paraná mission "about 200 miles inland." Lorenzana wrote that "we finally made it and we're O.K. The Tibiquari River is rising and the horse I brought with me drowned. The Indians came to meet us with great fervor and they fed us unsalted beans, cassava bread, and corn."[36] Lorenzana thought that the land around the Tibiquari was beautiful, with its undulating fields interspersed with little islands. Lorenzana then alluded to what was to become a major issue dividing Jesuits and Spanish settlers and one that Hernandarias was to regret, the Jesuit adamant opposition to the Spanish demands on the Guaraní for Personal Service, the *Servicio Personal* controversy. "This is the most important mission," wrote Lorenzana, "because the Paraná Indians control the entire Paraná waterway and have blocked the Spaniards who attempted to use it. The Indians have always claimed that they were exacting vengeance from the Spaniards for the wrongs inflicted on them in unfair demands for Personal Service."[37]

Between 1610 and 1620 a thread runs through Jesuit correspondence from the reductions that describes Guaraní attempts to escape Spanish settlers' demands for forced labor on their farms.[38] Hernandarias had stipulated in 1598 that Indians work for Spanish encomenderos, a *mita sin sueldo* it was called, in return for religious instruction that was to take place in a church that the encomendero was to build. But instead of forming a bond between encomendero and worker, the opposite happened. Marcial de Lorenzana said in 1610 that the "*servicio personal* has driven many Indians away from the Spaniards."[39] And the Guaraní frequently asked Lorenzana if their encomenderos would come looking for them.[40]

In 1614 Fr. Pedro de Oñate's language was more colorful. He said that the Spaniards were "like wolves among sheep, seeking to devour the Indians."[41] Diego de Torres's Annual Letter described how Jesuit missionaries from the reductions of Loreto and San Ignacio actually confronted Spanish soldiers who were in the process of capturing Indians for service in Asunción. "The Indians came to the Jesuits to ask them to come and stop the Spanish soldiers from taking them from their village to serve them. They [the Jesuits] went quickly [*con mucha aprissa*] and walked day and night to confront the soldiers."[42]

It was partly this fear of Spanish roundups that caused many Guaraní to flee to the mountains, where the Jesuits then proceeded to round them up for the reductions. The Christian missionaries nicknamed themselves *cazadores del Señor*, the Lord's Hunters. Sometimes for months at a time missionaries from the reductions would scour the hill country to bring more Indians into the reductions. Fr. Diego de Salazar even hung up metal fishhooks on the trees in order to entice the Indians to come and listen to him. No luck.[43]

If the local cacique or headman wanted his people to integrate themselves into a Christian reduction, they went. He was the decision maker. But there were always the gifts, interestingly called *rescates*, distributed to the Guaraní—not only to the *cacique* but to the general public. Knives, scissors, shirts, fishhooks, and hats were always part of the missionaries' baggage. When the Jesuit Provincial, Nicolás Durán, visited the reductions in 1626, he had with him shirts, knives, and fishhooks, worth more than two thousand pesos. Durán gave away sixty shirts and eventually gave away his own, *"una frezada mia,"* and his legs were so puffed up with sores from chiggers that the Indians had to carry him in a hammock.[44]

The gifts were not mere frivolous trinkets flashing in the sun to attract the gullible. The Guaraní realized their importance. The iron fishhooks were more durable than the bone ones they were using; the iron knives cut through forest prey much more efficiently than stone tools; the European-made shirts gave the Guaraní the prestige of dressing like the Spaniards; and the potential use of guns, whose utilization would be realized in a short time, put into Indian hands a killing tool whose efficiency the Guaraní had never experienced. The gifts were not colored balls and bells but practical tools that made Guaraní life easier.

Arma Mágica

In the seventeenth century the Guaraní Indians needed "magic weapons" to battle their enemies. They found them. The arquebus became their *arma mágica* and the cross was erected in villages that accepted the new religion. The cross had a profound symbolic value. It meant that the village was under the protection of the Spanish Crown; that the village now belonged to the community of believers; that the community was guarded, defended, and supported. "To raise the cross meant to secure the land, to arrange the families thereon, to set a sign over them so that they would not revert to the past."[45]

Ironically, the Brazilian incursions from São Paulo created the Jesuit-Guaraní military alliances. The raids that had as their goal the capture of the Guaraní for the São Paulo slave market grew in such intensity that the Jesuit Provincial Congregation of 1632 called it the number one problem facing the reductions.[46] The Jesuits wrote to the king to report the damages inflicted on the twelve missions. "In the last four years," they wrote, "São Paulo has destroyed ten missions, entering churches, ripping children from their mothers, and burning houses."[47] In 1637 slave raids originating in São Paulo and Santos destroyed the reduction of Jesús María that held over twelve hundred Guaraní families. On Christmas day the church at San Cristobal was burned. The following year and within a period of eight months the reductions of Santa Teresa, San Carlos, Apóstoles, Martires, Candelaria, and San Nicolás del Pyratini were destroyed.[48] Several years later the approval arrived allowing the Guaraní to bear arms and for the Jesuits to store munitions in the reductions.

With *arma mágica* in Guaraní hands, the tide gradually turned. By 1641 the Spanish commander of Asunción was requesting Guaraní to defend his city. "If they can defeat the Portuguese," he wrote, "they can defend Spanish cities as well."[49]

From the middle of the seventeenth century, the government visits of the reductions listed the number of shotguns, bullets, lances, and other kinds of weapons that were stored "to defend themselves against the Portuguese."[50] But reduction Indians also did battle against other Indian groups. In 1657 the Spanish government used 236 reduction Indians, two hundred of their horses, and twenty of their canoes to punish rebel Indians. "Without Indians," General Cristobal de Garaz wrote on January 15, "the 50 Spanish soldiers would not have been able to invade and destroy the rebels."[51] In 1767, when the Jesuits were expelled from the reductions, the list of arms had grown. In the reduction of Nuestra Señora de Fe alone, there were fifteen canon, 159 rifles, thirty shotguns, thirty-four carbines, thirty-four pistols, 350 lances, "many" bullets, ten *arrobas* of powder, and 2,348 arrows.[52]

One of the conditions laid down by the Spanish home government in granting the Jesuits the permission to train Indians in the use of arms was that the Indian soldiers be available to the Spanish Crown. The Jesuits agreed and saw arming the Guaraní as a win-win situation. The reductions would be militarily protected while the crown would gain a native army. And what Mercedes Avellaneda calls "*espacio social*" would be created. The downside of it was the identification of the Guaraní army with the Europeans. There has been little scholarly work done on the Guaraní army, its makeup, organization, demographic effects on the reductions, nor on the local political and military effects of its activity.[53] By the eighteenth century, the Guaraní army was an essential part of the reductions. Fr. Bernard Nusdorffer, the provincial, ordered in 1747 that "every Sunday the exercise of arms will take place without exception, so that the Indians become proficient in using rifles and bow and arrow, in order that they can defend their lands, their wives, and children."[54] The army's presence created a stabilizing force within the reductions and was a positive feature that attracted the Guaraní.

However, security had a price. Toward the middle of the eighteenth century the Jesuit missionary, José Cardiel, wrote a long, rambling account of the Jesuit missions in Paraguay. He described the Guaraní as people who thought neither about yesterday nor tomorrow.[55] "Even after 100 years of steady evangelization," he continued, "they have the same lackadaisical attitudes towards life and work."[56]

Cardiel was not implying that no social changes had occurred within the Guaraní communities. They had. In fact, he described in great detail the new manual labor trades that were practiced in each Guaraní town. Blacksmiths, carpenters, silversmiths, weavers, hat makers, shoemakers, organ makers, tailors, painters, sculptors, and herdsmen were now active members of Guaraní society. The Indian had accepted a new division of labor with the acceptance of reduction life. The Guaraní exchanged an integrated belief system for a new concept of the divine, a new hierarchy of gods and holy people. A reorientation of the concepts of time, property, food, village life, construction, morality, economics, and personal responsibility was demanded of those who placed themselves under the protective umbrella of the Jesuit reductions. The newness of all of this was not apparent to the European agents of change. For them, the Guaraní were simply becoming civilized. They were accepting the standards of personal and religious behavior that civilized societies considered acceptable. Although Cardiel described the new manual trades with self-assuredness and the writer of the *Breve Relación* spoke of the twenty-year transition from "the most barbarous and bloodthirsty Indians in the universe" to "reasonable human beings in large towns,"[57] the Guaraní experienced the transition with an entirely different set of emotions. Their folk beliefs were turned into heresy; their religious shamans became objects of derision; the rites they had practiced to invoke the divine were condemned as evil superstitions; the interpersonal relationships that the Guaraní considered essential for maintaining their society were denounced as indecent. In brief, their value systems had been turned upside down.

The surrendered parts of the Guaraní culture system were replaced by Western elements considered not to be savage or uncivilized. The substitution took place immediately upon entrance into the reductions. At the top of the new structure was the representative of God, the priest. Beneath him in the reductions was not the new rulers of civil society, the Spanish, but a new hierarchy. The *corregidor*, the two *alcaldes mayores*, the *alferez real*, the four *regidores*, and the *alguacil mayor*, formed the new administrative hierarchy within the reductions. The regidores or town counselors probably held the most power, since they were the closest to the ancient council of elders who had ruled the group. Village elders selected the town counselors, but the priest always had approval or veto power over the selection. The corregidor or chief magistrate headed the entire *cabildo* or town council. The two alcaldes mayores were subject to the chief magistrate and the alguacil mayor was the policeman. The town council had its secretary, the *escribano*, who made sure that town business was recorded.

The selection of the officials was followed by a highly ritualized ceremony that took place yearly in front of the church, with priests, cabildo members, and singers participating. The newly designated officials received the insignia of their respective offices, whether staffs, *varas,* or clothing, from the parish priest who spoke briefly about the importance of maintaining order and authority within the reduction.[58]

The degree to which the new political order reflected the old has not yet been determined. It is unlikely that it reflected the old very much. But ostensible control, or at least the vehicle of direct control, remained in the hands of the village council, the native Guaraní, and this counted for much among the villagers. Just as the Jesuit missionaries were frequently told by the visiting provincial never to administer physical punishment themselves, but have the native Guaraní *alcalde* do it, so as not to be seen as the "bad guy," so the reduction political system was to be seen as controlled by the native Guaraní, although the de facto direction remained in the Spanish missionary's hands.

It is not coincidental that the author of the *Breve Relación* puts the political and economic management of the reductions under one and the same chapter heading. He titled chapter 5: *Cap. 5. Govierno Político y Económico,* as if to emphasize their mutual dependence. And in a real sense he was correct. The new political structure in the reductions reflected the new economic structure. The major crop, the *yerba del Paraguay,* was the same in that it existed and was used long before the Spaniards arrived. But the organization of the product's cultivation and the marketing methods used after 1620 were entirely new.

The Kingdom of God on Earth

What also reflects the changed order of life was the new village arrangement that each reduction followed. The sketches reproduced in Furlong's *Cartografía*[59] reveal a rigid type of town planning that literally followed the requirements set down in the *Leyes de Indias.* However, the layout of Furlong's town map is duplicated almost exactly by other reduction maps in the Jesuit archives. One in particular, the *Divujo de un Pueblo de los Indios Guaranis,* is a plan or visual representation reflecting deeply held convictions.[60] Its layout clearly displays the intent of the planner, which was to integrate God and man in the physical world of a Guaraní community. Use of the term *utopia* describes this ideal layout of towns that missionaries strived for. But whereas utopias are usually taken to mean the unattainable, the Jesuit reductions in Paraguay were concrete realities that held over three thousand inhabitants each.[61]

The central cluster of buildings, or reduction nucleus, in the *divujo* is formed by the church; the priest's house; the refectory; the great square in which community activities occurred; the two chapels, one for children and other for adults; and the crosses at the four corners of the plaza. On the sides of the central cluster are workshops, the offices of *mayordomo*, and the music and dance schools. In front of the nucleus and on its two sides are the houses of the Guaraní. Behind the nucleus is the garden and farm of the priest. Occupying large structures to the left of the nucleus are the granaries used for long-term storage. These granaries played key economic roles in the reductions. When times were bad, the town inhabitants were able to call on the products stored in the communal granaries. No walls enclose the town, at least none are in the plan.

The *divujo* details not only the physical arrangement of reduction buildings but also their design formation. But the *divujo* says even more. It reveals how townspeople, priests, and ideals were interrelated, how a group of buildings represented a deeply held conviction that the material and spiritual are bound together in a unified whole.[62] The European Jesuits wanted to create an earthly paradise in which God was served at the same time that the physical needs of the community were taken care of. The idea was the creation of a near perfect society, one in which both God and the mundane were satisfied. And it may not be too much of a stretch to imagine that the Jesuits conceived each if not of equal value then at least of equal virtue. To see God in all things, as Ignatius Loyola wished his followers do, did not mean a species of pantheism. For the Jesuit, since the redemption encompassed all creation, by consequence the earth and everything in it had a touch of the divine. The Fourth Week of St. Ignatius's *Spiritual Exercises* clearly states this, and the Jesuit's yearly retreat served to underline it. Therefore, it certainly is not beyond belief that the Jesuits in Paraguay were convinced that they were creating an earthly *civitas dei*, a man-made environment in which an almost perfect society could develop, a society in which both God and man benefited.

The artist of the *Divujo* claimed that while most of Native America lived in poverty, the over four thousand souls that lived in each reduction had streets and a plaza of one hundred sixty square yards. A great majority of the reduction buildings had *soportales*, or arcades to protect pedestrians from the sun and rain.

In the center of the reduction was the church, the *iglesia*. "The churches," he continued, "are very large, ordinarily 70 to 80 *varas* [yards] long, and 26 to 28 *varas* wide, and some are even 90 *varas* long by 30 wide. Each has three naves. They're constructed with stone one or two *varas* high at the foundations, and adobe brick throughout the rest of the building." On one side of the church was the town cemetery, divided into sections for men, women, boys, and girls. Within the church only ranking *caciques* or *corregidores* were interred. On one side of the church was the priests' house, the ante-refectory, the refectory, and the arms storehouse all of which looked out over a large patio or garden.

Alongside were storage rooms for community food products (called the *almacenes de la hacienda común*). Other workshops that faced patios held goldsmiths, carpenters, weavers, blacksmiths, and even rosary makers. Each reduction also had a House of Seclusion, a *casa de recogidas*, where young pregnant women could stay for the birth of their children, and some had a jail, a *carcel*, a juvenile detention house, *para delinquentes*, as well as an orphanage. An inn (*posada*) for Spaniards, Indians, or anyone (*de todas castas*) passing through was a feature of centralized reductions. And passing through was taken literally, since visits longer than three days by non-Indians were not encouraged.[63] The most space within the reduction proper, after the church, was occupied by the spinners of cotton who occupied seven or eight rooms, each of which was six by seven varas. An entire family, father, mother, and children, worked and lived in one room.

> The priest frequently visits the workshops in order to make sure
> they keep on schedule. The priest puts in each workshop the one
> who is most likely to do the best job and the Indian accepts this
> without contradiction. The tasks of drummer boy and flute player
> are taken by those who have this talent. Some reduction towns have
> ten or eleven of these. Two flute players accompany the drummer,
> and the flutes are highly polished reeds that can play fugues, arias,
> minuets, and other kinds of music. These instruments are so popu-
> lar that they accompany the river boats and the wagons, and during
> communal work they add a measure of joy to the labor.[64]

The communities were self-sufficient, which meant that each was independent insofar as basic needs were concerned. Fields that were for the benefit of the entire community, called *sementeras comunes*, in which were grown corn, vegetables, and cotton, were worked on Mondays and Saturdays during seven months of the year. Only weavers and blacksmiths were exempt from work on community lands. Cattle destined for community consumption grazed on community pasturelands.

Tea and Cattle

Following, perhaps a bit too closely, their founder's maxim to the effect that every spiritual work required a firm financial foundation, the Jesuit missionaries in the reductions rested their spiritual activity on the sale of *yerba del Paraguay* and the raising and sale of cattle products. Proceeds allowed reduction communities to pay the royal tribute tax assessed on each able-bodied

Guaraní, purchase church adornments, and even buy incidental articles for the Guaraní.[65] The process whereby this was done created controversy and in a real sense overshadowed the unique accomplishments of the Jesuits in Paraguay, forcing them continually to look over their collective shoulders to protect their backs.[66]

The *yerba del Paraguay* was later popularly called Jesuit tea, and it is still marketed under that name in the United States. The Jesuit Annual Letter of 1626 referred to it as a kind of "laurel leaf called *maracayu* that grows in certain mountainous places." The Indians, continued the description, "break the branches, toast the leaves over a fire, then grind them in mortars to powder [*polvo*]. It is then put into baskets and carried on their shoulders many leagues to the river for shipping."[67]

The inaccessibility of the growing areas was a challenge to the Jesuits. If tea could be grown in lowland orchards relatively close to the reductions, the tea could become a boon to both Indians and Jesuits. A larger income stream would be created and the Indian would not have to spend months outside of the reduction cultivating, harvesting, and carrying the tea down out of the mountains. A series of experiments were begun that would allow the Jesuits to grow the *yerba del Paraguay* on orchards nearer the reductions. The first plantings were unsuccessful. More experiments followed. The *yerba* seeds were as small as pepper grains and imbedded in a viscous, liquid-like substance. The local Jesuit botanist, whoever he was (and perhaps it was done in Spain), succeeded in separating the seed from the liquid and the seed was replanted. Success! However, trial and error showed that transplanting the seedlings was necessary and a second transplanting in other soil when the plant was more mature. Here it was irrigated and tended over a period of two or three years, and it was ready for harvesting after eight or ten years.[68] These experiments that were carried out over at least a decade and a half left the Jesuits with a certain proprietary attitude toward the tea that was grown in reduction orchards.

The tea became the most popular beverage in the Río de la Plata, Peru, and in Chile. Writing in the middle of the eighteenth century, Sánchez Labrador thought that the Spaniards used it for the same reasons that the Guaraní Indians did, "to feel the calmness in the bloodstream."[69] He goes on to say that:

> the Indians call the tea Caâygua and the Spaniards 'Mate.' Rarely do the Indians put hot water into it. Their customary method is to put cold water into the *Yierba* drinking it right before their most arduous tasks and in the warmest part of the day. I believe that the

Yierba contains little fire in itself [*poco fuego*] but it attracts and receives elements that inflame the blood and for this reason provides a certain alleviation for bodily heat. I have drunk it many times especially on trips and besides feeling a certain freshness in my blood, I noticed that the *Yierba* is a corrective to bodily liquid and does no harm even if one is sweating. Rather, a gentle perspiration follows, the senses are cleared, and one is relieved of the sun's heat. Even weariness disappears.

Spaniards and other *castas* in the cities are accustomed to take the *Yierba del Paraguay* by pouring boiling water into it, like Chinese tea is taken. The difference is because the *Yierba* is ground up and the powder does not boil in the tea kettle or heater, but it is put into gourd called a Mate, and there is added a little lemon or orange juice, or some sugar, or some other kind of sugary substance.

Taken in moderation, this beverage noticeably helps the body, producing perspiration, causing urination, and other notable benefits.[70]

By 1667 the Jesuit reductions were shipping almost six thousand arrobas of tea to Santa Fe and to Buenos Aires. Eventually a separate office, called the *Oficio de Misiones*, was set up in these two cities that managed the distribution of goods sent down from the reductions. Every year the pueblos shipped on large rafts, *barcos grandes*, a total of twelve thousand arrobas of tea that were received by the Jesuit procurators in the two cities. The twelve thousand arrobas sold for forty thousand pesos (in the eighteenth century), and the other goods, whether cloth, cotton, or tobacco realized another twenty thousand pesos. From this total, twenty-two thousand went to the royal coffers as tribute payment, three thousand for the *diezmo* tax on the shipped goods, and the rest was divided among the reductions, about 1,266 pesos for each. Knives and cloth for the Guaraní and ornaments for the church were purchased with this sum. And the Jesuit who wrote the report added cynically, "from which comes the million pesos sent yearly to the General of the Jesuits in Rome!"[71]

It is not difficult to pinpoint the source of resentment. By 1670 the Jesuits had taken the tea trade out of the hands of Santa Fe and Buenos Aires merchants, arguing that the Guaraní had not been given a fair price for their product. They themselves took over the sale and distribution of the tea. A royal order of 1675 repeated the charge that the Jesuits controlled the tea trade having put Spanish merchants out of the business.[72]

However, the complaint was premature. In 1671 and 1672, the reductions loaded a total of sixteen rafts with 6,178 arrobas of tea. The following year

10,531 arrobas were shipped and at this time the tea was valued at two pesos an arroba.[73] But the agitation grew and in 1679 Capt. Juan de Avila Salazar published an edict accusing the Jesuits of selling yerba, tobacco, and sugar without paying the *alcabala* tax. It was not the fruit of their inheritance, said the edict, but *propio trato*, business dealings, and they ought to pay. The goods came into the city (Santa Fe) on rafts and no declarations were made.[74]

The Jesuit response was swift. Valeriano de Villegas, the procurator of the reductions, stated before the governor that the edict should have mentioned that the proceeds from yerba sales pays the nine thousand peso yearly tribute sent to the crown. No yerba sales, no tribute. Villegas showed the governor a load of royal cédulas from the king in Madrid which allowed the Jesuits to conduct the tea trade for the Guaraní. In 1666 the Audiencia of Buenos Aires had passed a law authorizing the collection of the sales taxes on tea coming down from the reductions.[75] In short order, the Jesuits secured an exemption from the tax "since the tea, hides, and cattle is sold in order to support the work of the missions."[76]

This ability to respond rapidly stung the local bureaucracy. The obvious influence of the Jesuits in Madrid and the order's capacity to wage legal battles in America labeled the Jesuits arrogant.

Although the Jesuit reductions were restricted to the yearly sale of twelve thousand arrobas of tea, their trade network throughout Latin America enabled them to ship quantities to Santiago de Chile, to the silver city of Potosí in present-day Bolovia, and to Lima, Peru. In 1734 two major categories of tea were distinguished, *yerba caamini* that was sold for three pesos an arroba, and *yerba de palos*, which was of inferior quality and sold for two pesos an arroba. More than eighteen thousand arrobas of the former were produced on the reductions and twenty-six thousand arrobas of the latter.[77] Tea commanded higher prices in Santiago and Lima and hence the eagerness to distribute to those places. The yerba caamini sold for seven pesos an arroba in Santiago but for only four pesos in Buenos Aires.[78]

Tea distribution and sales involved the initial producers on the reductions, the Jesuit procurators in Santa Fe or Buenos Aires, and lay distributors such as Miguel Tagle, Alonso de Moreyra, and Felix del Bono.[79]

The contract between the Jesuit procurator's office in Córdoba and the distributor Andrés Lascano stipulated that Lascano was to transport 3,296 arrobas of yerba caamini to Lima. There he was to buy with the proceeds six bundles of good cloth, six sacks of sugar, two sacks of indigo, a case of strong tobacco, and a box of chocolate. For security reasons Lascano was to divide the shipment into two. And he was further instructed to purchase high quality gold in Chile, if necessary with a letter of credit.[80]

These were the kinds of arrangements that cast a dark shadow over the European Jesuits in Paraguay, and the Jesuit provincial, Jaime Aguilar, warned about them in 1735. In his parting report to the College of Paraguay he wrote:

> I want you to finally do away with every occasion for the discredit
> that we are suffering because of our reputation as merchants in this
> city and province. Therefore, I strictly order that no Jesuit sell or
> exchange any goods or valuables belonging to this college ... and so
> only the fruits and goods produced from our haciendas and slaves
> can be sold. I allow you to buy animals for the hacienda and for the
> support of our family with the cotton cloth we produce.[81]

Of equal importance in the economic scheme of things was the cattle raised on the reductions. They provided a source of food and of income for the Guaraní. Cattle was slaughtered and the meat eaten by the Guaraní. This raised their caloric intake but it reduced their reliance on hunting.[82] Cardiel speaks about a weekly distribution of meat and Nusdorffer visiting the reduction of San Borja saw eleven head of cattle slaughtered daily to feed seven hundred families and four hundred widows. He ordered that the number of cattle slaughtered be raised to fifteen a day, thereby increasing the daily intake from three to four kilos.[83] The author of the *Breve Relación* said that the reduction of Yapeyu was accustomed to slaughter thirty or forty a day, about ten thousand yearly.

> In Yapeyu which as I have said is the largest of the reductions, they
> are accustomed to slaughter 10,000 cows a year for food, which
> comes to 30 and sometimes 40 daily. The cattle are driven by horse
> from the large ranges as I described above. Cattle from the new
> range is sold to other towns. San Miguel does this. Whoever is not
> familiar with the things of America may not believe how a range 50
> leagues long can exist, or that 10,000 head are slaughtered for a
> town numbering 1,700, or that each head of cattle is priced at 3 sil-
> ver *reales*. But this is another world, vast and abundant. Cows here
> are much bigger than those in Spain; there are 6,000 *varas* to a
> league; the pastures and *estancias* of Yapeyu and San Miguel are the
> largest. The others are eight, ten, or at the most twenty leagues
> long.[84]

Understanding the author's tendency to exaggerate, he makes a good point. America and Europe *were* world's apart. While the Spaniard, European mis-sionaries included, viewed cattle primarily for their export value in hides, the Guaraní ate the beef.

Only eight or ten towns had herds large enough to feed each family with four or five pounds of beef daily. The other towns supplied their inhabitants with meat three or four times a week. What was called the *ración* was handed out in the patio of the workshops after recitation of the rosary which was usually an hour after sunset. A woman from each family was summoned by a drum roll that signaled the beginning of the day's distribution. Everyone received the same amount of beef "except the wives of those who brought in the cattle and the *principales*. They received a double *ración*."[85]

Cattle however were raised not just for beef. Cows (*lecheras*) were distributed to the Guaraní for a regular supply of milk. To make sure that the herds were maintained properly the priest was ordered to visit periodically the reduction ranches that were usually sixty to one hundred miles distant.

The total intake of calories and proteins from animal and vegetable products per year per person on a reduction in 1767 has been calculated to be 2,509. Since the Food and Agriculture Organization of the United Nations recommends three thousand calories for each adult, the reduction number compares favorably with contemporary levels in Paraguay, Brazil, Uruguay, and Argentina.[86] But protein levels must be balanced against the overall effect on the native habits of food acquisition and consumption. While on the one hand, protein levels increased, on the other something was lost by abandoning traditional food sharing practices. Food foraging as a way of life was eliminated when the reductions became major cattle producers and beef became a major food for the Guaraní.

Cattle were introduced to the reductions in the seventeenth century by way of Asunción and the environment suited them. Herds grew rapidly.[87] In 1728 the reduction ranches of Concepción had 7,772 head of cattle and 15,748 sheep, besides mares and stallions. The sizes of herds on other reduction estates varied considerably, between ten and twenty-four thousand head. Concepción also had 1,190 *bueyes de la gente*, or oxen for draft work on the farms.[88] At the time of the expulsion of the Jesuits from Latin America in 1767, the Guaraní towns had more than seven hundred thousand *vacas*, 44,183 oxen, 240,027 sheep, 28,204 horses, and 15,234 mules.[89]

Although the reductions used beef as food, something that the pampas later rarely did until the introduction of refrigeration in the nineteenth century, the sale of hides from slaughtered cattle was a major source of income. Shipments to the *Oficio de Misiones*, whether in Santa Fe or Buenos Aires, were regularly made at the same time as the yerba was transported.[90]

Besides tea and cattle, tobacco and cotton played minor but significant economic roles. The Guaraní word for tobacco was *peti* and the Spaniards used the leaf not only for smoking and snuff but also for medicinal purposes. When a smallpox epidemic struck, and they did so frequently, the patient was fed tobacco. "When the smallpox hit the Guaraní missions, Fr. Francisco de Acevedo used this remedy in Itapua with great success. Of the 638 who were sick, only 23 died."[91] But the most effective remedy was flight and hiding in the forests. The fevers were as violent as any in Europe, affecting Indians and *castas* more than Europeans "either because of the weakness of their humors or because of the poor care they received once they catch the disease."[92]

Cotton was grown and it too had a medicinal use. The Guaraní word for cotton was *mandiyu*. It was first fluffed then spun into cloth. But if the sprouts were soaked in water then drunk, the mixture was a successful antidote to scorpion bites or to other kinds of poisonous stings.[93] Ground branches spread over wounds was also a remedy. Grains also helped kidney problems, prevented dysentery, and stopped coughing. The oil extracted from seed grains relieved skin rashes. It seemed that there was little that the cotton plant could not do.

From Folkways to Heresy

In 1635 Fr. Pedro Nola wrote that in the reduction of Jesús María a group of shamans were tied up, beaten, dragged around the town, and offered to the priests as slaves.[94] The youth of the village laughed at them. A major conflict pitted a thousand armed Guaraní supporting the new religion against the forces of the *hechiceros*, the adherents of the old ways.[95] This extraordinary struggle represented a reversal of religious belief occurring less than two generations after the arrival of the Spanish missionaries. Native opposition to Christianity was always laid at Satan's doorstep. The *demonio* was the one who clouded the minds of the Guaraní. He was the one who had been adored and who placed obstacles in the way of the missionaries, as the annual report of 1635 recounted.

> The missionary found a partly burned footstool in a hut where the
> devil had been and in whose honor a candle had been lit in front.
> Three sticks forming a triangle and painted with carbon had on top
> of them a jar with water that the devil had brought. The Father
> burned down the entire hut but he punished lightly the boy who revealed its presence. Never again was the hut used because the devil
> fled once he was exposed.[96]

The European missionaries in the reductions did not view themselves as outsiders intruding on the culture of the Guaraní, but as God's vehicles offering the keys to everlasting life. God wanted cultural change to take place among the Guaraní and they were there to make sure it happened. A culture survives only if it can resolve basic problems. It has to provide for the production and distribution of goods. Members will adhere to the culture only if it offers a means to biological continuity. The culture must be able to maintain its adherents in reasonably good order and see to their survival. And finally, it must be able to change.[97] What the Jesuits attempted in Paraguay was not a modification of the belief system but a radical alteration of an entire way of life. The Jesuit brought with him from Europe what he believed was absolute truth, not only about the divine but also about how civilized man should behave. Military conquest supported an immediate reversal of belief and behavior. Political motivation was part of this equation since docile Christians subservient to missionary and crown were more apt to provide labor and taxes. The changes that occurred, however, not only were imposed from outside but they had some degree of acceptance from the conquered society itself. What Nwoye in Chinua Achebe's *Things Fall Apart* called "the poetry of the new religion," must have likewise affected at least some of the indigenous peoples of Paraguay. How many conversions were authentic is difficult to say. But as the Guaraní culture broke down, key elements of a new belief system were adopted.

What the Guaraní had considered sacred, the gods they had worshiped, the groves and forests that were consecrated, the rites that were venerated and respected, the entire belief system that had held sway since time immemorial was now to be considered worthless. In its place the Jesuit put a collection of religious ideas and beliefs held by European Christians. The three persons in the trinity, the godhead, angels, the Virgin Mary, heaven, the redemption, and the afterlife were presented to the Guaraní in the form of stories. While condemning the folk myths of the Guaraní, Fr. Ruiz de Montoya saw no contradiction in placing a "piece of St. Ignatius's cassock in a jar" to ward off evil.[98] Apparently the folk Catholicism of sixteenth-century Europe was more true and effective than the folk beliefs of the Guaraní!

As early as 1614, just a few years after the founding of the first Jesuit reductions, the Guaraní in Todos los Santos would gather before dawn for prayers in their own houses. When the sun rose, they went to the church for catechism lessons, called the *doctrina,* and afterward Mass was held. When the adults left the reduction for work in the fields, the children, boys separated from girls, studied more catechism. After evening dinner when the bell rang, the town gathered for recitation of the rosary in the church and hymns were sung.[99] As the years passed, the rites and rituals became more elaborate. Processions, choirs, musical instruments, pageants, all modeled on European Catholicism, captivated the Guaraní audience.[100] Andrew Greeley suggests that

Catholicism's stories, i.e., the birth of God's son in a stable with angels singing and shepherds adoring, the miracles of Christ, the Resurrection and its accompanying details, Mary as Mother of God, plus others, provided a convincing and satisfying motive for adhering to a new belief system. Christianity's stories were "better" than the other guy's stories![101]

What had been considered wrong or right in Guaraní society before the coming of the Europeans was the reverse afterward. The Jesuits did not share the "anything goes" attitude of cultural relativism. They did not hesitate to condemn Aztec human sacrifice in Mexico or to root out the "compassionate cannibalism" of the Guaraní. However, the references to eating human flesh are relatively few. They appear in the first half of the seventeenth century. Father Joseph Orregio wrote that a *cacique* named Erouaca came to Santa Ana with his wives, parents, and children. "He ate human flesh. He stayed a league from the reduction. He ate his wife, his sister, another wife and his child. We saw the bones."[102] But Diego de Torres's statement probably sums it up. "Drunkenness is common but there's almost no reports of anybody eating human flesh."[103]

What occupied much more attention was the polygamy of the Guaraní *caciques*. "They [the *caciques*] have several wives and when they [the *caciques*] become Christian, they marry one and the other women work their fields."[104] The early Jesuit missionaries were told to ease up on the demands of Christianity but with polygamy they held a very tight line, requiring a Christian *cacique* to be married to only one woman.

When Ruiz de Montoya was the parish priest of the reduction San Ignacio, one of the *caciques* married but soon wanted to take another woman as his wife. The *cacique* was "attracted to a woman, nor for her beauty but her noble status . . . his life was exceptionally scandalous as he had a large number of concubines, with the full consent of his pretended wife."[105] Ruiz objected and he interpreted the *cacique's* refusal to accept this objection to mean that the *cacique* resented the "purity and modesty" of the Jesuits. "Our own purity and modesty was an offense to him; he disliked our obliging the sick and those who wanted to be truly cleansed through baptism to give up their concubines."[106] The *cacique*, wrote Ruiz, became so bitter that he said:

> The devils have brought us these men, for with new teachings they
> want to take away from us the good old way of life of our ancestors,
> who had many wives and servant women and were free to choose
> them at will. Now they want us to tie ourselves to a single woman. It
> is not right for this to go any further; we should drive them out of
> our lands or take their lives.[107]

Ruiz de Montoya was not aware, nor should he have been, that polygamy was closely related to economic opportunities and community relationships in that it gave broader landowning opportunities and prestige to the *cacique* while intergroup relationships and marriages cemented peace. Some *caciques* were so dissatisfied over Jesuit demands for monogamous relationships that they founded their own reduction in Corrientes modeled on the old way, permitting *caciques* to maintain a plurality of wives.[108] It did not survive.

Several methods were used to insure adherence to the new morality. Public embarrassment was one. The reduction *fiscal* read aloud in public the names of those who missed religious services. Children were encouraged to tell the priest of their parents' shortcomings, which must have produced considerable stress within families and groups. The children, acting as morality policemen, drove a wedge between those family members who accepted the new belief system with its behavior corollaries and those who wanted to adhere to the old ways.

Physical punishment was meted out to those who deviated from the new morality. Homosexual behavior was put on the same level as bestiality, which if either were proven was punished with three months in the reduction jail and four whippings of twenty-five lashes each over the three months. However, the prisoner was permitted to attend Mass. If a victim of poisonous herbs died, the perpetrator was jailed for life. If the victim did not die, three months jail time was the punishment. Incest and procuring abortions were punished by two months in jail with three whippings, twenty-five lashes each. No Jesuit was allowed to administer physical punishments. Village *fiscales* were the executioners. "And you should never cut anyone's hair off without the permission of Father Superior."[109]

All decisions regarding reduction life were the responsibility of the priest. He was on top of the new hierarchical pyramid. He was the new intermediary between the Guaraní and the Divine. He was the one who had the power to bring God's blessings or wrath down upon them. He held the keys of the kingdom. He could summon the Spanish army to destroy them. He was the one who sat in a large chair on January 1 and distributed the symbols of authority to the newly chosen corregidor and to the new cabildo.

Every morning the corregidor and the cabildo received the orders of the day from the priest and they in turn gave him a list "of those who did wrong." The orders of the day consisted of the tasks that the village had to perform and where each villager would work. The symbolism and message of who was actually in charge was clear. Each cabildo member was given an entire fatted cow (*vaca gorda*) at fiesta time, along with a basket of bread, a packet of honey, yerba, and tobacco. Beneath the cabildo and corregidor was the *fiscal* who enjoyed the confidence of the priest. He was his assistant; the one who orga-nized the children's doctrina lessons, the one who prayed with them in the morning and at night; he was the one who accompanied the priest on visits to the sick; the person who informed the priest about absences from religious services. The *cacique* who had previously enjoyed absolute sway found his power diminished. However, he did receive special treatment. His meat ration was greater than that of the commoner. Physical punishment was never ad-ministered to him within view of his people. And although the prestige he once enjoyed carried over to the new dispensation, it was a prestige without power.

Traditional Guaraní religion did not survive. Traces were carried into the European-derived culture, but the old was superseded by the new. However, its collapse was not inevitable. No cultural laws were at work, only the very real presence of invaders, both Portuguese and Spanish. Their presence forced the Guaraní to make adaptive choices involving their very existence. Whether the Guaraní would have adapted to "modern" times if they had been left alone is pure speculation. But they probably would have.[110]

7

Art, Architecture, and Theater

Colonial art and architecture have been the subjects of several excellent studies.[1] Styles, forms, models, architects, and materials have been examined in reasonable detail. However, less attention has been paid to the specific iconography and architecture of Jesuit churches and buildings, at least until Arellano's work in 1991 and Bailey's in 1999.[2] Even less attention has been paid to colonial art and architecture as a didactic form used to reinforce a belief system. The same is true of theater, especially in Jesuit colleges. The latter was almost exclusively the prerogative of the elite, sons of Spaniards who were thought to be the future decision-makers in Latin America.

Old Forms in New Settings

When the first missionaries arrived in Mexico in the sixteenth century, they brought with them European models of churches and iconography. Convents and monasteries were constructed just as in Spain but early on new features not found in the Old Country were added, necessitated by the new evangelization. The open-air atrium accommodating hundreds of Indian worshippers and used for instruction was one distinct contribution to early American religious architecture.[3] Some early Mexican churches had a fortress-like look because they served the same purpose as the Norman churches in eleventh-century France, protecting villagers from armed assaults.

They were usually built in the Romanesque, Gothic, or Renaissance style of Europe with a single nave.[4] The church was the only stone construction in the vicinity able to withstand a protracted attack of arrows and weaponry. The plateresque style in Latin America appeared after the discovery of the great silver mines of Guanajuato, Mexico, and Potosí. Carved ornaments with delicate tracing was characteristic of this style. By the seventeenth century the Baroque style had made its entrance into the capital cities of Latin America. The standard interior design of the Latin cross was preserved with the nave bisected by a transept, thus separating the sanctuary from the section of the church reserved for the faithful. Marriages and baptisms were recorded in a *cuadrante* or register room. The church cloister was usually associated with the *convento* or priest's house. It was spacious with gardens, flowers, and greenery.

What follows is not a history of Jesuit architecture in America. Not found here are the technical aspects of the buildings with the dates of when they were constructed, which artists and architects were responsible for which works, with an accurate dating of when various parts of the churches were built. What is present in this chapter, however, is a sense of what the colonial churches and their iconography tried to say to the multitudes who saw them. Architecture and art is an expression of energy. It speaks in a language of form whose meaning must be deciphered.

Houses of God

Jesuit churches were frequently associated with their colleges. The Society of Jesus did not staff parishes in a city because that was the prerogative of the secular clergy, but alongside their colleges was almost always a distinctively constructed church. The church in Santiago de Guatemala, for example, is almost a replica of rural fiesta art. The façade is extraordinarily busy. Twelve saintly figures peer out from their niches, scallop-like designs fill three-quarters of the façade, four belltowers stretch above the three entrances, and three colored glass windows are above each door. The center window, which is above the main church entrance, is filled with pieces of transparent bone. Topping the entire façade and looking down over those entering the church and those in the courtyard, because the church faces not a street but the college courtyard, is a monstrance. One usually associates the Sacred Species with a monstrance, used to bless the faithful at benediction services and in Corpus Christi processions, but in this monstrance is the Jesuit symbol IHS (symbol for Jesus), which is found on much of Jesuit iconography. In the single niche below the monstrance is a crucifix of the dying Christ.

As most Jesuit churches, this one in Santiago de Guatemala, later called Guatemala City, was built over several decades. Funds dribbled in each year from college-owned estates and real estate, funds that had to be shared by other demands associated with operating an urban institution. The society in Mexico from which Guatemala was governed assigned a Jesuit full time to church construction, Fr. Ignacio Lopez de Azpeitia. The province catalogue described him as: "*Praeest Fabricae*," or as we would say today construction manager. This was the third Jesuit church in the city. The first proved inadequate, the second was destroyed in an earthquake, and this third one was built near the Plaza Mayor, the center of the city.[5]

The church was physically attached to the college precincts to enable easy access of students and Jesuit faculty. It is unclear whether others had unlimited access to the church or whether it was considered a "college" chapel. The interior had a free open space with nave and sanctuary but no transept. A sanctuary where the altar was located was set apart from the rest of the nave. The plans we now possess do not elaborate on the details of the interior. Only the façade is drawn in detail. And it is a unique example of colonial art. It conveys the feeling of a family shrine not overwhelming one with its size. It appears flat and wide, almost as if hugging the ground, no doubt deliberately so constructed in order to protect against earthquakes.

Generally speaking, the number of statues looking down from the façade of the church was calculated to impress the viewer with the magnitude and plenitude of the Communion of Saints. They are all there, each with an assigned task waiting for the faithful to call upon him or her to invoke power, protection, and assistance. Just as in early Europe where the rosary replaced the talisman, or the statue replaced the household god, or the Mass replaced pagan rites, so too in Mexico, and elsewhere in Latin America, the saints replaced the powers that ruled the daily lives of the Native American. Now the Native American had the Christian saint to pray to. No matter that the Indian prayed to both, refusing to cast aside centuries of belief in a local god. The faithful, both Spanish and Indian, were reminded of this reality by the plethora of saints visible in their niches. Although San Lucas has fourteen statues looking down from the façade, their number does not compare with the 300 cherubim and saints on the façade of the Jesuit church at Tepozotlán, Mexico. This once was the church of the Jesuit Novitiate house in Mexico and it has been called the most beautiful baroque church in Latin America.[6]

A major question arises about what the European missionary imagined that the Indian thought of all these figures. For the Spaniard, the Baroque was beautiful, and the swirling columns and elaborate decoration and cherubim heads were a direct response to the stark emptiness of the Protestant reformer's place of worship. The Baroque architecture in Europe was a similar response. In Latin America where the Protestant Reformation meant very little, the elaborate façade was simply another design. The Indian saw the church at Tepozotlán as an icon to the new belief system. Whether it was "beautiful" did not matter. His notion of beauty was different from the European's. The Baroque style in Latin America was a projection of the European's universalist sense. But even the Baroque church at Tepozotlán combines American and European features. It was not totally European. The Indian craftsmen who molded the statuary, designs, and the icons that still grace the façade and interior left Indian features on the saints, Indian symbols both within the church and on the exterior.

The façade of Tepozotlán is carved in stone, in a Churrigueresque style. The stone changes color depending on the shadows that fall on it during the daytime. Jesuit iconography, St. Francis Xavier, the society's symbol IHS, and St. Ignatius Loyola dominate. St. Francis Xavier, who was revered within the society as the missionary par excellence, was the patron of the church because the Jesuits were originally entrusted with the town of Tepozotlán in 1591 to act as missionaries for the Otomi Indians and to educate the sons of the Indian leaders. The bell towers have the traditional Mexican *estipetes*, pilasters that look like inverted pyramids.

The construction of the church began in 1671 and was completed around 1740. The church dome throws light on the five gilded altarpieces. The magnificent craftsmanship of the altarpieces is a tribute to the Indians who brought their ancient talents to bear on behalf of the new religion. St. Francis Xavier has a place of honor in the sanctuary to the left of Nuestra Señora de Guadalupe who is in the center. To her right is the founder of the Jesuits, St. Ignatius Loyola. Along the nave walls are St. Joseph and the Virgen de la Luz. Two of Miguel Cabrera's paintings are in the lower choir, *El Patrocinio de Jesucristo a las Almas de Purgatorio* and the *El Patrocinio de la Virgen María a la Compañía de Jesús*.

A small interior room decorated in a Baroque style is used to change the gowns of the Virgin, an indication of the degree to which Spanish realism had been integrated into and accepted by the indigenous population. The statue, whether the *Virgen de Guadalupe* or San Francisco Javier, is considered more than just a representation of the individual. No one would say that the statue is the person represented, but neither would a Spaniard or Mexican admit that it is simply a little plaster object with lifelike features. The dressing room is an example of how the concrete was preferred to the abstract in Hispanic culture.

The cloister with its gardens, fountain, and graceful arches, the kitchens near the patio, and the smaller Domestic Chapel with its brightly decorated mirrors, relics, and paintings, were used exclusively by the Jesuits, intended primarily for the novices seeking admission to the Society of Jesus in the Mexican Province.

Spaniards and Indians viewed the churches differently. But on some level the effect was the same. The Spaniards were reassured that the rites and rituals into which they had been born were observed in the New World. The American-born European was likewise reassured in his cultural heritage. But as alluded to above, the churches were neither Spanish nor Indian. They were American. The blend of European fundamentals with Native American designs and shapes produced a third quality that was distinctively American. No church complex in Spain ever looked like the Sanctuary of Nuestra Señora de Ocotlan in Tlaxcala. Nor did any approach the gilded façade of Santa María Tonantzintla, Puebla, or have tiled domes like the ones on the church of Carmen in Mexico City. So although the European and American-born Spaniard were reassured by familiar religious surroundings, the surroundings bore a distinctly American flavor. For the Indian, the church structure and its related buildings were a symbol of power, a "powerhouse" as all large structures, whether civil, religious, or private, are intended to be. The Indian was never excluded from the Spaniard's church like the black slave in the North American South was excluded from the white man's place of worship. The Indian was not a slave but he was on the lower end of the social pyramid. Nevertheless, he partook of the festivities, rituals, and processions that the European priests introduced into the calendar. The religious fiesta was by no means simply an opportunity to revel. The saint whose feast day was celebrated was considered truly the appointed guardian of the city or town whose presence and protection had to be assured, primarily against the wiles of the devil. There was a social as well as deeply religious motivation operating beneath the dancing and drinking of the yearly fiesta. Therefore, the Indian saw the physical attributes of the church, the statues standing in protection of him, the patron saint watching his every move, the Virgin or Christ observing all, the decorated façade, the church interior whose walls were hung with colored pictures and paintings and murals, the thick church walls and the atrium, as the tangible manifestation of God's presence working through the priests who ministered to him. The massive church also meant power, influence, and domination. In Mexico City the great Christian churches were frequently constructed on top of the ruins of the Aztec temples to demonstrate once and for all the obliteration of the old religion. In the rural areas of America, it was not so easy and Christian missionaries came to a gentle accommodation with the old native rites.

The silver mines of Guanajuato and Taxco as well as the great haciendas and ranches were the primary sources of the funds that built ornate churches and paid craftsmen to decorate them. While Mexican colonial churches tried to outdo each other in ornateness and size, farther south, in the Andes, the religious orders constructed a number of extraordinary religious sites and shrines employing native craftsmen to decorate and create the iconography. The Jesuit church in Quito is a prime example of massive Baroque construction in an urban, Andean setting.

The Jesuits arrived in Quito from Peru in 1586 but it was several years before serious church construction was begun. Popularly referred to as La Compañía, the Jesuit church in Quito has a long construction history, from 1605 to 1765, intimately connected with the college complex and associated buildings.[7] Property adjacent to the college was purchased for a church in 1605 for 6,500 pesos, and by 1613 a suitable edifice was opened for public worship. In 1636 the Italian Jesuit architect, Marcos Guerrero, arrived in Quito to direct construction of a more elaborate church. Interior and exterior refinements were added and by 1666 the interior of the church was completed as was the general architecture of the square block that held the Jesuit church, residence, college, and university. Guerrero supervised construction of the college building, the library, and the church, and also much of the sculpture. The famous façade was not begun until 1722 nor completed until 1765. The cost of construction materials and labor was high.[8] The cost of the Jesuit church in Lima was about a million pesos and Quito's could not have been too much less. When added to the costs of building the college, university, library, lecture halls, theater, cloisters, living quarters, dining room, and general offices, the sum was almost two million pesos. The piece de resistance was the gold leaf plating of the church's interior. To plate just one of the side altar tabernacles cost six thousand pesos. How much the main altar *retablo* (usually a statue) cost, or the other side altars can only be guessed. The *cofradías* bore much of the financial burden for the side altars.

A long-time resident of the Jesuit house in Quito in the eighteenth century characterized the residence as truly regal, with magnificent paintings, gardens, cloisters, spacious living quarters, and dining room decorated with the most lovely paintings.[9] The façade of La Compañía is truly remarkable both for the exquisiteness of detail and the form of the design. The eight statues looking down from their niches is not overwhelming. And four of these are looking toward the center portal. The five swirling pillars pull the onlooker's gaze upward. On the topmost part of the façade is an inscription to Ignatius Loyola, founder of the Jesuits, and atop this is the monstrance. Although not immediately apparent, the church is similar to the Gesù in Rome, the grand Baroque Jesuit church whose interior is encrusted in gold topped by a fantastically painted ceiling that flows down over the pillars to become almost three-dimensional, merging with painted stucco figures in a swirling composition glorifying the Jesuit saints. However, the façade of Il Gesù is nothing like the La Compañía's. At Il Gesù no swirling columns greet the visitor. No cherubim heads and bodies are suspended. No square pillars are lavishly decorated. No Jesuit symbols are in evidence. One has to enter Il Gesù to see these. La Compañía announces them beforehand and tells you what to expect inside.

The interior of La Compañía is cavernous. Vaulted ceilings move on to a windowed dome throwing light on the sanctuary. The entire church is gilded and decorated with finely worked designs. Six side altars are exquisitely done in gold and silver. The *retablo* dedicated to San Francisco Javier is exceptionally elaborate. The saint's statue is flanked within the niche by five angels, with other angels along the *retablo's* border. To the left of the statue is a carving depicting the saint's death on the Island of Sancian as he was on the point of entering China. On the other side of the statue another carving depicts the saint baptizing a dark-skinned person, probably an Indian. The entire side altar and retablo is painted in gold.

The side altars are matched by the magnificent pulpit that is topped by a statue of St. Paul preaching to the Gentiles. Other saints, including St. Ignatius Loyola, are in niches around the circumference of the pulpit. The colors are lively but not glaring. Blue, red, amber, and gold predominate, all coordinated to produce a pleasant effect. However, gold is the dominant color. The relative simplicity of La Compañía's exterior contrasts sharply with the interior. Here, especially in the sacristy, the wall paintings and the dome recall the dome of the Jesuit church in Quito. The four evangelists, Matthew, Mark, Luke, and John, are joined by the traditional martyrdom of St. Stephen and the Resurrection of Christ. Little Indian flavor here! Only the archangels above the horn of plenty in the dome are Peruvian-style angels. The polychrome and wooden statues near the sacristy doors are more local.

For the European and the Native American gold was a precious metal, the *most* precious available. Therefore, a church gilded in gold represented to both Spaniard and Indian a degree of unsurpassed affluence. Driving the penchant for more ultra-Baroque decorative churches was a sense of competition among the religious orders. The stated motive for the expense of decoration was that the building was for God and no expense should be spared for this purpose. However, working alongside this motive was the fact that the religious order up the street had to be outdone. The history of religious orders in Latin America is dotted with rivalry, competition, and resentment. The Jesuits came in for their fair share of criticism and were able to dispense it with equal vigor. The basis of the rivalry was the mystique that the Jesuits brought with them from

Europe to America. They were the Catholic Church's answer to the problems that Trent tried to correct. They had the reputation of having the most intelligent members, the best trained, and the most successful. The rivalry and competition might have been played out over minutiae: who walked first in processions, the right to grant degrees at a local college or university, the administration of certain churches. But in reality the cause was deeper, the past and present resentment of the Jesuits for their perceived superiority and for what they had accomplished. The reason for the extraordinarily decorated Jesuit churches in the Andes and in the major cities of America was in part but not wholly due to a desire to outshine the rival religious order. The churches also sent a message to Indians and to the European world: superiority is manifest in the material as well as in the intellectual world. The Jesuits felt that great churches meant more prestige for Christianity vis-à-vis the indigenous American.

In Andean Peru a slightly less degree of affluence is evident in the colonial churches. However, Cuzco was an exception. This was the ancient capital of the Incas, the city at which Francisco Pizarro's men stared in disbelief. The palaces of Atahualpa's rival, Huayna Capac, the Temple of the Sun, even the houses of the common folk were unlike anything that the poor Spaniards in Pizarro's army had ever seen. The chroniclers of the conquest of Cuzco compared Cuzco to Santiago de Campostella or to Seville, so grand was it. When the dust of conquest settled, the religious orders went about building their own monuments to their God. The Jesuits who arrived in Cuzco in 1593 constructed a massive church on the foundations of the old palace of Huayna Capac. Deliberately? Conveniently? A message that the old had been destroyed for good? In any event, comparing the Cuzco sacristy with the sacristy of the Jesuit church in Lima, San Pedro, one is struck by the latter's greater number of paintings and the greater wealth of detail.

The two wide bell towers of La Compañía appear slightly out of proportion with the main portal since together they are wider than the entire façade. They seem like anchors holding the church into the ground and they may well have served exactly that purpose. Earthquakes are frequent so this may have been a colonial form of earthquake proofing. The squat, hugging-the-ground appearance was designed to ensure survival.

The hugging-the-earth motif is also exemplified in the Jesuit church complex in Arequipa in southern Peru. The city lies at the foot of the big cones of the maritime cordillera in the Chili River Valley at an altitude of 2,400 meters. Its wealth during colonial times was based mainly on sugar and wine production in the Pisco, Nazca, and Ica valleys to the north. The Jesuit church in Arequipa has an elaborately decorated façade with an equally handsome cloister and attached buildings. The architecture of the complex is unique. The white limestone exudes a sense of purity and almost subtropical warmth. But the flatness of the entire complex reflects a reasonable concern with the frequency of earthquakes. Not a spot remains empty on the façade, almost as if every square inch had to be filled with an elaborate design. This kind of design, where bunches of grapes are prominent, reflects the native folk-art *retablos* of Indians dancing and people in general engaged in a variety of fiesta activities. The scene is busy yet it remains pleasant to behold.

The wildly carved seventeenth-century façade of Arequipa is an introduction to the decorative motifs within. St. Ignatius Loyola is the centerpiece of the main altar, featured in a gold-leafed cedar carving along with Jesus and Mary. St. Ignatius also has a side chapel whose walls are exuberantly painted with birds, warriors, the four Gospel writers, Matthew, Mark, Luke, and John, tropical fruits, and flowers.

On the walls of the chapel are paintings of Ignatius, the Virgin and Christ Child, Christ bound to a pillar, and the Risen Christ all done in the eighteenth-century Cuzco style. The figures in the paintings all have gentle, almost child-like expressions on their faces. The pillars of the Jesuit cloister are all decorated. Grapes, papaya, and pineapples are motifs repeated on each pillar. Here as well, the squatness of the construction is a reminder of the closeness of the snowcapped volcano, El Misti, just north of Arequipa. An earthquake is always a possibility.

The church and entire complex is certainly less ornate and less affluent than the Jesuit churches in Cuzco or Quito. The decorative motifs give us a clue as to why. The audience that the structures played to were Indian as well as Spanish. Arequipa was remote from Lima, semi-isolated by the dry coastal desert, almost tropical in its whiteness. Much of the construction materials for houses came from the white rock, the *sillar*, found at the base of the volcano, El Misti. The Jesuit complex abounds in it. The whiteness of Arequipa contrasts sharply with the grey fog, the *grua*, of Lima. No wonder, then, that the Jesuit church is filled with the bright colors of the tropics carefully and painstakingly worked by native artists.

The Great Estates

Jesuit institutions and colleges were supported by large-scale ranching and farming operations.[10] The ranches themselves frequently had significant structures including church or chapel. The ranches and farms in Andean Cuzco varied as to size and importance. Many of the ranches were not simple economic entities and they affected the social and religious life of the surrounding area. The hacienda was a complement to the colonial city in that it achieved the same goals as the city but in a rural setting.[11] In Andean Peru the hacienda was linked closely to a town or village primarily because the village frequently supplied labor for farm and ranch work. However, the Cuzco hacienda buildings, if one can judge by extant maps and sketches, were not as dramatically large in size as those in Argentina or Mexico.[12] In Argentina, for example, the Jesuits left behind several complexes of magnificent hacienda and farm structures. They are architecturally interesting as well and help to define the rural landscape of colonial Latin America.

Santa Catalina estate, a little northwest of Córdoba, along with nearby Jesús María, Caroya, and Altagracia, became the nucleus of the college of Córdoba's landholdings and provided the lion's share of the college's yearly income. After the Jesuits' departure from Latin America in 1767, many of the estate buildings fell into disrepair, but some survived and were purchased by other rural landowners. Santa Catalina's main structures survived and they reveal more than just the shell of rural economic enterprise. They tell us a great deal about what the Jesuits attempted to do in rural Córdoba and what their goals were.

The estate of Santa Catalina was dominated by a large, expansive church connected to which was the major residence looking out onto a large patio. The Jesuit superior of the group lived here, the religious instructor, the lay rancher and usually a Jesuit lay brother. Large orchards were enclosed by a stone and adobe wall serving not only as a boundary marker but also to keep out wild animals and ensure privacy. A *tajamar* or man-made reservoir supplied water for the apparatus of a small textile mill. The slave population was housed in the *ranchería* (laborers' quarters) that still stands today (2006). The ranges spread out around the cluster of hacienda structures.

The average annual slave population on Santa Catalina during the eighteenth century was about 321, a large number given the cost of purchasing and maintaining them. Almost all were used for the mixed ranching and farming operations of the estate. A strong emphasis was also placed on raising mules for the annual fair in Salta.[13]

Construction materials on rural estates reflected utility and convenience. Jesuit buildings in Tucumán used stone, adobe, lime, and lumber. The floor of the one-story slave *ranchería* was made of well-spaced rectangular stone. The pillars and even their bases were made of brick. Possibly because the *ranchería* building was only one story, a stronger base was not needed. Facilities for construction materials were Jesuit-owned and located near Córdoba. Santa Catalina was a large, imposing complex of structures that stood out on Tucumán's rural landscape. The church especially stood out, in height, size, and quality of decorative arts. A protruding portal stands between the two-towered façade of the Santa Catalina church. The central pediment is characterized by graceful, undulating lines, echoed in the belfries above. There is an emphasis on rounded shapes—in the finials, balustrade, the decoration on the belfries, and on the windows in the towers.[14] Two Italian Jesuits, Andrés Blanqui and Juan Bautista Primoli, were primarily responsible for most Jesuit construction in the area.

Off the church, connected but to its rear, is an enormous patio, a major construction feature reflecting a Spanish Andalusian influence. "Make me a patio, and if there is space left, some rooms," went the sixteenth-century Spanish saying. The patio was surrounded by cloisterlike passageways common to the great religious monasteries of Europe. The high arches and long corridors give the place a quality of majesty and affluence, contrasting sharply with the naked brick vaulting and square pillars of the nearby slave quarters. The latter seems like a medieval dungeon, which of course it was.

The Jesuit rural constructions in Tucumán lacked the decorative detail and embellishments found on Mexican and Peruvian structures. But their great size conveyed a feeling of power. And that was a major point. The large rural house was in reality a "powerhouse," a showcase, an image-maker displaying visible evidence of wealth and power. This was the church militant and triumphant. Local Jesuit provincials tried to moderate the tendency toward massive structures and in 1710 an official visitor, Antonio Garriga, actually put a stop to all construction, "in order to avoid the excesses introduced in these times of overly large buildings and other signs of excess wealth that should be foreign to our profession of religious poverty."[15]

Jesuits were divided about the extravagance of construction. Those in favor cited the Jesuit General Oliva who promoted all types of artistic expression, especially in construction. Oliva made the distinction between Jesuit residences that should reflect holy poverty and Jesuit churches that should "try to reach up to the sublimity of God's eternal omnipotence with such appurtenances of glory as we can achieve."[16]

The architecturally significant Jesuit rural structures used local artists working through European forms. Thus there developed a blend of Native American art and Spanish forms. This was true of all Jesuit architecture. The result was unique. It was neither Indian nor Spanish but a blend of Baroque and American. Workshops were set up to train indigenous artists and craftsmen. In Santiago de Chile, the German Jesuit, Karl Haimbhausen (1692–1767), founded an arts and crafts academy by bringing over from Germany a boatload of fifty artists.[17]

In the rural world large churches alongside agricultural and ranching enterprises demonstrated that the human side of ranching and farming contained a spiritual dimension. The church, the cloister, the refectory for eating, the rooms for storage, and associated farm and ranch buildings were a reflection of the Kingdom of God on earth. Both secular and religious functions were integrated demonstrating what an ideal society on earth should be.

"Palaces in the Desert"

The Jesuit structures of Peru and Quito are equally matched by the structures that the Jesuits raised in the Paraguay reductions. Not all of the thirty missions that dotted the banks of the Paraná and Uruguay rivers were lavishly constructed, but several were endowed with magnificent churches and buildings, the ruins of which are today (2006) major tourist attractions.

San Ignacio Miní is perhaps the most widely known for the splendor of its architecture. Only the shell and ruins of what was a magnificent complex of mission buildings exist today. The mission church itself was a massive structure with two high pillars on each side of the entrance. Two human-sized angels guarded the entranceway from above the pillars. A smaller entrance with only one pillar on each side was to the right of the main portal.[18] Within the church native Guaraní craftsmen filled the side altars and the main *retablos* with well-carved statues of saints and the Trinity.

The entire mission complex was a didactic exercise designed to instruct the Indian neophyte in the Christian belief system.[19] The plethora of statues and religious architectural symbols in the mission complex, many of which are today preserved in the Museo Histórico of Buenos Aires, were more akin in purpose to the stained-glass windows of the medieval cathedral than to the gilded decorations of Lima and Quito churches. The gold leafed decorations were aimed more to impress than to teach. But for this very reason, the building construction of the Jesuits came under serious criticism from their own central administration in Rome, prodded by local unease. From 1645 on, a steady stream of cautionary letters was written, warning against ostentatious construction especially in the missions of Paraguay. In 1714, the Jesuit General Michaelangelo Tamburini wrote to Juan de Zea, the provincial of Paraguay, describing the missions of the Paraná as "palaces in the desert." "Of what use," he wrote, "was a patio of 300 square feet, a dining room 50 yards long with a gold-leafed ceiling, or a forty-foot terreplein, other than to demonstrate a great lack of poverty."[20]

Tamburini's remarks were inaccurate on two counts. First, the Paraná River missions were surely not in a desert. The beauty of the landscape, the temperate climate, and the fertility of the soil are legendary. But for the European, America was an empty desert! Second, massive construction had its cost, but it was a cost borne by the "institution." It did not reflect the individual poverty that the missionaries experienced. Each missionary lived on about 290 pesos a year which accounted for food, clothing, shelter, and travel.[21] In all fairness to the Jesuit superior, however, Tamburini was referring to the appearance of extravagant wealth. The massive stone edifice of church and rectory and associated ranch and farming structures with outlying fields and grazing land was property only owned by the rich and powerful. The Jesuit was surrounded by the symbols of wealth, and sometimes the symbols of excess wealth, therefore, he was considered wealthy. The distinction made between institutional and individual wealth fell on deaf ears and could not dispel the obvious, that the Jesuit belonged to an institution that owned vast amounts of land and that possessed political and economic influence.[22]

By extension, the large, elaborately decorated Jesuit churches in Mexico, Quito, and Peru were exposed to the same criticism. But were they simply extravagances that should not have existed amid the poverty of the Indians? Or is this too simplistic in that it ignores more profound cultural and psychological explanations? Although it can be argued, and frequently is, that the symbols of affluence juxtaposed against poverty simply cause resentment and outright hostility, it is also argued that they are a form of escapism offered to the impoverished. The didactic element, however, cannot be understated. Both directly and indirectly, architecture and art was committed to both the reinforcement of the new religion and the new political reality that came after the conquest.

Jesuit Theater

Christian missionaries in the Americas had as their goal the building of the church in America. Even the political geography reminded them of the newness of their endeavor. It was a *New* World, a *New* Andalucia, a *New* Spain, a *New* Granada, that Spaniards were founding. North it was a New England, a New Amsterdam, a New York. So too the church in America was starting from a tabula rasa. The core values and rituals would be universally respected but the cultural layers surrounding them would assume a decidedly American flavor. The mindset that the Jesuits acquired in America would be quite different from that of their brethren in Europe. European Jesuits were busy *restoring* a weakened ecclesiastical institution to preeminence, recovering what had been lost and making sure it would not be lost again. After the Council of Trent they assumed a defensive mode whereas in America they demonstrated an aggressively optimistic manner. The Jesuits in America were part of a concerted effort to build a new church among neophytes as new to Christianity as the longshoremen to whom St. Paul had preached a millennium and a half before.

Although the entirety of Spanish activity in America was a new endeavor, the Spaniards recreated features of the Old Country that possessed universal value. But the colleges that sprang up in America were not quite duplicates of those found in Spain or Italy. They had distinctively local attributes that were in great part dictated by physical and cultural surroundings. Among the key features uniquely found in American colleges was the presence of the sons of the native Indian elite. Jesuits in Mexico and Peru were of the opinion that native-born Indians had every right to attend their colleges. However, the Jesuit superior general in Rome thought otherwise and eventually the native born Indian was excluded or made to attend schools that were "separate but equal."[23]

One feature of European colleges that was wholeheartedly embraced was the theater. Jesuit theater in Europe, especially in Central Europe, and to a lesser extent in Italy and Spain, offered an excellent vehicle for achieving what Jesuit pedagogues strove to inculcate in their students: *Eloquencia Latina*.[24] It taught the student to appear advantageously in front of an audience, how to convince, how to move. It helped to instill a sense of self-confidence in a young boy and also gave him the principles for acquiring the personal self-control and discipline that future leaders needed.[25] It helped the student acquire a resonant voice, as well as learn the importance of gestures when delivering a talk. It also helped do away with the fear of public speaking. In short, the Jesuits in Europe saw the theater as an excellent and novel way of instilling aspects of leadership and personal qualities they thought their students should acquire. The medieval precedent for the play, the Mystery Play, was present, and wandering players were increasingly performing in European capital cities, but the Jesuits in Italy, Spain, and Central Europe raised theater to a position that made it a respected form of popular culture in a local college. Not only did theater instruct and develop students but it reached out to the public thus serving a didactic purpose as well as a public relations opportunity by offering a local community a form of free entertainment.

This raised ecclesiastical eyebrows because it was a radical departure from the way the monastic orders traditionally portrayed religious beliefs. Most, but not all, of Jesuit theater was religious in content. This was because the secular theater adequately covered the themes usually associated with the theater: love, death, humor, murder, greed, and interpersonal relationships. It would have been considered inappropriate for the Jesuit theater to concentrate on love, for example, rather than on the characteristics they, as men of religion, were attempting to inculcate in their students.

Jesuit theater in Latin America was by no means an absolute innovation. Indigenous groups had a long tradition of symbolic portrayal of religious and secular events.[26] What the Spaniards brought into the picture was the European tradition of liturgical dramas that were presented around the time of religious festivals. These early presentations had an instructive nature to them and served as a substitute or as a supplement to catechetical instruction that Indians received. These early presentations were called *Autos*, or Acts, and had a religious connotation to them. They were usually associated with teaching some aspect of the sacraments.

Garcilaso de la Vega mentions that the Jesuits in Peru presented comedies for the Aymara Indians.[27] The theme was the enmity between the Blessed Virgin and the devil. This type of presentation was in line with the educational Franciscan theater of Mexico. Bernabé Cobo describes another kind of presentation that the Jesuits in the College of Lima put on in 1599. In addition to music and song, the Jesuits placed on the stage old skeletons and mummies from the indigenous *huacas* in order to help portray what would happen on the Last Judgment Day. The packed house gasped at this audacious display of realism.[28]

Up until 1604 the plays of Calderón and Lope de Vega were acted on the Jesuit stage in San Pablo. The actors were students, the plays amateur productions, and the audiences were first and foremost the college community but also the city populace. The presentations at the college became enormously popular, probably because there were few other kinds of theatrical presentations available.[29]

Few texts of Jesuit college plays have survived. One, however, has, and is carefully preserved in the National Library of Lima, Peru.[30] *Santa María Egipciaca* was probably written by Fr. Vicente Palomino who was the author of several other texts and plays. Examining the text of the play enables us to draw a little more closely to what the Jesuits in Latin America intended with their emphasis on theater. The play is symbolic of the Jesuit philosophy of education in that it encompasses the *totus homo*. Its aim is to enhance the intellectual and spiritual life of the actors and the audience, keeping in mind that the college existed not only for students but also for the local community. The college was basically an urban phenomenon in the Roman tradition in the sense that it was firmly believed that only in the city did the most important intellectual, educational, and artistic activities take place.

The religious ideas current in seventeenth-century Peru are essential in understanding the importance of *Santa María Egipciaca*. The post-Tridentine church sincerely believed in the ability of the individual to turn away from evil and accept the grace of God. Why the person had originally rejected God was laid at the doorstep of human frailty. It really did not matter. What mattered was the return to God in the manner of the Prodigal Son. The intercession of Mary also remained a major belief in the post-Tridentine church. The ability of the Virgin Mary to intercede before God the Father was denied by the reformers in order to re-establish Jesus Christ as the only true intercessor. Spanish Christianity, however, steadfastly held to the role of Mary as Mother of God and as an all-powerful intercessor with special divine influence. There are many reasons for the steadfastness of this belief. As early as the third century A.D. the church in Europe placed Mary in a prominent position, a position that only increased over time, such that by the thirteenth century few of the great cathedrals had divine patrons other than the Virgin Mary.[31] Every great church had a Lady Chapel. Few churches in Spain and Italy placed Christ in a prominent sanctuary location. Mary or a saint usually held this distinction. When questioned by the sixteenth-century reformers, it was argued that "tradition" had placed Mary and the saints as intercessors before God the Father right along with Jesus Christ. The reaction to the reformers was to assign Mary an even greater and quasi-essential role in the divine hierarchy.

In the play *Santa María Egipciaca* the heroine is named María and the Virgin Mary is the major intercessor for her before Christ. She appears to the protagonist very briefly but her role is central in the development of the play. The Virgin Mary is given an active part in Egipciaca's turn away from sin and her acceptance of Christ.

The play has six characters, the protagonist, Santa María Egipciaca, Alejandro and Chaparro, two characters representing the dark side of society but injecting some comic relief into the action, a good angel, and Luzbel, a bad angel. What the text calls *Música* is actually a Greek chorus, cautioning the actors, commenting on that action, and advising the audience about the morality of the play's actions.

The action takes place in May on the Feast Day of the Holy Cross. The chorus encourages all to hurry to the fiesta, even the shepherds and shepherdesses of the valley. Chaparro warns Alejandro about what awaits him. The *dama del infierno* will be there to destroy him.

> ¿Tienes los ojos cerrados o
> que demonios te han hecho?
> ¿No ves que estás destruido y
> de más a más debiendo

> muchos miles, que ha tragado
> essa dama del infierno? y
> aunque mude mas galanes
> que un Duque vestidos nuevos,
> estás echando la baba,
> ¿todo aquesto no es muy cierto?[32]

Chaparro hesitates but Alejandro encourages him to go along. The chorus reminds the audience that Christ has already redeemed souls. Luzbel enters and doubts whether María Egipciaca, an old worn-out whore (*la ramera*), can entrap youth any more. But Luzbel decides to use the old sinner as a hook to catch a big fish for hell.

> Esa Egipciaca, ramera es,
> de quien esto profiero, cuya
> extremada belleza, en
> Palestina es anzuelo que me
> ofrece grande pesca de
> almas para el inferno.[33]

So all go to the fiesta and Egipciaca makes her first appearance in the play. (No doubt a young male student played the female part of Egipciaca since no women were allowed to appear on a Jesuit stage.)[34]

Egipciaca finds herself alone on stage. The usual crowd of military men with their plumed hats and black capes, the students, the clerics, the friars from the conventos, the nobles and rural farmers, and all the possible clients that a prostitute can have, have all gone to the fiesta. Egipciaca decides to go too and she hopes to catch ten or twelve lovers.

> Hermosa es la variedad de hombres galanes, compuestos unos
> a lo militar, con plumas, otros de vestido negro, unos de capotes ri-
> cos, otros de espadín, en cuerpo. Colegiales, monigotes, Frayles de
> todos conventos, hombres nobles y plebeyos. Yo juzgo están en la
> fiesta, porque aquí a nadie veo, pues alcanzar no e podido a los que
> engañar pretendo; boyme a entrar por el concurso, porque yo solo
> intento sacar diez o doce amantes.[35]

Egipciaca sees the church, wishes to enter it, but some inner force prevents her from doing so. The chorus tells us why. "Pecadora atrevida. Limpia tu alma, si quieres que Dios las puertas te abra; pues tus culpas te cierran las de su gracia."[36]

At this point in the play the Virgin Mary appears, although she is not listed in the characters of the play. Egipciaca sees her and calls her the "Divina Aurora Celeste," the protector of sinful souls, the door to heaven for her afflicted slave. Then the crucified Christ appears, also not mentioned in the play's characters. The chorus tells Egipciaca to approach him, who is the key to salvation. She does so and prays.

> No sois, dueño mio,
> como otros amantes
> que nunca perdonan
> si injuria les hazen;
> pues de Vos no dudo
> que por perdonarme,
> estais rebentando
> por quinientes partes.
> En pies, pecho y manos
> he visto señales de que
> deseais nuestras
> amistades; ea, hermoso
> dueño, ea, rico amante,
> libradme un destello
> que mi pecho abrase.
> Galan de mi alma, mi
> Dios, perdonadme, a
> que de tus pies a un
> desierto baje, a hazer
> penitencia de mis
> culpas graves, por toda
> mi vida; sin perder
> instante que mis ojos
> sean copiosos
> raudales.[37]

The biblical references to the repentance story of Mary Magdalene and to Christ as the shepherd seeking the lost sheep are evident. Egipciaca, however, speaks the sensual language of the prostitute. Christ now becomes her *dueño* (master), her *amante* (lover), the *galán de mi vida* (beau of my life). She also turns to her new "lover" out of her own free will. No one forces her to repent. No one makes her change her way of life. Egipciaca wanted to enter the church but she could not until she herself cleansed her soul through repentance. She speaks about her *voluntad* being that of Christ's. This element of free will is a major Jesuit contribution to their theater and it is emphasized in the play.[38]

God is present. His assistance is offered through grace, but the individual must freely accept it. The individual can reject or accept God's grace. Human action is essential if man's destiny is to be fixed. Thus, human freedom remains intact. Man's liberty is secured. This important theological point, the effectivity of grace while preserving free will, so hotly debated in the seventeenth century, was not lost on the audience.

Once it is clear that Egipciaca chooses to accept God's grace, the good angel comes to her side to help her along the path to righteousness. She tells Egipciaca that Christ has sent her to guide her steps. "Y me ordena que te guie, y a tí que sigas mis pasos hasta donde es su gusto que vivas, desagraviando con singular nueva vida su respeto soberano" (He has ordered me to be your guide, and you are to follow my footsteps to wherever they may lead you, disregarding your own wishes).[39]

The chorus tells the audience to weep, to repent of its sins and dispose itself to receive his rewards. Egipciaca bids farewell to the world of her past, to its hypocrisy, its pomp, its delights, its pride. She no longer needs the world as a friend; she no longer follows its footsteps.

Luzbel drives off Chaparro. Egipciaca is still fearful of God's wrath but the good angel assures her that God wishes to reward her good works. The angel says: "Contigo seré María, hasta llevarte a los cielos" (I will accompany you, Maria, even as far as heaven).[40]

Both Alejandro and Chaparro also turn to God and ask for grace to live a good life. Alejandro hears celestial music and he is told by the good angel that Egipciaca has caused it by turning to God. The angel urges Alejandro to imitate her virtues, flee the risks of offending God who although good and holy is also rigorous and severe. Both Alejandro and Chaparro ask for God's grace.

Dádnos vuestra gracia
porque seamos buenos.[41]

The play ends with all, actors and audience, asking God to pardon their sins.

TODOS. Pidiendo disculpa
de nuestros defectos.[42]

There was no room in the Jesuit scheme of things for fate. Nothing happened by chance. The individual chooses and upon that decision rests his future. Evil is present to pull one away from good, but evil succeeds only if the individual allows it to. Man's ability to conquer evil remains a major characteristic of the individual. Man is not a helpless creature beneath the weight of nature's massiveness. This blend of Renaissance individualism and Tridentine theology was a major contribution of the Jesuits. The audience may or may not have realized the theological import of what they were viewing. A staged spectacle, an elaborate performance with props, costumes, songs, music, and sometimes dance, overwhelmed but never eliminated the didactic element in Jesuit theater. Actors, stagehands, audience, and community looked upon the theater as entertainment with a purpose. The Jesuit theater was a microcosm of what the Jesuits themselves wanted to inculcate in their students. They wished their students to be articulate, committed believers, learned in all forms of secular knowledge but with the realization that they were on a journey toward a more permanent homeland. How they behaved and lived in this life would determine the nature of the reward or punishment in the next.

8

The Beaver and
the *Fleur-de-Lis*

In New France where missionaries followed fast on the heels of *habitants* and trappers, a large number of Huron Indians became Christians. What made them forsake ancient traditions? Conversion to Christianity was muddled by accompanying commercial advantages with the French. Colonial Christianity was compromised by trading relationships, alliances with Europeans, and tribal rivalries, each playing off the other to the eventual detriment of the Native American.

The Land Between the Lakes

Between the northwest rim of Lake Ontario and the southeastern edge of Lake Huron (now called Georgian Bay) lies a seventy-mile strip of fertile, gentle rolling hills. Stands of maple, elm, and birch rise peacefully between lakes and ponds that dot the area. In the summertime the temperature reaches 85 °F to 90 °F. In July the humidity rolls off the lakes and the bay and the abundance of lush green foliage is reminiscent of subtropical Brazil. The winters are bitter cold. Winds whip down unimpeded from Hudson's Bay. The temperature plunges below zero in February and seventy-one inches of snow falls each year. This four-hundred square-mile piece of land was home for thirty thousand Hurons in the early seventeenth century and it was here that many of the Jesuits who volunteered for the missions of New France were posted. The Hurons were stable agriculturalists, members of the Iroquoian-speaking peoples, trading allies with the French, and ideal targets for conversion to Christianity.

From 1634 to 1650 missionaries worked to convert the Hurons. After 1641 the missionary focus was on the Hurons and by 1648 almost 10 percent of them had become Christian. Two major obstacles worked against the Europeans. One was disease. Influenza, smallpox, and measles periodically swept through the land and the Indians suspected that somehow the French were responsible. They were correct. Whereas the European's immune system resisted these viruses, the Indian's could not. They became killer epidemics. Between 1636 and 1640 the Huron population fell from thirty thousand to fifteen thousand.[1] In 1640 the Jesuits baptized 1,200 dying children, which only served to confirm the Hurons' worst suspicions. And this was the European Jesuits' second obstacle. Ironically, doing what they had come to the New World to do, convert Native Americans to Christianity, drove a wedge between themselves and the Indians. The Jesuit rushed to the dying because he believed that only with baptism would the soul go to heaven. In the Indian mind the Blackrobe became the harbinger of death.[2] Baptism killed. The Indian believed that the Jesuits had a secret pact with the disease since the Europeans remained healthy and full of life. Where the Jesuit went, death followed. Thereby, the Jesuit became an evil shaman, tolerated only because he was a key link with the French who provided the trading goods the Hurons sorely wanted. Disease, death, and a new religion the Indians did not need were what the French Blackrobes had to offer.

In 1650 the rival Mohawks, Onondagas, and Senecas destroyed the Huron villages and drove the French missionaries back to Quebec. The missionaries' attempt to make stable agriculturalists out of partial hunters and gatherers had failed. The Jesuits eventually became convinced that assimilation (trying to make Frenchmen out of Indians) was impractical. Allowing the Indians to remain Indians, what is called today *indigenization*, was a more reasonable approach to Christianization. But the realization was gradual. In between was a series of stops and starts demonstrating hesitancy and doubt. Eventually, the easy acquisition of liquor and the perceived licentiousness of French frontier life convinced the Jesuits of the correctness of this view.

Time and again the Jesuits complained about the devastating effects of liquor on the Indians of New France.[3] It not only wreaked havoc among the Native Americans but it prevented the missionaries from converting them. Because the sale of brandy was closely intertwined with the fur trade, no effective measures were ever taken to interdict the sale of alcohol.

The Indian did not have anything like alcohol in his pre-European food system so its introduction by the French was novel and destructive. The French soldier and trapper who returned from the wilderness and guzzled liquor until he passed out was probably the model that Indians followed. The Indian food feasts provided another avenue for drinking liquor. However, drinking bouts with brandy ended in fighting and sometimes murder. The Indian brandy feasts were often paid for with hides and furs not yet acquired, leading to a vicious cycle of drunkenness and debt.[4] Family members suffered physical violence, many families actually broke up, and liquor became an excuse for committing acts of violence.[5]

An additional use of alcohol that the Indians discovered was as a facilitator for their religious practice of dream interpretation. For the Indian, the dream was the vehicle used to receive instruction from the spirits about proper behavior.[6] But for the Jesuits, this kind of alcohol use was a major obstacle to conversion.[7] What made it all the more galling was that the Christian French were the brandy suppliers and although the home government paid lip service to stamping out the trade, it never really had its heart in stopping it. The alcohol trade continued because on it, argued the French fur traders, depended the trade in beaver furs.

The situation was similar to that faced by the Jesuits in Paraguay at almost the same time, only the product the Spanish traders wanted was not beaver furs but yerba mate. The Spanish middlemen in Buenos Aires bought the tea at a pitifully low price from the Indians. The Jesuits stepped in and not only began to act as brokers for the Indians but set up storage houses in the city and in other key locations, thus successfully driving the Spanish middleman out of the tea business.[8] The Jesuit response in Paraguay to colonial exploitation was to isolate the Indian in self-sufficient towns called reductions. This achieved several purposes. It kept the Indians away from what the missionaries considered the harmful influences of alcohol and sexual promiscuity; the Indians were taught crafts, animal husbandry, and agrarian techniques that would allow them to remain economically self-sufficient[9] and, most important of all, the stable Indian community permitted the missionary to indoctrinate on a regularly scheduled basis. So, the Jesuit missionaries exposed themselves to the charge that *they* were exploiting the Indians and reaping the financial rewards of the *yerba mate* trade.

Government support and resources were available to the Jesuits and the economic and cultural climate (for want of a better phrase) almost guaranteed success in the reductions. In New France, on the other hand, the Jesuit missionaries faced the problem of liquor and its perceived corrosive influence, but they were marginally successful in establishing mission towns. Those that were developed did not last long and were not nearly as controlled or effective as the Jesuit reductions of Paraguay.

The Jesuit mission town of St. Joseph de Sillery, about ten miles west of Quebec on the St. Lawrence River, was established for the same reasons that the Jesuits of Paraguay established the reductions: to isolate and indoctrinate.[10] In 1638 the Jesuit superior, Paul LeJeune, moved two Christian Indian families onto land that he had acquired from the Duc de Sillery family. Other Montagnais Indians moved onto the periphery of the village. LeJeune was hopeful that the Indians would "become sedentary and . . . believe in God."[11] A smallpox epidemic scattered the inhabitants in 1639 but by 1640 the village had a hospital and a Jesuit residence. Four one-room houses were constructed for the Indian families and a chapel was erected. Agricultural lands were cleared on the outskirts of the village but the Jesuits were hard put to convince the Indians to abandon their traditional hunting traditions. Disease, fire, Iroquois attacks, and cultural tradition combined to empty the village of the 120 Christian Indians that lived there in 1646. By the 1660s, the Jesuits in Sillery were caring for the French settlers of the village, the Indians having long abandoned the site.

Notre Dame de Lorette was more successful. Situated on the Jesuit lands of St. Michael about ten miles south of Montreal, the mission village held over three hundred Iroquois and Huron Christians between 1669 and 1674.[12] Thirteen cabins formed a quadrangle with a chapel in the center. In one year, twenty-seven Iroquois were baptized. The Onondaga Iroquois were persuaded to leave their own lands and live as Christians "to escape the drunkeness and disorder" of their own villages.[13] No drinking was permitted in the villages and no Frenchmen were allowed to settle in their environs.

La Prairie de Madelain, about one hundred miles east of Sillery was the other mission village the Jesuits erected. All three villages tried to create an environment reminiscent of a European town. Church, civil government in Indian hands, a school, sedentary agriculture, and monogamous families, all under the watchful eyes of the French missionary, were the major features of the villages. But the seed did not germinate. The Jesuits hoped that the example of sedentary agricultural life would act as catalyst among the Indians and persuade large numbers to join what they believed to be the better and more civilized way of life. But too many factors militated against the Indian accepting the new religion as long as it was covered in a European cloak.

The monogamy and revised courtship practices demanded by the missionaries were opposed and eventually led to uproar and confusion. Christian males denounced non-Christian females and demanded that they be imprisoned by the French. Public flogging of young women by village officials became a common sight.[14] The traditionalists bitterly opposed the Christians and in the end the old lifestyle and customs prevailed. Many Indians were not persuaded that sedentary agriculture was for them and they looked upon the mission village as a convenient base camp for the winter hunt.

Sillery and the mission villages failed to be successful agents of Western civilization. "We are well as we are," was the response that summed up the general feeling of the Montagnais, Huron, and Iroquois.[15] The initial encounter between European and Indian and the following century of contact was insufficient by itself to persuade the Indian to accept the new culture. The Jesuit missionaries on their part, at least those near Quebec and Montreal, were unwilling to modify their theological message. Not only was the message wrapped in layers of culture-bound elements (e.g., the Jesuits insisted that the Indians cut their long hair) but the proximity to the administrative centers of Quebec and Montreal made the missionary more sensitive to the criticism of adapting too easily to Indian ways. The Chinese Rites controversy in which the Jesuits were embroiled in the seventeenth century further reduced their zeal to fully accept Indian ways. Cultural relativism was not in the Jesuit quiver. Cautious adaptation was.

Politics, Culture, and Religion

Unlike the Spanish Jesuits in Florida, the French Jesuits in North America were not considered essential to the political and economic aims of their government. France did not need a pliant, obedient Christian native population as a work force, only one willing to trade. French interest in North America was not imperial in the usual sense of the word. France had no designs on Indian lands or native labor. The French were interested in commerce. This meant trading for beaver furs, pelts, and hides, with beaver by far the most important commodity.[16] Beaver fur made the smoothest and most stylish hats in Europe, commanding high prices.

The French in New France erected their apparatus of government around trading companies that took furs from the Indians in return for iron tools, kettles, fishhooks, liquor, and guns. The Stone Age clashed with the most modern of the Western world's technologies. The pull for the Indians was irresistible.[17] Life became easier for the Indian by using an iron instead of birch bark kettle. Bullets were more lethal than arrows; iron fish hooks more durable than bone. Liquor allowed the Indian to conjure his dreams and his gods in a matter of minutes.

While a handful of Frenchmen traded for beaver, the Jesuits tried to win more adherents to Catholicism. In the age of conquest and colonization, state and church were partners in a great enterprise.[18] In the realm of the spiritual mission of the church in New France, the Jesuits had sole authority for over twenty-five years. Priests did what they could to assure that the state achieve its secular goals while at the same time demanding that the state support the spiritual (and sometimes physical) conquest of the Indians. There was no contradiction in pointing out to the state that by helping the church achieve its mission, the state benefited as well. The Jesuits were good salesmen.

The first Jesuits in New France were Pierre Biard and Ennemond Masse who landed in Port Royal on June 12, 1611. Gilbert du Thet, a laybrother, followed. In the spring of 1613 George Quintin arrived. Mt. Desert Island in present-day Nova Scotia was the scene of the French Jesuits' first attempts at New World evangelization, but the Indian language was difficult so they made little progress. To make matters worse, the English colony in Virginia would have no truck with the French. Samuel Argall led a force of twenty-nine fighting men from Virginia in 1613 and scattered the settlement. Masse was set adrift in a boat and Biard and Quentin were taken to Virginia.

Samuel de Champlain persisted.[19] In 1615 he and some Recollect Fathers settled inland along the St. Lawrence. Ten years later at the Recollects' invitation, the Jesuits returned. Masse, who somehow got back to France in his boat, Charles Lalemant, and Jean de Brebeuf were in the contingent along with Anne de Noue and François Charton. Their task was to work in the trading stations along the St. Lawrence at Three Rivers, Quebec, and Tadoussac. As French immigration grew and the desire to convert the Indians increased, the Jesuits refined their goals and their methods.

In 1629 an English force took a French supply ship and starved Quebec into surrender. By 1632 the French reoccupied the settlement and the Jesuits returned. It was precisely the triangular claims of politics, church, and economics that caused confusion in assessing the role and effects of the Jesuits in New France.[20] The missionaries could evangelize only if peace reigned in the Indian world. By introducing Old World goods into Indian economies, the Europeans made certain it did not. The balance of power was severely disturbed. The Mohawks raged against the Huron because they did not have enough furs to trade with the Dutch; the Algonkins battled the Mohawks who searched out more furs in the Algonkin territory; the Jesuits who were allied with the French threw their weight on one side, then pulled back to the other, encouraged treaties only to see them broken, acted as peacemakers, middlemen, agents, all in an attempt to smooth the way for proselytization. To the Indians the Jesuits were foreign sorcerers who brought disease and destruction and were tolerated only because the flow of European goods might be interrupted if they were harmed; to the French fur traders, the Jesuits were meddlesome men who prevented them from trading liquor for furs; to the French government, they were haughty and independent. At the foundation of it all was the seventeenth-century version of European colonialism that conquered or traded with New World cultures but never considered them anything close to equals.

Message and Response

How did the Indians of New France respond to the Christian messengers? Their social and religious systems were every bit as complex as those of the Florida and Mexican Indians. However, the European influences were different. Competing colonial interests pulled the Indians of New France in different directions. The French missionaries took up residence not only as representatives of the European God but also as unofficial colonial agents. Thus, Christianity was filtered through what the Indians saw as a quasi-political screen.

The Jesuits who came to New France did not arrive under the protective shadow of colonial troops (soldiers came later). They realized that they had to make major adjustments in order to convey their message. They had to speak the Indian languages and they had to understand Indian ways. This meant that each had to experience another novitiate, an apprenticeship that would allow the Jesuit to penetrate if only for a time the veil that separated European from Indian. In the beginning, these apprenticeships took the form of Jesuits living alone with Indians over a period of time—not instructing or criticizing but learning. In 1633 the future superior of the Jesuits, Paul LeJeune, spent a winter with the Montagnais Indians. The experience turned out to be a microcosm of Jesuit-Indian relations in New France. Conflict, struggle for power, opposing world views, misunderstanding, cultural chasms separating two worlds, were all present.

The Hunt

Paul LeJeune's world had turned upside down. Less than two years before, the Jesuit priest's voice echoed in the cavernous church of Dieppe, France, where hundreds of the faithful listened to him in silence. On October 18, 1633, he stood silently by the water's edge at the foot of the French settlement of Quebec watching three Montagnais Indians carefully load the two canoes that would carry him and his hunting party to a remote part of the North American wilderness. They would all search for food.[21] But LeJeune did not feel the satisfaction of accomplishment. He would become a burden to the Indians in the coming months even though Mestigoit, the hunter and leader of the small group, had invited him. LeJeune's two fellow Jesuits, Anne de Noue and Gilbert Burel, tried to dissuade him from going. He was their superior, they said. They relied on him for guidance, so he should stay with them in Quebec. Even the governor of the French settlement, Samuel de Champlain, warned him of the dangers of committing himself to so dangerous an expedition. It would be a struggle for survival, not a journey to the next village. LeJeune told his brethren that he wanted to learn the Indian language and that this was the best way to do it. But he knew it was not the language he sought. He had been learning that for the past year. What he really wanted to learn was how these Indians, "nos sauvages" he called them, survived in so harsh an environment. He wanted to get inside their minds, to be able to think as they thought and sort out the values that moved them. If he were going to convert them to Christianity, he had to be able to enter their door in order to lead them out through his.

LeJeune watched the sacks of biscuits, ears of corn, the flour, the prunes, parsnips, and wine being placed onto the two rafts that would transport them down the St. Lawrence River. The birch bark canoes were the last to be loaded. They were fragile. A chunk of floating ice could rip the thin bark and cause disaster. He felt inadequate and humbled. The skills of philosophy and theology, of oratory and learning that were considered so important in his French Jesuit world were useless here. The Indians laughed at him because he didn't know how to paddle a canoe.

At last all was ready.

Twenty Indians, men, women and children, and the sole Frenchman, the Jesuit priest, Paul LeJeune, settled in their places. The rafts' sails caught a gust of river wind and the tiny fleet swept into the rapid current of the St. Lawrence River heading east. The massive rock on which the tiny settlement was perched moved farther and farther away.

Every winter the Indians hunted. In November and December, when the snows were light, the beaver, porcupine, and rabbits were stalked. When the heavy snows prevented the large game from running, the elk and moose were the prey. In bands of twenty to forty, the Indians fanned out in a ten-mile radius careful not to intrude or poach on another group's hunting ground. Mestigoit, the most skilled hunter of his lodge, invited LeJeune to go with them. LeJeune knew why he wanted to go but he was not sure of the Indians' motive in inviting him.

The Indians brought along their shaman, Carigonan, whose skills at forecasting the weather, bringing good luck in the hunt, and warding off sickness were essential. Did they think that two shamans were better than one? There might have been another reason. When an Indian got drunk on the wine LeJeune brought, he blurted out that they had allowed the priest to come only because they thought he would give them food upon their return to Quebec. "In vino veritas," was LeJeune's comment to himself. After that, he harbored no illusions about why they asked him to join them.

The tiny fleet glided past the Island of Orleans. Toward late afternoon it put ashore on one of the river islands. The rituals of setting up the bark lean-to and preparing the evening meal began, ones that would be repeated daily for the next six months. In several other respects, that first evening portended what would follow.

Carigonan realized that LeJeune was a rival, one who tried mightily to discredit his powers before his own people. LeJeune believed that if he could discredit the shaman, then Christianity would have easier access. The Indian priest held a status and power in Indian society equal to LeJeune's in his. The Christian priest held the keys of the kingdom, the power to deny or allow entrance into eternal life, the power as sole intermediary between God and man. So too did Carigonan. He interpreted dreams, drove the evil spirits away with incantations, healed the sick, and attracted prey for the hunters. Carigonan and LeJeune engaged in a battle over minds and hearts.

Before that first evening's meal, Carigonan and LeJeune clashed. The shaman's brother got drunk on the wine that LeJeune had brought. He threatened to kill the Frenchman and was stopped only when Mestigoit, LeJeune's host, threw a kettle of hot water into his face. Other Indians protected LeJeune. LeJeune wrote in his journal:

> As the night was coming on rapidly, I retired into the woods to es-
> cape being annoyed by this drunkard. While I was saying my
> prayers near a tree, the women who managed the lodge of my host
> came to see me; and gathering together leaves of fallen trees, said to
> me, "Lie down there and make no noise," then having thrown me a
> piece of bark as a cover, she went away. This was my first resting
> place beneath the moon whose rays covered me.[22]

LeJeune, like his Jesuit brethren in Florida, saw nothing but the devil in Carigonan. For him he was a sorcerer (*sorcier*) or a trickster (*jongleur*) who was deliberately deceiving the ignorant savages for his own benefit. But LeJeune was puzzled because after careful and continual observation, he could not see him speaking with the devil. He even began to doubt Carigonan's devilish qualities. When the pagan priest was sick, he asked the Christian priest for assistance. When the healed Carigonan rejoined the group, there was "nothing but feasting in our cabins. We had only a little food left, but these barbarians ate it with as much calmness and confidence as if the game they were to hunt was shut up in a stable."[23]

The hunting band island hopped for the following two weeks, at night using the sails from the rafts as a roof for the lean-to. When no game was caught for a meal, pieces of LeJeune's biscuits were divided among the twenty. On October 27 some snow fell. The crisp October air gave way to November's chill. There were other hunting bands in the area so Mestigoit decided to turn north. No sooner had they done so when hunters coming from that direction dissuaded them. The hunting was not good in the north, they said.

They turned south again. On November 12, the band pushed the rafts and canoes ashore on an island and headed inland into what is today upper New York State. "Now," wrote LeJeune, "we were going to invade the Kingdom of the wild beasts, a country far broader in extent than all France."[24] The hunting group had grown to forty-five, three lodges in all, of nineteen, sixteen, and ten members. LeJeune was amazed at the generosity of his hosts. They divided their food, no matter how little they had, with all newcomers. On several occasions the Jesuit was the object of their generosity. They gave him mittens to keep his hands warm, bark with which to cover himself, food, and encouragement. "Harden yourself, resist hunger, you will sometimes be two, three, or four days without food. Take courage. When the snows come, we shall eat," Mestigoit told him.[25]

One day LeJeune expressed amazement at their wisdom and love for each other. On another he berated them for their incivility. LeJeune used Aristotelian logic to categorize the Indians. According to the Greek philosopher, LeJeune wrote, the world had gone through three stages. The first was when people were content with being alive, the second stage united the agreeable with the necessary, and the third and highest stage allowed people to contemplate natural objects and reflect on beauty and goodness. LeJeune placed the Indians in the first stage of the world. "They eat so as not to die . . . politeness and grace has no place here."[26] Yet, the Jesuit was fascinated with the complexities of their language, the way they cared for each other, their houses and clothes, the indigenous medicines, everything that a modern ethnologist would delight in recounting.

The hunting band pushed into the deep forest. The women went ahead carrying the supplies. When the snow was deep, "they make sledges of wood which splits and which can be peeled off like leaves in very thin, long strips. These sledges are very narrow because they have to be dragged among masses of trees closely crowded in some places, but to make up for this the sledges are very long."[27] LeJeune measured one sledge. It was about nine feet long.

"They fasten their baggage on these sledges and with a cord which they pass over their chests, they drag these wheelless chariots over the snow."[28]

When there was something to eat, the day started with breakfast. The young ones went ahead, each carrying a load.

> We did nothing but go up and go down. Frequently we had to bend halfway over to pass under partly fallen trees and step over others lying on the ground whose branches sometimes knocked us over. If it happened to thaw, Oh God what suffering! It seemed to me I was walking over a road of glass which broke under my feet at every step. The frozen snow would collapse and break into blocks into which we sank often up to our knees or waists.[29]

When the hunting party reached the predetermined place for a camp, the men cleared away the snow and the women set up the bark lean-tos. LeJeune waited until the work was finished. He shivered for hours and "I was so frozen that fire alone could thaw me." The Indians were surprised at how severely the cold affected the white man. At first they did not believe that he was freezing. "Give us your hands," they said, "that we may see if you tell the truth." And "finding them frozen they were touched with compassion and they gave me their warm mittens and took my cold ones."[30]

But the battle with the shaman Carigonan continued. One evening before a meal of beaver stew, the shaman grew furious, tore at the poles that held up the lean-to, rolled his eyes like a man out of his senses, and screamed at the crowd to hide their weapons, for he was about to kill the priest. He cried, laughed, sang, howled like a wolf, screeched like an owl "and every moment I was expecting him to throw himself on me." LeJeune outwardly paid no heed. "I continued in my usual way to read, write, and say my little prayers, and when my hour for retiring came, I lay down and rested as peacefully through his orgies as I would have done in a profound silence. I was already accustomed to go to sleep in the midst of his cries and the sound of his drum, as a child is to the songs of its nurse."[31] The shaman went through the same trance the next night. LeJeune approached him this time, found his forehead without fever, and was convinced that his behavior was feigned for "he thus drew upon himself the compassion of all our people who in our dearth were giving him the best they had."[32]

After several days when no more beaver or porcupines were found, the band moved on. The heavy snows began but the bad weather did not slow down the hunting party.

Each evening the shaman beat his drum and in LeJeune's words "howled as usual." This time, however, he was ill and the Jesuit recognized a sick man.

He conversed with him and told him that beating his drum would only deafen him. LeJeune proposed an agreement. Stop beating the drum for ten days, the Jesuit said, and I will pray to my God for you. If you are cured, call together everyone and burn your drum and ritual paraphernalia and renounce your gods. The shaman would agree only if the Jesuit's God cured him first. No agreement was made.

The hunting was poor. The Indians used tobacco as an appetite suppressant.

> Our savages having no food for a feast here made a banquet of
> smoking tobacco. Each inviting the others to the cabin, they passed
> around a little earthen plate containing tobacco, and everyone took a
> pipefull, which he reduced to smoke, returning his hand to the dish
> if he wanted to smoke any more. The fondness they have for this
> herb is beyond all belief. They go to sleep with their reed pipes in
> their mouths. They sometimes get up in the night to smoke. They
> often stop in their journeys for the same purpose and it is the first
> thing they do when they reenter their cabins.[33]

By the end of the December the lack of game frightened even the Indians. On Christmas Eve the band had one porcupine to share among the twenty now in the group. The others had left for another hunting ground. On Christmas Day LeJeune gathered all the Indians in a circle and made them repeat prayers to his god, prayers to help them in the hunt for food. Even the shaman knelt in prayer to the foreigner's god.

That afternoon beaver and porcupine were caught and the tracks of a moose were found. In two days the moose was killed with bow and arrow and an eat-all feast was celebrated. LeJeune could never understand why the Indians stuffed themselves so. But within a week, the specter of starvation reappeared. The band ran into other hunters, gaunt and weak from lack of food.

On January 10, another moose was slain "at which there was general rejoicing." The celebrating was cut short by the arrival of four emaciated Indians. "They looked most hideous, the men especially more so than the women, one of whom had given birth to a child ten days before in the snow, and in the famine had passed several days without eating."[34] LeJeune was amazed at the love that the Indians showed for them. These new guests were not even asked why they had crossed boundaries. They were received not with words but with deeds, without exterior ceremony and not without charity. They gave them large pieces of the moose that had just been killed without saying another word but *mitisoukou*, or "eat."

February and March passed without hunger. The woods were thick with moose and other game that was easily trapped by the hunters. LeJeune fell sick and did not recover his health until he returned to Quebec. The shaman said that his god was punishing him and LeJeune countered that it was just bad food and weakness that afflicted him.

The hunt was almost over. LeJeune, Mestigoit, and Sasousinat, the Montaignais Indian whom the Jesuit referred to in his journal as the renegade (he had been baptized but reverted to his old religion), traveled together slowly, behind the others as they made their way to their final rendezvous by the Riviere du Loup

> On the thirteenth of the same month [March] we made our eighteenth stop near a river, whose waters seemed to me sweet as sugar after the dirt of the melted snow that we drank at other stops out of a greasy and smoky kettle. I began here to experience the discomfort of sleeping upon the ground, which was cold in winter and damp in Spring. My right side upon which I lay became so numb from cold that it scarcely had any sense of feeling . . .[35]

The Indians thought that LeJeune was dying so Mestigoit and Sasousinat decided to bring him back to Quebec immediately.

LeJeune's baptism of fire had concluded. At three in the morning on April 9, he arrived at the Jesuit residence of Notre Dame des Anges. LeJeune's hunting trip with the Montagnais was a microcosm of the missionary experience in New France. The North American environment, whether winter's snows or cold, or summer's heat and humidity, was an all-pervasive enemy. Finding a decent comfort level was a continual struggle. European clothes were inadequate to repel the howling winter wind and in summertime the black flies bit through the Jesuit's thin cassocks. The New World possessed extreme climatic features not present in the Old.

In addition, the native peoples were intransigent, unmoved by the ideas of the new religion. Satan, it seemed, worked through the native shaman, actively seeking to prevent the Jesuits from touching hearts and minds. The Indian shaman correctly saw LeJeune as one who threatened his social existence within Indian society. If the Jesuits were successful in undermining the peoples' belief in their own religion and in their native clerics, the entire fabric of Indian society would collapse.

Future Jesuits would make the same kind of a trip that LeJeune made. Jean de Brebeuf spent time with the Montagnais. Pierre Marquette learned the language and was initiated to the New World by living several months at Sillery. It was a form of initiation, another novitiate that the Jesuits felt was needed to make a transition to a world of different values and attitudes. On his own trip

LeJeune learned about the people he had come to America to convert, about the cultural and physical obstacles that stood in his way, and probably most important of all, he learned a great deal about himself.

The belief system of his hosts became clearer.[36] LeJeune had pestered his fellow hunters to reveal the concepts about creation and spirits that gave their lives meaning. They believed that Atachocam had created the world. It was then destroyed by a flood and Messou had restored it. Messou went hunting one day with lynxes instead of dogs. But the lynxes went into a great lake and were held there. Messou looked for them. A bird told him that he had seen them in the lake and he followed them into the lake, but the lake overflowed and covered the whole earth. Messou sent a raven in search of a little piece of ground with which to rebuild the earth but he could not find a piece of dry land. He next sent an otter but the otter could not find land. A muskrat did and brought back a little piece of dirt and Messou used this to rebuild the entire earth.

Every animal, man and beast, had his brother somewhere in the forest. The brother was many times larger, a prototype. If anyone saw the brother of the beaver in a dream, he would have a good hunt.

Nipinoukhe created the spring and summer. Pipounoukhe produced the winter. The Indians were not sure whether they were men or animals but they knew that they were living and they could be heard in the woods. The world was their dwelling place, one half for Nipinoukhe and the other half for Pipounoukhe. When their period of stay in one part of the world was over, they went to the other. Nipinoukhe brought with him the heat, the birds, the grass. He restored life and beauty to the world. Pipounoukhe laid waste everything and destroyed it with the snow. This passing from one side of the world to the other was called *achitescatoueth*, meaning that they passed reciprocally to each other's places.

The spirit world was inhabited by *khichikou*, which meant light or air. These spirits could tell the future and were consulted frequently. Only the shaman had the power to control them. They could tell the priests where the elk were, how successful the hunt would be, when the enemy would strike. The Indian placated the khichikou by tossing grease into the fire with the words, "Make us find something to eat."

The wife of the *manitou* (the devil) caused evil in the world. Her husband was the origin of evil but she was the destroying she-devil. She caused diseases. She killed men, fed upon their flesh, gnawing them from the inside. Her gorgeous robe was made of the hair of the men and women she had killed. She sometimes appeared like a fire, a roaring flame, but her language could not be understood.

All living creatures had souls. All souls were immortal and they ate and drank. That was why food was placed in the grave with the dead. Indians believed in an afterlife. Souls of the dead traveled very far away, to a large village where the sun set. The souls went on foot, fording river and stream. It was a hard journey and the Indians were afraid to make it. On the journey the souls hunted for the souls of beaver, porcupine, and moose, "using the soul of the snowshoe to walk upon the soul of the snow."

Prayer invoked the spirits. In famine and sickness continual song and the beating of drums and reciting loud prayers echoed in their cabins. A sneeze meant sickness. It was met with the reply, "I shall be very glad to see the spring."

The moon, the sun, thunder, and the world all found meaning within the Indian's idea of life. Paul LeJeune realized that he faced complex layers of beliefs that were interwoven with behavior. It was "dust in their eyes" that had to be removed in order to see "the beautiful light of truth."

The harsh reality of life among the Indians was far from the romantic visions LeJeune imagined years before when he listened to the veteran Canadian missionary, Fr. Ennemond Masse, speak about America. The Indian physical world was almost beyond the limits of the genteel French Jesuits who had been raised in the most delicate of middle-class surroundings, making the most simple physical hardship a herculean task. For men who considered physical work beneath their dignity, schooled on the idea that others should do the menial tasks to free them for more important duties, the crude lifestyle of the North American frontier was an obstacle in itself. But after spending six months with the Indians on a hunting trip, life in the tiny Jesuit residence of Notre Dame des Anges with some of the niceties of Old France must have seemed luxurious. The extremes of heat and cold, the lack of appropriate housing, the dietary changes, the strange illnesses, and the absence of creature comforts created in Paul LeJeune's mind a place that was an enemy to be fought against and conquered. The place itself was an antagonist.

The problems of evangelization were just as difficult. After his journey with the Montagnais, LeJeune was convinced that the only lasting success the Jesuits would have with the Indians would be among those nations that were sedentary, who had fixed agricultural lands, who would not pick up and leave, making the missionary go with them. Stability was a perceived requirement for achieving success.

Learning the Indian language was equally important. LeJeune was annoyed by his inability to make himself understood and he grew impatient with himself for not being able to comprehend what they said about him. He kept a little book in which he wrote down new words he heard and he pestered Mes-

tigoit and the others for translations of phrases. He would later insist that all
Jesuits new to the missions spend time learning the language.

LeJeune's prolonged stay with the Indians gave him a deep appreciation
for their kindness to each other and to him, their capacity to survive in a harsh
and hostile environment, and their willingness to tolerate his presence. But he
could not accept what he considered their gluttony, their brutality, their stoi-
cism, many of their social customs, and their reliance on the shaman. Try as
he might, he could not penetrate their religious secrets. He learned bits and
pieces, what they chose to reveal. Unknown to him were their most secret
beliefs about dreams and their role in the Indian world, the power of the spirits,
the integration of spirit and material universe. LeJeune sensed the presence of
an impenetrable wall between him and his hosts. It would take more than
preaching to penetrate it.

The initial reaction of the French Jesuits in New France was similar to that
of their Spanish counterparts in Florida half a century before. As Europeans
with clear ideas of what an ideal society should be like, their task of re-creating
one in hostile environments seemed unattainable. However, the Spanish had
no available and convenient economic hinterland from which to draw European resources. Although wheat farming was attempted in Florida, it came to
nought. In New France, the trading posts of Quebec, Tadoussac, and Three
Rivers grew in size and became convenient staging and supply posts for the
missions. A New France was more quickly created on the St. Lawrence than a
New Spain in the Caribbean. Florida had been quickly abandoned for the readily accessible and attractive territory of Mexico. Not only did the Jesuits of New
France lack the option to move their mission to one with more promise, it is
unlikely they would have done it anyway.

Legacies

In a controversial but significant book on the Indians of the Northeast, Calvin
Martin proposed a theory about the Indian's attraction to European tools, guns,
and material goods.[37] Instead of a materialist explanation for why the Iroquois
became enamoured of the guns and iron kettles of the Europeans, Martin
posits a theory that supposes a clash between the Indian and the spirit world
of the beaver. A unique relationship between the hunter and the animal had
been disturbed. In developing his argument, the author states that Jesuit missionaries in Huronia and among the Mohawks contributed to the decimation
of the beaver population by encouraging large-scale, periodic hunting.[38] Martin's creative and important approach to Indian studies will remain standard

fare for years to come. His assertion about the Jesuits, however, raises further questions. Just how deeply did the Jesuits affect Indian life and culture and how long lasting were the changes? What was their legacy in New France as agents of Christianity?

The Indian and European borrowed and learned from each other.[39] Some artifacts became permanent cultural possessions. Most ironic and lethal, of course, was the exchange of tobacco for liquor. Both Indian and white thought that he was getting the better deal. Appropriate dress for the North American frontier, new foods, and a few Indian words that remained part of North American French are readily identifiable Indian contributions. Liquor, guns, metal cooking equipment, and hunting tools became essential to Indian life. But where the Jesuits hoped to make their greatest impact and contribution was in the area of religion and behavior. Only relics of the attempt remain. The Jesuit mission of Ste. Marie-des-Hurons in Midland, Ontario, was resurrected as a tourist attraction, as was Auriesville, New York, site of a Jesuit mission to the Mohawks. Remnants of an Indian Christian community still survive near Montreal. These are important reminders of a remote past but are now either government or church attempts to benefit financially from cultural or religious curiosity.

In Indian villages the Europeans used painted pictures to teach the key points of Christianity. They understood well, however, that the Indian would not be converted to the new religion "by showing them a crucifix."[40] The Europeans were convinced that the devil was behind the Indian refusal of Christianity. "Le diable qui es le seul maître de cette barbarie . . ." is a phrase continually repeated in various forms in the missionary correspondence in New France.[41] It was the devil who prevented the Indian from accepting the Europeans's teachings. The response to the "superstition, error, and barbarism of the native" was to be fourfold, according to Paul Le Jeune in 1638. Missionaries were to learn the native languages in order to oppose the error. Because of the prevalence of disease, a hospital should be built immediately. Since youth was the hope of the future, a reduction, or "seminary" was to be set aside for the Hurons, Algonquins, and the Montagnais. And above all, LeJeune thought, the savages have to be stopped from wandering.[42] A fixed place was essential. Using a military metaphor, as was common to the Jesuits of the time, these were the batteries that would destroy Satan's empire in New France. In fact, the military metaphor was fairly commonplace in the Jesuit accounts. The Jesuits were soldiers of Christ and they were laying siege to the ramparts of Satan in America; or they were "liberating" the Native American from the hold of Satan.[43] At other times they were "laying siege and capturing the field" and their knowledge of native languages would be "arms required for the war."

The liberation from Satan was only marginally successful. In the 1680s Claude Chauchetière described Mohawk life of the 120 to 150 Indian families in the mission village near Montreal. Sexual mores were regulated. The Indians retained their long-standing practice of winter hunts, in addition to farming. But the church bell ruled, calling them to rise, to pray, to work, and the women practiced an extreme mortification of the body.[44] The compromise was reached. The European missionaries soon switched their tactics and methods when they found out that Indian indifference, ridicule, mockery, and violence was the response to their attempt to alter long-standing traditions and customs. Only by keeping the Indian in the New France equivalent of *reducciones*, could the European missionaries claim that their mission was successful. On his part, the Native American was partially successful in retaining his identity, in that he retained his native religion. The Seneca Indian, Red Jacket, summed it up: "We also have a religion which was given to our forefathers, and has been handed down to us their children. It teaches us to be thankful, to be united, to love one another! We never quarrel about religion."[45]

Go Left at the Gila River

The Jesuit reports from New France are invaluable today in reconstructing the early history of the Europeans in the New World. The European missionaries were the first to spend the most time with the native population. Through this contact they became "privileged observers." Language was the key. With it, they were able to go beyond being mere describers of the material world of the Native American and plunge into the belief system and political life of the Indian.[46] And they did not stop in New France.

Jesuit missionaries pushed west through the Great Lakes and down the Mississippi. In Mexico they came north into Arizona. What drove Marquette,[47] Eusebio Kino,[48] or Claude Allouez to explore unknown rivers and arid deserts? One of the obvious reasons was their interest in discovering new groups of North American Indians for evangelization. This was the motive that prompted Marquette's superior to assign Marquette to accompany Jolliet to find the Mississippi. During their journey both Marquette and Jolliet went out of their way, hiking six miles inland, to visit a Peoria Indian village. There Marquette announced to the Indians that God had sent him to help them acknowledge his existence.[49] After his voyage of exploration, Marquette returned to the Illinois Indians whom he had described as gentle and peace loving. The same motive is evident in the land and river explorations of other Jesuits in North America. Kino's explorations through the southwest and over the barren hills of Baja

California were all undertaken with a fundamentally evangelical motive.[50] Paul du Ru's diary of the exploration of the Mississippi from the mouth of the river north is likewise sprinkled with references to the Indian groups that he encountered as potential converts.[51]

When the missionaries found a tribe, the day would begin with the Jesuit explorers saying Mass, the essential Catholic ritual, to ensure God's blessing on their enterprise. In many cases, the explorer would not wait to return to begin evangelizing, but would briefly instruct and then leave with the Indians an upright cross, the visible symbol of Christianity. The missionary-explorer would give a condensed version of the catechism, touching on the redemption, Christ's life and death, and the need for adherence to the missionary's instructions. On his return, the other tangible images of Christianity that were important in winning converts could be presented to the neophytes.

The Jesuit explorers also inquired wherever possible about other Indian nations and other appropriate sites for missions. When Allouez travelled more than five thousand miles in 1666 through the Great Lakes, he wrote in his journal that "this lake [Superior] is the resort of twelve or fifteen distinct Indian nations who come from the North, the South, and the West. They come to fish in the lake . . . but God's purpose is to proclaim the gospel to these wandering tribes."[52]

The religious motive of Jesuit explorers was supported by the more practical political impulses of the colonial government, whether Spanish or French. The missionary explorers always described themselves to the Indians as messengers of God and King, for very practical reasons. Powerful rulers, they claimed, protected them. Kino's forays into northern Mexico and the French Jesuits' voyages differed significantly in that Kino frequently had a troop of Spanish or Mexican soldiers with him. Marquette and Allouez were never accompanied by armed guards. The Jesuit frontier missionaries were never able to convince the Apaches to lay down their arms so they remained a constant threat. The Apaches were in continual revolt against intrusions and occupation of their lands. On the other hand, French fur traders and voyageurs never threatened the Indian with occupation of their lands so the missionaries were never viewed as an advance column for white land grabbers. It is impossible to imagine what the Indians assembled in Sault-Sainte-Marie in 1666 thought of Fr. Claude Dablon's panegyric of the King of France and the French proclamation of ownership of all the land that stretched "from Montreal as far as the South Sea."[53] After singing hymns and hearing speeches by Dablon and the French ambassador, they returned to their homes and life did not change. On the other hand, a similar proclamation in New Spain would have been followed by settlers, mission construction, land occupation, and possibly a garrison for soldiers. The frontier in New France was never pushed back in the same sense that it was occupied and expanded in New Spain. The mission was not a frontier institution in the north the way it was on the Mexican frontier.[54] The frontier of Northern Mexico was an organized Spanish, mestizo, and Indian society that had distinct social and economic traits. It was a developing region in flux that was characterized by changing land ownership, and most important of all, Indian relocation from less accessible areas to the organized structures of the mission village. It was this transfer, so eagerly espoused by missionaries, that resulted in social upheavals for the Indians and frequently in armed rebellion.[55] The Indians in New France did not consider the missions and the church as agents for white economic and political control. There was an attempt to relocate them into mission villages, such as Sillery or Lorette, but the French colonial government never forced them to remain relocated. Hence, the missionary was considered much less of a threat.

The economic objectives of the explorers differed from the economic objectives of the political patrons of the explorations. Mines of precious metals were of great interest to the French patrons of du Ru when he sailed up the Mississippi.[56] He himself thought of other ways of channeling the work of the Indians. Talon's interest in copper was at the bottom of his support of Marquette. Kino wished to improve the lot of the Pima Indians and those in Baja California. He tried to do so by bringing in cattle, improving the methods of planting, growing, and using cottons and grains.[57] His Spanish patrons encouraged him because a sedentary, Christian Indian was a less troublesome Indian. Whereas Kino encouraged the Indians he encountered to move their homes to more fertile land, Marquette, Allouez, and du Ru simply returned to the Indians they found and put their villages into their missionary itineraries.

The French Jesuits had obviously developed a different sense of what an ideal Indian society should be. For them, relocation into European-style cultural units was neither appropriate nor feasible. It would have been demographically more efficient for the Jesuits but they realized that the Indian would never tolerate such confinement.

Of all of the motives that moved the explorer-missionaries, the most elusive but clearly evident was a Renaissance-like curiosity, a disinterested curiosity focusing on non-mission related objects. This was an attitude they inherited from the Renaissance, a period that raised the cult of the individual, extravagant daring, and indifference to pain and fatigue to a virtue.[58] It was not a scientific gathering and organization of data that the missionaries and explorers were after but a spontaneous, undisciplined, unsystematic absorption of knowledge. The Renaissance encouraged a more observant attitude toward natural history, and Jesuit reports and diaries are filled with descriptions of lakes and rivers, animals and people, bugs and flowers. The information was amassed rather than selected, arranged, and edited. By the same token, it was spontaneous and omnivorous.[59] Du Ru's journal of his voyage up the Mississippi River describes alligators and Indians, villages and trees, flora and fauna with equal zest. Du Ru also has the distinction of having written the only known ode to the Mississippi River.[60] There was no purpose to his descriptions, no set audience that he was trying to impress. He wrote the journal for himself.

What is also evident in the explorers' reports is the consciousness of taking part in great deeds. They shared in the somewhat exaggerated statement of Fernández de Oviedo that the discovery of America was the greatest event in mankind's history since the birth of Christ.[61] Whether the bounds of Christendom were being expanded, new peoples discovered for baptism, or rivers and hills mapped that had never been seen before, there was a sense of great accomplishment in the task. Nowhere is this more evident than in Marquette's reports of his voyage down the Mississippi, or Kino's repeated announcements that California was not an island but a peninsula that could be reached overland by turning left at the Gila River. They readily believed the Indian informants who frequently exaggerated distance or importance of the locality. Marquette thought that the Pacific Ocean was a stone's throw from the Mississippi, just across a plain that stood in his way. North was the water route to China and Japan, the long-sought and fabled Northwest Passage. Kino was convinced that the crowns of Spain and France would make contact through the Jesuit explorations down the Mississippi and north of Mexico. He had no conception of the vast spaces between the river and the northern Mexican frontier. Neither Marquette nor Kino were honored in their lives for their accomplishments. In the eighteenth century, the Jesuit provincial in Mexico City was still under the impression that California was an island. Marquette's feat went virtually unnoticed for decades.[62] But each knew what he had done and on some level was conscious of its importance.

The Jesuit explorers were propelled by a mix of motives. Decorum demanded that the religious motive take precedence. Politics required that due respect be shown the political and economic advantages accruing to the crown. But the mix included a large dose of Renaissance curiosity.

9

Maryland: "A Fine Poor Man's Country"

The French government was lukewarm over the support of the conversion of the Indians. They were more interested in commerce than in dominating Indians and occupying their lands. On the other hand, the British government was openly hostile to Roman Catholics in America and a fortiori to Roman Catholic Jesuits missionaries. Thus, the Jesuits in Maryland faced two adversaries: the Native Americans as object of conversion was the religious rival, while the hostile government was the political antagonist. In Latin America the Spanish government actively supported missionary work. Because circumstances differed in these three regions, Latin America, New France, and Maryland, the Roman Catholic missionaries in each had to deal with different issues.

St. Mary's City, 1634

When the Jesuit, Francis Parker, wrote to his provincial superior, Edward Knott, on July 26, 1640, asking to be sent to the recently opened mission in Maryland, he expressed the doubt that he "would not fare well in controversy with heretics having yett read but little in that kynde."[1] His reasons for going to Maryland were varied. He saw no hope in trying to convert his English relatives to Catholicism. Instead, he would imitate earlier Jesuits and seek conversions elsewhere.

"I will not rehearse my motives because I have almost infinite, amongst others, this is none of the smallest, that herein I shall soe neerly resemble glorious St. Xaverius, to whom above all other saynts I have ever since my conversion bine most especially devoted."[2]

Parker could not return to England because he was considered a traitor. The Reformation in England that began with Henry VIII's break with Rome in 1546 eventually split into two major camps, the traditionalist Church of England that recognized the king as the country's spiritual leader and the dissenters who were guided by John Calvin's purist theology. Both camps considered Roman Catholics to be devil worshippers, followers of the anti-Christ, the pope. Politics fueled the fires of intolerance. Spain was England's enemy; Spain was Catholic, therefore, a Catholic was by definition an enemy of the English crown, hence a traitor. Queen Mary's persecution of the Protestants and the madcap Catholic plan in 1605 to blow up the king and parliament gave added weight to the charges of treason. Therefore, it is not surprising that a Massachusetts statute of 1647 threatened death to Catholic priests.

Parker was part of the fourth generation of English Jesuits who were growing accustomed to spending most of their lives outside of England. To return to England was a death-defying act. Englishmen began entering the Society of Jesus in the time of Ignatius Loyola. One hundred fifty-five English and Welsh candidates joined the Jesuits between 1555 and 1585.[3] Most who entered had studied in Oxford or Cambridge and they joined the Society for a variety of reasons; security, whether spiritual or temporal, and spiritual desires, predominated. The median age of entering candidates was twenty-five. From such a pool were volunteers for the Maryland mission drawn.

The mission had unique origins that were far from Maryland's shores. George Calvert, the First Lord Baltimore, had been privy councilor and secretary of state to James I. He received a permit from the king to begin a plantation in Newfoundland.[4] In 1628 he transported a boatload of settlers to that location. The local clergy was both surprised and chagrined to discover that the settlers were mostly Roman Catholics, complete with their own priest. Lord Baltimore had hoped that his Catholic settlers would be able to not only live side by side with Protestants and Anglicans, but even share a place of worship where both the Mass and services would be offered at different times. Lord Baltimore was ahead of his times. Both Catholics and Protestants objected. Lord Baltimore ended up battling French marauders and his own intolerant countrymen who were not quite ready for his version of religious freedom. Other reasons worked against the success of his Newfoundland plantation. The land was cold, there was little food and, "his house had been a hospital all winter."[5] Lord Baltimore tried to move his Catholic settlers to Virginia but the governor there would not allow them to land. Maryland, north of Virginia, named after Charles I's queen consort, Henrietta Maria, was the alternative. Lord Baltimore received another permit to begin a settlement in Maryland. He probably did not realize it, but he was helping to end the arrangement that had guided European monarchs since the time of the Reformation, namely that the religion of the king would be the religion of the people: *cujus regio ejus religio*. His were the first steps toward recognizing the individual right to profess politically unacceptable religious beliefs. Lord Baltimore died in 1632 but his son, Cecil, continued to advance the principles that were the foundation of the Newfoundland experiment.

Lord Baltimore's charter for his Maryland settlement, published on June 20, 1632, contained several clauses that would buttress an authoritarian and aristocratic regime.[6] Maryland was a royal gift, a fiefdom that resembled land grants made by Spanish kings to the conquistadores. The lord proprietor answered only to the crown. He received rents, taxes, and fees, appointed all officials necessary to enforce the law, and exercised final judicial and political authority. He was given the liberty to erect, found, and act as patron of all churches and chapels; he was exempt from all Laws of Mortmain. And all of these powers belonged as an inheritance to the lords Baltimore for all time. By the time Lord Baltimore received the Maryland charter, he had already become a Roman Catholic making the royal concessions all the more interesting, and alarming, in some quarters.

Cecil Calvert, the second Lord Baltimore, asked the Jesuits to accompany the settlers to Maryland. Why is not clearly known. Perhaps he admired the Jesuits' reputation as missionaries or their dislike for the episcopal jurisdictional claims in London.[7] Whatever the reason, Calvert thought he recognized an ally. The Jesuit provincial in England, Richard Blount, passed the request on to the Jesuit general in Rome, Mutius Vitelleschi, who expressed great misgivings about the project.[8] Vitelleschi's major concern was that England might be trespassing on Spanish claimed territory and the Spanish government would be harshly critical of Jesuit participation. Nevertheless, Vitelleschi allowed Blount to use his judgment if he thought the plan a good one. However, he cautioned the English provincial about the type of men he should send to America.

> ... in the choice of those whom you think of sending forth on that
> new expedition, you [must] not only make much account of their in-
> clination and desire, since, if people are unwilling or are not so well
> disposed for a long voyage like that, no great good can be expected
> from them, but also that you scrutinize most diligently their virtue,

prudence, and zeal, especially in the case of those who are to lay the foundations of the mission; that they be such as the others who come afterwards may look up to walking in their footsteps and following their example as a rule and model of action.[9]

The Jesuits who eventually accompanied Leonard Calvert, brother to Cecil, to Maryland were Fathers Andrew White and John Altham and Brother Thomas Gervase. From the very beginning it was clear that the relationship of these Jesuits to the colonizing group was quite different from the role of other Jesuit missionaries who went to America with French or Spanish colonists. They would not receive any recompense or support for their labors from the proprietor of the colony but were to work the land like other colonists and be totally self-supporting.[10] Calvert's Condition of Plantation awarded two thousand acres of land for every five men brought to the colony, so the Jesuits who brought with them thirty men as indentured servants stood to receive twelve thousand acres. In some sense this was similar to land grants awarded religious orders in other parts of America. Without laborers to work the land, large grants were of little value. So the beneficiary had to hire laborers or purchase slaves. In early colonial English America, indentured servants played major roles in the labor market and the Jesuits had a ready supply. But the difference was considerable. The Jesuits received no more land than any other lay colonist who transported men to America. They were not considered economic or commercial rivals and so the resentment that built up against the Jesuits in Spanish and French America was not immediately or universally present in Maryland. In Maryland a de facto separation between church and state would exist which eventually developed into the American Catholic tradition of religious liberty.[11] Catholics would be a minority in colonial Maryland and the governor, Leonard Calvert, was instructed by his brother, Cecil, that they "suffer no scandall nor offence to be given to any of the Protestants, whereby any just complaint may heereafter be made, by them, in Virginea or in England...."[12]

On March 25, 1634, the Jesuits and the two hundred colonists on the *Ark* and the *Dove* landed on St. Clement's Island at the mouth of the Potomac River.[13] Before making a permanent settlement, Calvert and a small group sailed upriver at least eighty miles, made contact with the two *tayacs*, or regional headmen, of the area, and the Jesuits had the opportunity to engage in their first attempts at evangelization. Calvert decided to stay downriver, closer to the anchorage near the sea. According to Fr. White, the land was good, the air wholesome, and the river afforded a safe harbor for ships of any burden. Fresh water and wood was plentiful, "and the place so naturally fortified, as with little dificultie, it will be defended from any enemie."[14] The Yoacomacoes who lived there sold Calvert about thirty miles of land in exchange for axes, knives, and some cloth, agreeing to share the town with the Englishmen. The Indians even agreed to leave at the end of harvest season. Father White pointed out that the Indians were anxious to have the Englishmen nearby in case the Susquehannocks began raiding.[15] On March 27, 1634, Governor Leonard Calvert took possession of the town and named it St. Mary's. Cattle, hogs, and poultry were brought in from Virginia, a water mill for grinding corn was built, and "within the space of six months, was laid the foundation of the colonie in Maryland."[16] So much corn was available that the *Dove* sailed to Massachusetts in July with one thousand bushels and returned with salt-fish, the beginnings of a lucrative intercolonial trade.

Jesuits and Indians

One of the attractions for Jesuits who volunteered for the Maryland mission was the opportunity to convert the Indians. Although the English Jesuits were few in number and limited in resources, they were enthusiastic about converting the Indians. White identified conversion of the Indians as Lord Baltimore's primary reason for organizing a colony in America[17] and he fully intended that the Jesuits who would accompany the colonists and those to follow would have this as their primary task. White himself established a mission at Kattamaquindi, the capital of the Piscataways, and baptized their chief, his wife, and their son. White became sufficiently proficient in the Piscataway language to write a catechism and translate some prayers. Elsewhere in Maryland, Ferdinand Poulton, the religious superior, converted the chief of the Anacostans, and Roger Rigby lived with the Patuxent and learned their language. Most Jesuits, however, used interpreters in the early years of contact.

The tribes living within Baltimore's grant were members of the Algonquin family.[18] Farming, fishing, and hunting furnished food. They lived in hamlets. Less than fifteen hundred lived on the eastern shore of the Chesapeake, where they formed the Choptank, Nanticoke, Pocomoke, and Asseateague tribes. Patuxant and Mattapanients occupied villages on the western shore. On the Potomac River there were clusters of Canoy subtribes: the Choptico, Potapacos, Piscataway, Yaocomaco, Pamonkey, Mattowoman, and Anacostank. The western shore counted about fifteen hundred Indians. The Susquehannocks lived about forty- to fifty miles up the river that the Marylanders named after them. Baltimore's colony arrived as the Susquehannocks were in the midst of conducting raiding forays into the Chesapeake region.

Despite fairly extensive contact during the first five or six years in Maryland, Jesuit descriptions of the people or the places they encountered are almost nonexistant. In sharp contrast to the French and Spanish propensity for letter writing, describing in detail the flora and fauna of America, the Maryland Jesuits seemed almost reluctant to put their ideas and impressions on paper. There were several reasons for this.

The irregularity of communication with Europe was one reason. Unlike Spanish America and New France that dispatched regularly scheduled packet boats to Spain and France soon after arrival in America, Maryland did not have nor did it need regular communication with England. Lord Baltimore in London had his sources of information about his plantation's progress, but no government entity required regular reports. Another reason was that the Jesuits were not in the frame of mind to commit to paper what was still technically illegal business and extralegal activity. Their caution about what they did and with whom they did it was reflected in the paucity of written records. The French Jesuits encouraged their missionaries to write lengthy accounts, some pious, some political, which were then edited and used for recruitment and public relations purposes in Europe.[19] The religious and political atmosphere in England, however, made this type of correspondence from America impossible. During the seventeenth and eighteenth centuries the Jesuits played a lethal cat-and-mouse game with the government and the generally accepted rule of behavior was to make as little noise as possible lest the cat awaken. This remained the accepted norm of behavior long after the need for total silence was necessary. As a result, we have little from the Jesuits in Maryland that describes in detail what they were doing or what the people with whom they worked were like.[20] The little they did write was frequently worded in a readily identifiable code. Parishioners were "customers," rectories were "houses," priests were "gentlemen" and they even had to use aliases (e.g., Fr. Thomas Copley was "Philip Fisher" and John Altham used the name "John Gravener"). Even more curious is the lack of any complaint about the situation. No doubt it was stated verbally, but never was it committed to paper where it might be used as evidence of disloyalty. A paralyzing culture of fear enveloped the Jesuits. White's first report from Maryland to his superiors in Rome stated explicitly that the purpose of the expedition was "not only to work among the colonists, but also to devote themselves to procuring the conversion and salvation of the barbarians."[21] The Jesuit report from Maryland in 1638 stated that "the rulers of this colony have not yet allowed us to dwell among the savages" because of the prevalence of disease and because of perceived hostility.[22] The phrase leads one to believe that they wanted to live in Indian villages and within a year the Jesuits actually succeeded in doing so. In 1639 White was living in the village of Maquacomen, the tayac of the Patuxants, whom he had converted. Altham lived on Kent Island in the Chesapeake Bay, sixty miles north of St. Mary's. Poulton and a lay brother lived on the plantation of Mattapany, which had been given to the Jesuits by the tayac of the Patuxents.

White had little success with Maquacomen and was soon living with the Piscataways. Kittamaquund, their tayac, insisted that the priest live in his lodge and his wife cooked bread and meats for the Jesuit. The need for English support against his tribesmen was one reason for Kittamaquund's affection. Another was the Jesuit's appearance in a dream along with Leonard Calvert and a beautiful god. Also increasing the priest's prestige was his healing powers. When Kittamaquund fell ill, the Indian shamans could not do what White did—cure him. White bled him and gave him a mixture of "a certain powder of known efficacy mixed with holy water." The tayac recovered, immediately accepted baptism along with his wife and two daughters and was forever grateful to the priest.[23] The illnesses at this time that struck Indian and white alike were not the deadly epidemics of smallpox and influenza. These came later. They were the "Maryland fevers" for which the Chesapeake was noted, probably malaria. One Jesuit ascribed them to the "hot and sultry summers and the treacherous climate." Another thought that "the fresh water marches whither the salt water could not penetrate" was the culprit.[24]

The Jesuits had to be satisfied with what they called "excursions" into Indian country searching for converts. The Chesapeake Bay region was characterized by waterways and inlets that effectively prevented a gradual land penetration of Indian territory. Instead, the missionary first identified a target community and then set out in a pinnace with interpreter, manservant, and supplies. "We take with us a little chest of bread, butter, cheese, corn, cut and dried before it is ripe, beans and a little flour—another chest also for carrying bottles, one of which contains wine for religious purposes, six others for holy water for the purpose of baptism; a box with the sacred vessel, and a slab as an altar for the sacred function; and another casket full of trifles, which we give the Indians to conciliate their affection—such as little bells, combs, knives, fish-hooks, needles, thread and other things of this kind."[25]

A translator always accompanied the Jesuits on their excursions and this troubled the missionaries. They were never comfortable with the fact that the concepts of their religion had to be conveyed without them knowing exactly what was being said. The Annual Letter of 1642 lamented the fact that only Fr. Rigby had succeeded in making progress with the Indian language and that "none of us can yet converse with the Indians without an interpreter."[26] Rigby eventually wrote a catechism in Piscataway and White also wrote one, now lost. However, it seems that the Jesuits in Maryland set no special store in learning the Indian languages before attempting evangelization, possibly because they did not have the luxury of time to do so. The mission stations needed immediate staffing and the Catholic settlers immediate attention. In addition, the events of 1645 onward crystallized the Jesuit mission in Maryland as one that served almost exclusively the white Roman Catholic settlers of Maryland.

Politics and Religion

The rise of Puritan influence in England was eventually felt in America. Maryland had never been a Catholic colony in the sense that it had been founded for and peopled by Roman Catholics. Members of the Church of England and dissenters had always been in the majority in America and the three groups lived side by side with reasonable but varying degrees of tolerance.

In 1645 the tolerance ended. Richard Ingle, a self-proclaimed champion of the Puritans, ransacked the Jesuit farm buildings and residence in St. Mary's, took two Jesuits captive with him to London, and drove three other Jesuit priests into Virginia where they remained in hiding until their deaths.

Ingle had been a familiar figure in St. Mary's, a merchant-trader who supplied the innkeepers and the gentlemen-farmers with whiskey and English manufactured goods. In 1644 he arrived in St. Mary's on his ship appropriately named *Reformation* with a more noble mission: to excoriate King Charles I and acclaim the virtues of the Parliament. He was arrested and returned to England where he set about obtaining Letters of Marque from Parliament to be used against those who had seized his ship in Maryland and against the city that was the hotbed of Papists and the enemy of Parliament.[27] He was empowered to take all ships and cargo owned by interests opposed by Parliament. With the assistance of Governor Claiborne of Virginia, Ingle returned to Maryland and launched an attack against St. Mary's. He and his men burned down the Jesuit farmhouse of St. Inigoes and the priests's residence, pillaging as many Catholic homes as he could find. Tobacco crops were seized, livestock driven off, and servants urged to revolt. Ingle tried to arrest the governor, Leonard Calvert, but he escaped to Virginia. The Jesuits were not so fortunate.[28] Fathers Copley and White were put into chains and sent to London. Roger Rigby, Bernard Hartwell, and John Cooper escaped to Virginia where they died. The Jesuit Indian mission in Maryland ended.

Ingle was no mere freebooter, his attack no aberration. It was borne out of a traditional suspicion and a smoldering anger against Roman Catholics that needed little to push it to the surface. Lord Baltimore's original instructions to the Catholics who travelled to Maryland displayed a circumspection toward Puritans and Anglicans bordering on a nervous fear that in fact had a basis in reality. In 1606 an "Act for the Better Repressing of Popish Recusants" had levied a fine of £20 each month on all over the age of sixteen who refused to attend the services of the Church of England or, in lieu of a fine, to suffer forfeiture of two-thirds of their lands.[29] Anyone discovering Mass being said or relief being given to a Jesuit priest was to receive a reward of one-third of any fine imposed or one-third of any property forfeited. No Catholic who refused to conform to the new laws could seek redress in court. He could not hold public office nor be an officer in the army nor could he practice law or medicine. Any Catholic not married in the Church of England could not own property, his or his wife's. Catholic children sent to foreign Catholic schools forfeited their inheritance to their Protestant next of kin. Anyone could enter a Catholic home under pretext of enforcing the penal law. Conformity followed the Catholic even to his grave. He could only be buried in ground of the established church. At times the enforcement of the penal laws relaxed but they were always there, hovering like gray ghosts. Catholics had no church to attend and could only worship in secret. All the more curious was that by the time of Ingle's raid in Maryland, the Jesuit province of England had 338 members, perhaps spurred on by the execution of sixteen of its members as traitors.

The cloud of fear, suspicion, and hatred that characterized relations between Catholic and Protestant moved across the Atlantic and settled on Maryland. The almost feudal relationship between the proprietor and the colonists fanned the fires of discontent. The Baltimores' reign was authoritarian, the model one of royal absolutism that did not sit well in a changing political and religious atmosphere. The governor's council was composed mainly of Catholics.[30] A thin line divided Catholic domination and political absolutism. And it was bitterly resented by the Protestant colonists. Ingle's attack on the Jesuits and on Catholic property met with nods of approval.

One unforseen and unintended result of Ingle's raid has been a clearer picture of the physical environment that the Jesuits created around them in the Maryland mission. Thomas Copley sued Ingle in London for the return of Jesuit property. He never received compensation but the list of goods that the Jesuits claimed to have been pillaged or destroyed by Ingle's men reveals how their houses and farms were furnished.[31]

The Jesuits returned to Maryland in 1648 but by the time they got back the Indians whom they had evangelized had been driven off in a series of clashes with white settlers. Numbers were still small, only Copley and Francis Fitzherbert returned immediately, so the Jesuits became gentlemen-farmers working exclusively among the white immigrant colonists.[32]

In the midst of Cromwell's ascendency, the Maryland legislature passed an extraordinary set of laws that directly contradicted the Puritan concept of

how the ideal state should relate to religion. The Puritans held the very traditional belief that the state and the Christian Bible should be institutionalized
and shine as a beacon to all who had not accepted the truth; in brief, the state
became a quasi-theocracy where the ministers of government were also ministers of the word, or close to it. Much of the rest of the world at that time
followed the same idea. The old Roman Empire, the Islamic world, and the
Christian West all held to the idea that religion and politics were distinct but
not separate. The Maryland legislature moved in a much different direction.
Church and state would exist side by side, each with its own set of laws and
chain of authority. What has been commonly termed the Toleration Act was
approved in 1649. These laws allowed all Christians (Jews and other believers
were excluded) to publicly practice their religion, whatever that might be. "No
person," the law said, "shall be in any waies troubled, molested or discounte-
nanced for or in respect of his or her religion nor in the free excercise thereof
within this province."[33] Even the use of inflammatory words like heretic, popish
priest, Jesuitical Papist, Lutheran, Calvinist, or Roundhead was punished with
a fine of ten shillings. Within five years the act was repealed by the Puritans.
By a twist of logic, the right to toleration became the right to be intolerant.
Nevertheless, the Toleration Act was important because it demonstrated a general tendency that eventually came to dominate feelings toward religion in
Maryland.

    After Cromwell's rise in 1655, a ten-man Puritan council ruled Maryland.
The Toleration Act was repealed, a pamphlet war broke out between Lord Baltimore's followers, and the Puritans destroyed the proprietor's forces in a naval
battle on the Severn River. But by 1657 in one of those sudden reversals of
form dictated by economic necessity, Cromwell helped restore Baltimore's pro-
prietorship, the Toleration Act was dusted off and put in place, and the violence
and divisiveness ebbed.[34]

    The Catholic population in Maryland at mid-seventeenth century was
around 2,300 out of a total of twenty-five thousand settlers. Jesuit-operated
schools opened; the one in St. Mary's began in 1649, Newtown in 1653,
and schools in Bohemia Manor, St. Thomas Manor, and St. Inigoes later.[35] The
school in Newtown was for "eyther Protestants or Catholikes." Chapels were
erected in Port Tobacco and Newtown. It is evident that the Jesuits took advantage of the lack of Protestant ministers and schoolmasters. They preached their
own version of Christianity wherever they could and they frequently paid the
consequences. In 1658 Fr. Fitzherbert was summoned before the Provincial
Court in Calvert County and accused of "treason and sedition" because at a
general muster of townsfolk he did "endeavour to seduce and draw from their
religion the inhabitants there met together." He also "rebelliously and mution-

ously sayd that if Thomas Gerard Esq. [of the council] did not come and bring his wife and children to his church, he would come and force them to his church."[36] The court decided that Fitzherbert's argument, that "he shall not be molested for or in respect of the free exercise of his religion," carried enough weight to warrant the case's dismissal. The court accepted preaching and teaching as part of the free exercise of religion. Fitzherbert was either a reckless firebrand or he felt reasonably comfortable in preaching to a crowd at the musters and at St. Clement's across the river from Newtown, probably the latter. The Jesuit was turned in not for preaching but because his preaching "caused several inhabitants of this province to refuse to appear at musters that they shall thereby be incapable of defending the peace." The objection was not against Roman Catholic preaching but against its perceived result, with which the judges did not agree. Years later when the Penal Laws were resurrected, the accusations would not be so indirect.

Between 1650 and 1688 the farm of St. Thomas Manor served as the Jesuit administrative center where the superior of the mission resided. The nine or ten Jesuits in Maryland preached to their congregations (and to Anglicans when they got the chance), organized a network of Roman Catholic families, said Mass, and tended their farms.[37] But as far as most Catholics were concerned, it was a period of disquiet and apprehension. The house of Baltimore had regained its proprietory rights from Oliver Cromwell's government, thus allowing power shifts to occur from economic and social ranking. Catholic landowners and tobacco farmers were among the most prosperous settlers. In 1681 William Calvert, a Roman Catholic, commanded the foot soldiers of the St. Mary's County militia. Vincent Lowe and Henry Darnall, also Catholics, commanded the foot soldiers and horsemen of Talbot County, Charles County, and parts of Calvert County.[38] But although Catholics were prominent in the colony, they were suspect, and continually accused of conspiring with the French and Indians to massacre the Protestant population. Preoccupation with the Indians on the fringes of the Maryland frontier intensified. The Susquehannocks and the Senecas were pitted against the Virginians and Marylanders.[39] Rumor spread that Catholics conspired with the Senecas to massacre the Protestants and ally themselves with the Catholic French in Upper New York.[40] In 1676 John Yeo, a Church of England minister, pleaded for more ministers of Maryland to confute "the soe many profest enemies as the Popish priests Jesuits who are encouraged and provided for."[41] Yeo was concerned about the numbers of Anglicans who were converting to Catholicism. In 1681 Capt. Josias Fendall testified in a deposition that Catholics and Indians were out to kill all Protestants.[42] But he was hard put to explain how or when this massacre would happen.

The religious politics of the home government again upset the delicate balance among Catholics, Anglicans, and dissenters in Maryland in 1688. The Glorious Revolution drove the Catholic James II from the throne, William and Mary began to rule, and the Penal Laws against Catholics were restored. Catholic attorneys were disbarred by an oath prescribed in 1692. The Test Oath in 1699 barred all Catholics from official positions in Maryland. In 1704 an act was passed "To Prevent the Growth of Popery" that declared the practice of Catholicism a penal offense.[43] Priests could not say Mass, nor could a Catholic teach in or keep a school. In December of the same year, legislation was passed allowing Catholics to attend religious services only in a private home. Thus began the custom of building chapels connected to houses where Catholics gathered to celebrate their rituals. They were called Mass-houses. Taxes were imposed on Catholics entering Maryland. In 1717 the duty was doubled from twenty to forty shillings per "Irish Papist."

Despite the proliferation of laws against them, the Catholic population kept increasing. By 1759 their numbers had risen.[44] "In the neighborhood," stated Thomas Greaves, "there are two Catholic families for one Protestant one." Greaves, a carpenter who worked for the Jesuits, reported that the "papists said that they would wash their hands in the blood of Protestants and that Catholic priests would soon preach in Chaptico Church."[45] More serious, Greaves thought, was that "the Jesuits were back country with the French, they had a public chapel and were building a Popish Chapel in St. Mary's County." Schoolmasters were papists and taught Protestant children publicly. If Greaves was correct, and he probably was, it says little for the government's inforcement of the Penal Laws.

But the laws were in fact always there and the Jesuits were frequently reminded of them. In 1745, the Jesuits Livers, Molyneux, and Herne were summoned before Governor Thomas Bladen. The governor made a long, rambling speech about how dangerous it was for Negroes or royal subjects to congregate under pretense of attending Divine Worship. He then made the extraordinary suggestion that the Jesuits conduct services without congregations.

> As nothing can give greater alarms to His Majesty's well affected
> subjects than frequent meetings of people and negroes under pre-
> tence of Divine Worship, I cannot discharge my duty if I do not ac-
> quaint you it is expected your religious duties be complied with (as
> they surely may) without concourse of people as may give suspicion
> of something else being designed than a bare exercise of religion.[46]

The governor did not forbid Catholic services. He did not even scold the Jesuits for organizing them. He suggested the illogical almost as if to be able to report to the home government, if he ever had to, that he had shaken his finger at the Papist Jesuits.

Governor Sharpe's spirited defense of Roman Catholics in 1756 might have allayed some minds. He inquired and scrutinized "into the conduct of the people of the Romish faith" and came up with the conclusion that none of them had "misbehaved" or had given just cause of "offence."[47] But the anti-Catholic and anti-Jesuit feeling increased, if anything. Although the law was not enforced, Jesuits were forbidden from owning land. Catholics again were accused of supporting the Indians against the English settlers.[48] The lower house of the Maryland Assembly, bitterly anti-Catholic, was in favor of using the oaths of William and Mary's period as a test of loyalty. To which the upper house (always pro-Catholic) responded that "if the example of the Mother Country in the Article of Religion were to be imitated in the British Colonies in North America, what an infinite confusion there would be!"[49]

In the midst of the Maryland Assembly's anti-Catholic tirades, the Catholic community organized, worshiped, and prospered. The lower Assembly might not have reflected the feelings of the majority. More and more Catholics married Protestants and Anglicans. The dynamics of farming, the tobacco trade, commerce, and nature itself drew Catholics and Protestants into business and personal relationships. The commercial and business imperative especially helped the formation of a pluralist society.

The Jesuits themselves gave no hint of the antagonistic conditions under which they worked. A young Jesuit, John Lewis, wrote a 144-line iambic pentameter poem about his trip from the Patapsco to Annapolis in 1730 in which he imagined himself in some ethereal Garden of Eden where the moon, stars, animals, flora and fauna existed harmoniously without the harmful intrusion of man. The land unfolded before him stretching toward the Blue Mountains to the west. He wrote:

> Now looking round I view the outstretched land,
> O'er which the sight exerts a wide command,
> The fertile vallies, and the naked hills,
> The cattle feeding near the crystal rills;
> The lawns wide op'ning to the sunny ray,
> And [mazn] thickets yet excludes the day.
> A while the eye is pleased these scenes to trace,
> Then hurrying o'er the intermediate space,

> Far distant Mountains drest in blue appear,
> And all their woods are lost in empty air.[50]

The Turner-like landscape put into poetry by the Jesuit says something about his frame of mind. He pre-dated the Lake Country Romantics by over a century, and the fact that Lewis could have so turned his attention to the beauty of his surroundings without even alluding to the persistent persecution of his brethren is remarkable. Perhaps it was something with which he had learned to cope, a part of the environment with which he had to interact. His fellow Jesuit, Joseph Mosley, who worked in Charles, Talbot, and St. Mary's counties from 1758 to 1787 seems to have felt the same. In his letters to his sister spanning most of his time in Maryland, he alluded only once to religious intolerance and that only indirectly.[51] Mosley had a parish with fifteen hundred souls. "I am daily on horseback," he wrote, "visiting the sick, comforting the infirm, strengthening the pusillanimous, etc. And I enjoy my health as yet as well, as if I were breathing my own native air."[52] The people of Maryland seemed poor to him. Maryland for him was "a fine poor man's county." Grain was abundant, food plentiful, but there was no bread, only a kind of "mush," a hasty pudding made of Indian corn. The forests were vast, the horses magnificent, the work tiring, but Mosley considered himself "as content as a King, and never shall desire a change if I can keep my health and be of service."[53] He said nothing about religion, cautiously referring to his fellow Jesuits as "Gentlemen," writing "p..t" for priest and calling parishioners "clients." His only complaint was that indentured servants had to take the oath on landing, "a law invented to prevent the importation of Catholic servants."[54] Aside from this one comment, one would not know from Mosley's letters that the Penal Laws existed. In his final letter to his sister, written in 1772, Mosley complained of failing health. After a long ride to Philadelphia, he was seized with violent fits. "If I can't ride," he wrote, "I shall be here an unprofitable servant." But he gave himself a longer life trajectory. He asked his sister to send him "a pair or two of men's buck-skin gloves."[55]

Mosley and Lewis may not have been representative of the entire Jesuit community in Maryland. But throughout the eighteenth century there were only fifteen or twenty Jesuits active at any one time. The Penal Laws seemed more a nuisance than a hindrance to their labors.

Farms and Manors

On the eve of the supression of the Society of Jesus in 1773 the Jesuit mission in Maryland was thriving. Their churches and communities went as far north as Philadelphia. There were twenty Jesuits in Maryland and over ten thousand Catholics. The economic base of the Jesuit mission was a complex of farms that yielded tobacco for sale, livestock, and farm products.

The Jesuits as an institution ranked alongside the small number of merchant-planters who dominated the Maryland economy in the middle of the eighteenth century. These merchant-planters lived in two-story brick manor houses surrounded by other estate buildings supporting associated farm activities. In 1733 the 2.3 percent of the landowners in Talbot County, Maryland, who owned slaves and land worked anywhere from one thousand to twenty thousand acres each, and much of it was leased to tenants.[56] Each of the Jesuit farms had its manor house but contemporary descriptions do not paint a portrait of lavish accoutrements. When Joseph Mosley set up the mission of St. Joseph's in Tuckahoe, Talbot County, in 1764, one of the major criteria for a site for the manor house was proximity to Roman Catholic homes. When he found the appropriate location (his five congregations were ten, twenty, twenty-four, twenty-two, and twenty-two miles away), he purchased a piece of land that already had three buildings on it, "a miserable dwelling house, a much worse for some negroes, and a house to cure tobacco."[57] He described his manor house as "nothing but a few boards riven from oak trees, not sawed plank, and these nailed together to keep out the coldest air; not one brick or stone about it, no plastering and no chimney; the bricks I was obliged to buy and cart above five mile."[58] Mosley brought four male and four female slaves from the Jesuit estate of White Marsh to help in cutting down the woods and opening the plantation. The estate apparently had fallen into disrepair under the prior owner, a Parson John Miller whom Mosley paid £260 10 s. for the land.[59] Inside the main house (a "sort of a house" he called it) Mosley put a table, a desk, some chairs, paper and ink, and candles. Within a few months Mosley had hogs, sheep, cows, turkeys, geese, and other fowl. The speed with which the Jesuit had set up an apparently thriving farm with slaves, cattle, and buildings might have been at the root of the bitter resentment voiced by Protestants against the Jesuits in eighteenth-century Maryland. The "Jesuits," complained the Freeholders of Calvert County, "accumulate great wealth, the best estates, [and] extensive possessions."[60]

Mosley was able to purchase Miller's farm because he drew the £260 from the General Fund that the Jesuits called the *Arca Seminarii*. Each Jesuit estate in Maryland was assessed an annual prorated sum that totalled £200. Major purchases were made from this General Fund.[61] Every residence kept at its own expense a "public meeting place of Divine Worship," that is, a chapel. Farmhouse, clothing for workers and slaves, building reparations, everything except bread and meat, was supplied by farm income.[62] Those residences that did not have sufficient income to pay their way were supported by those that did.

Land purchases were serious matters and could not be undertaken without the advice and consent of the Jesuit superior. When James Green sold Fr. George Hunter three acres called the Strife (each tract had a name) "on the Patuxant north of Isaac's part of Jacob's Hope" for twenty shillings, a complex process of approvals had to be undergone. The Maryland Jesuits' internal regulations stressed not purchasing land without permission from the Provincial, contracting debts and obligations *ex justicia*, and any sort of house construction without leave.[63] Intermediaries were frequently used by the Jesuits for land purchases. On April 22, 1754, John Lewis, the Jesuit stationed at Bohemia Manor, paid Peter Lowber £42 15s. 4d. "for a tract of land purchased by Mr. Poulton [Fr. Thomas Poulton, the Jesuit Superior] of J. Cain and *uxor* [wife] lying in Kent upon Delaware in Motherkill Hundred called Addition to Cavilridge layed out for 100 & twenty acres. see the papers . . . capital & interest thereof from the year 1745, 19th of October."[64] Lowber was the intermediary in the purchase.

The existence of a General Fund that must have grown considerable over time enabled the institution to finance a variety of activities and expand its missionary work into Pennsylvania. It also permitted the institution to make purchases when prices were depressed and allowed the individual Jesuit farmer to absorb temporary losses. Crops could be kept off the market until prices improved. Unfortunately, we do not have a series of Jesuit production and sales records that would enable one to determine how and to what benefit the Jesuits used the central financing at their disposal. It might have worked somewhat like the Jesuit farm complexes in Peru and Brazil.[65] However, one gets the sense from examining the extant farm records that the Maryland Jesuits did not have nearly as much time, money, or personnel invested in the estates as did their brethren in Mexico or South America, possibly because the stakes were much higher in Mexico and South America. Major physical plants such as large colleges and universities and the construction of massive churches depended financially on the Jesuit sugar estates of coastal Peru. The Jesuits in Maryland did not have nearly as much riding on the farms they owned. However, the General Fund in Maryland permitted the individual missionary-farmer to dedicate a generous part of his resources to capital improvements and better living conditions on his own farm.

By the eighteenth century the Jesuits were purchasing land on their own. When they first arrived in Maryland, they did not have to. Because Thomas Copley made arrangements for a number of Jesuits and indentured servants in 1633, he requested 28,500 acres of land from Lord Baltimore according to the formula laid down by the proprietor. He didn't get it. But he did receive two thousand acres at a place the Jesuits called St. Inigoes, one thousand acres on St. George's Island, four hundred acres of townland in St. Mary's, and about two thousand acres at Portobacco.[66] These original grants were added to and other purchases made over the years. Another source of Jesuit lands was inheritances from pious Roman Catholics who willed thir lands to the Jesuits. Donations of this kind were very popular in the seventeenth and eighteenth centuries, assuring the donor a place in the prayers of the priests and a reward in the afterlife.[67]

A considerable part of each Jesuit farm was leased. Between 1735 and 1740 John Jackson paid 3,500 to 4,000 bales of tobacco as rent to the Jesuit owners of Bohemia Manor for a tract of land. For a tract on the same farm, Darby Donlevy paid three thousand bales yearly from 1736 to 1740 and two thousand from 1741 to 1745. He rented another tract for which he paid ten pounds yearly.[68]

Tobacco was the major product of the Jesuit farms. When Ingle raided the Jesuit farm of St. Inigoes in 1645, he made off with twenty thousand pounds of tobacco, besides corn, cattle, and beaver skins. The local superior contracted with shippers who sent the produce from Jesuit farms to England for sale. Lading receipts also indicate that in the 1750s and 1760s the Jesuits had an agent in London who received direct shipments from the Jesuit superior in Maryland.[69]

The large farms of St. Thomas Manor and St. Inigoes included a building for the resident Jesuits, gardens or orchard near the house, mill, stables, barns, and surrounding tobacco, corn, or wheat fields. A Jesuit managed the farm but each farm had an overseer. Indentured servants and slaves were quartered near the blacksmith's shop and storehouses. Hogs, cattle, and sheep were part of the farm's associated activities. Fr. Joseph Mosley's Day Book carefully records cattle slaughtered and hogs killed. "We killed six hogs," "We killed a cow," "Hung up to be smoked 32 gammons & 56 shoulders 7 midlings," "We had the first lamb," was written in January and February of 1765.[70] The meat was for the Jesuits, their servants, and slaves.

Besides some tobacco, Bohemia Manor produced a large amount of wheat annually. In 1750 of the 339 bushels harvested, only 16 went to the house. Thirty-one went to "the landing" for shipment elsewhere, nine went to "Lilly," and the rest was sold to four individuals for £60.[71] Corn was also a major product. However, in 1755 only 46 barrels were harvested (St. Inigoes harvested 140). Fr. Lewis noted at the bottom of that year's account that "it was an exceeding dry year from March till September."[72]

The Jesuits observed the rhythm of the agricultural seasons. Their crops were diversified with associated stocks of cattle and swine. In April the corn was planted. In May the tobacco was planted. In August tobacco was cut and housed. In November the corn was gathered. In February the tobacco was stripped. Each activity involved a specific number of tasks that the Jesuit-manager supervised.

Income from the farms varied annually. Table 9.1 shows an annual average income per farm of £99 but the disparity between Portobacco (£188) and Queenstown (£18) was considerable. The smaller farms and smaller income-producing units were begun not with profit in mind but for their geographical proximity to Roman Catholic families. More productive units supplied what the smaller needed.

The income shown in table 9.1 is net income after expenses were deducted from the gross. In 1750 gross income at Bohemia Manor was £260, mainly from the sale of wheat and corn.[73] Seventeen percent of this income was spent on labor services (both slave and free), 23 percent on capital improvements, 42 percent on house and farm expenses, and 9 percent on the resident priests' expenses. Labor-related expenses included food and clothing for the farm slaves and salaries to periodic workers. Capital expenses were improvements to the farm that generated additional income. For example, a mill was built in 1749–1750 for £70. Neighboring farmers used it for a fee. House maintenance and farm expenses meant anything from buying a cow (for £4, 19s. 5d.) to replacing some clapboards on the barn (£1 6s.).[74] Bohemia Manor, as did all the other Jesuit farms, had fixed expenses that were paid yearly, or semi-annually. "Public Dues" of £7 18s. 11d. were paid to the local sheriff each year. Charitable donations increased after 1740. The Bohemia Manor ledger records alms to "a poor woman," a poor man, an Irish gentleman, and so forth, which might indicate an increase in mendicancy in the Chesapeake area or that the Jesuits

TABLE 9.1. Jesuit Farms in 1765

Farm	Jesuits	Acres	Slaves	Annual Income
St. Inigoes	1	2,000	20	£ 90
Newtown	3	1,550	29	88
Portobacco	3	4,400	38	188
White Marsh	2	2,100	65	180
Deer Creek	1	127	7	24
Queenstown	1	200	7	18
Bohemia	1	1,500	26	108
TOTAL	12	11,877	192	696

Source: "Missiones in Marylandia 23 Julii 1765," MPA 57 (1).

were simply easy touches. The Jesuits purchased barrels of wine, which was used for Mass but also could have been for personal consumption. As far as one can make out from the ledger of one large farm, the Jesuit missionaries had adequate food supplies from their own farms and purchased other needed goods and services.

The large Jesuit farms of the Chesapeake were not self-sufficient estates like those of the Jesuits in Mexico or Peru. Houses were made of brick or clapboard. When the Jesuits needed new living quarters on St. Thomas Manor they contracted with a local carpenter "to build a dwelling house with 2 rooms below 2 above with a gable and 2 chimneys of brick and have it with a lease for 21 years at the rate of 10 sterling and 16 hundred per year of tobacco."[75] Diet included bread, lamb, corn, pork, vegetables, cheese, wine, liquor, coffee, and tea.[76] They travelled by horse. Frs. Lewis and Poulton each had a wig for formal occasions. Poulton's cost 15s. but a Mr. Fitzpatrick charged Fr. Lewis £2 10s. for his. Newspapers were delivered regularly to Bohemia Manor from Annapolis. Fr. Mosley's remark: "I can now almost live with some comfort, as I begin to have things grow about me," could have been echoed by the other Jesuits in the Maryland mission in 1770.[77]

The religious and political confusion of the times made the Jesuits fear for the retention of the farms they had so carefully nurtured, the economic base for their missionary work in Maryland. The Penal Laws that forbad Roman Catholic priests from owning property were easily skirted but their very existence made the Jesuits cautious. Despite their vow of poverty, circumstances demanded that property ownership rest nominally with individual Jesuits. In times of emergency land was sometimes deeded to fellow Roman Catholics. However, in normal times the lands were bequeathed to the Jesuit superior at the time of the owner's death. When Fr. George Hunter, the Jesuit superior, died, he left in his will to Fr. James Walton of Newtown in St. Mary's County all twelve tracts of land that the Jesuits owned.[78] The extant Jesuit wills left estates and personal belongings "to my well beloved friend," whoever the Jesuit superior might be. An internal Jesuit regulation circulated in 1759 required that wills be made out in favor of only one person, "the better to preserve from danger our lands and settlements."[79]

Maryland Missionaries

Although Jesuit evangelizing activity with Native American groups in the Maryland region ended soon after 1645, their activity continued with Roman Catholics who came to Maryland in the seventeenth and eighteenth centuries. They performed the rituals attendent on the life cycles of birth, christening, marriage, and death. These communal gatherings offered opportunities to socialize and bond with one another. The chapels where these rites occurred became social centers in the true sense of the word. The missionaries in Maryland did not extend the frontier. They followed it. Unlike the Benedictines in Europe who pushed back the frontier in the Dark Ages, cultivating farmland that became pockets of Christianity in the wilderness, Jesuit farms and their related activities functioned for the institution with no grand cosmic design aimed at civilizing a frontier. Their agrarian activities were more participatory than innovative. In Maryland, the Jesuit missionaries after 1645 had no new language to learn, although their past confreres did, no exotic foods, clothing, or housing to adapt to. They did not live in primitive conditions. On the contrary, the Jesuits recreated a lifestyle reminiscent of rural England. They had farms, servants, and slaves. They spent hours managing their lands, drawing up accounts, and making purchases. They viewed this as essential to their primary role, tolerated in order to accomplish their task in Maryland. In so doing, by the middle of the eighteenth century, they had become country gentlemen who also served as religious ministers.

IO

Retrospective

In his insightful study of the first European encounters with other civilizations, Hecter Macedo discusses how Europeans "recognized the unknown." They projected their own feelings, fears, ideas, phantoms, superstitions, and in short, their own imaginary, onto the things and people they encountered.[1] The Jesuit missionaries in Florida, Sinaloa, Julí, and New France were able to "understand" what they experienced of Indian culture only by projecting their own preconceived notions of what they were seeing or experiencing. Thus, they succeeded in recognizing the unknown.

Jesuit missionaries in America continually faced the unknown. Never before had Europeans come face to face with different belief systems nor with such a wide variety of believers. How deeply the beliefs were interwoven into the Native American social fabric affected the manner of proselytization employed, whether benign or aggressive—or whether it was considered possible at all to change a belief system that already had provided spiritual and emotional satisfaction to its adherents.

Both Indians and European Jesuit missionaries brought to their encounter sets of dynamics that impacted the acceptance of Christianity. On each of the frontiers examined in this book the Indians had experienced varying degrees of spiritual security and emotional satisfaction from their traditional religions. What then was Christianity's appeal? Was its association with the conquistadors the major factor in the Christianization of Mexico? Aggressive, truculent prose-

lytization? (Although massed, forced baptisms soon gave way to more traditional means of evangelization.) To what degree were conversions to Christianity free from social and physical coercion? Did the Indians of Sinaloa, New
France, and *La Florida hear* the same thing when Jesuit missionaries spoke
about God, creation, or heaven and hell? The agents of Christianity on the
American frontier did not offer indigenous America different versions of their
belief system but emphasized different aspects of Christianity.

Unlike the spread of early Christianity that probably appealed mainly to
the common people and the poor, the European missionaries in the New World
targeted the elite classes—the spiritual leaders—first, expecting all others to
follow. With a different spin on the European *cujus regio ejus religio* (the king's
religion is the people's religion), the local cacique frequently led the way in
accepting the new religion. If *he* accepted Christianity, then his village followed
along without complaint. But added to the formula, and confusing the issue
as well, was the presence of the European military, as well as the less tangible
elements of the white man's world. A conquered society could climb a social
ladder only if it assumed the elements of the conqueror: his religion, his food,
his education, and all that accompanied these colonial features.

The military presence was paramount, however. The conquest (in Mexico)
and presence (in New France) gave missionaries free rein up and down the
social hierarchy. In other parts of the world, the Jesuits had different experiences. In India the Jesuits were only successful with the poorest of the poor
along the Cape Comorin Coast. The upper classes were inaccessible. However,
the same was not true of China, where Matthew Ricci enthralled the literati
with his maps, mathematics, and astronomical observations. Chinese converts
came from the educated classes.[2] Nor was it true of Japan where many
sixteenth-century converts to Christianity were not "rice" Christians who benefited from Jesuit largesse, but intellectually convinced, upper-class Japanese.[3]

To cultivate an economic foundation for their evangelization of America
and to ensure government support, the Jesuits launched a massive public relations campaign originating with the missionaries themselves. The goal was
to make the educated and the rulers of Europe aware of the political, economic,
and religious importance of the wider world. Books, sermons, pamphlets, and
speakers circulated throughout Europe, describing the peoples and cultures of
America and Asia. Jesuit-authored books about China struck the most resound-
ing chord.[4] Europe became fascinated with Chinese education, government,
language, art, and religion. The writers were obviously empathetic toward the
Chinese and this affected the European attitude toward China.

While Jesuit writers described almost a near parity between European and
Chinese religion, such was never the case with Jesuit interpretations of Amer-

ica. America in the minds of Europeans was a land of wild men, vast spaces, and massive mountains.[5] The environment was portrayed as hostile, dangerous. DeBry's sixteenth-century sketches made its inhabitants just as threatening. No Jesuit sketches appearing in their books on China approach in goulishness the portrayals of the Florida Indians, the Aztecs, or the Incas. Cannibalism, maiming, excessive cruelty, and diabolical religious rituals became the accepted version of indigenous America. The widely read *Jesuit Relations* with their periodic portrayals of cultured, educated, European missionaries struggling against the forces of nature and Satan in the snow-bound reaches of North America confirmed Europe's worst suspicions about the Indians of the Americas.

The *Jesuit Relations* were a major source of information about the land and peoples of New France. They were widely circulated and translated into several languages.[6] In a typical *Relation*, for example that of 1636, one is hard put to find empathy and flexibility toward the Indians of New France.[7] Instead, a description of the Indians' major vices is predominant. "Liars, ill-tempered, gluttons, and lazy," are their major characteristics. These vices were said to be genetic, passed from one generation to the next. Although the land was described as fertile, the general environment was depicted as threatening, both inhibiting activities and disrupting religious and social activities.

The *Relations* portrayed the Jesuits as preferring short-term adjustments to long-term adaptation. This was the case even though the individual missionary accepted a mission assignment with the understanding that his post was to be his new home with ordinarily no possibility of returning to his native land. The commitment to place was designed to ensure a commitment to the work of the mission, but in fact there was a return of Jesuits to France for a variety of reasons. Most, however, remained until death.

Stories about the conversion and baptism of Indians occupies 40 percent of the *Relation* of 1636. Another 40 percent describes political events and Jesuit activity along the St. Lawrence. Ten percent is given to "Remarkable Events" in New France, which meant descriptions of Indian behavior and customs.

The *Relation* makes no attempt to reconcile the status of the Indians' religion with Christianity, no suggestion of an Indian-Christian synthesis. Quite the opposite. No evident attempt was made to "understand" Indian religious beliefs in the way that Ricci studied Confucianism. Only Jean de Brebeuf's lengthy account of Huron burial practices written with respect and empathy approaches a sympathetic portrayal of the Indian. "Our savages are by no means savages in so far as their natural respect for the dead is concerned," he wrote. The Jesuit was sorry that fifteen or twenty Christians were buried alongside the "*infidèles*," but "we say a *De profundis* for their souls along with the firm hope that if God continues to bless this land, this feast of the dead will no longer be or will only be for Christians who perform holy ceremonies rather than foolish or useless ones." However, Brebeuf was adamant in opposing the burial of Christians in Huron burial grounds. On the Indian Day of the Dead, the burial grounds were "an image of hell. The great open space was filled with fires and flames and the air filled with screaming shouts of the barbarians."[8]

Even Brebeuf's admiring description of Huron burial practices cannot avoid also painting a picture of diabolical frenzy. Brebeuf concluded the 1636 *Relation* doubting whether the Indian would ever be capable of living the Christian ideal. "I have great apprehension," he wrote, "about the time I will have to tell them about their customs and to teach them to rein in the flesh and live within the integrity of marriage . . . I fear that they will grow uneasy when I ask them to put on Christ, to bear his livery, and live as good Christians." Brebeuf was echoing a doubt that would continue in Jesuit *Relations* about the inability of the Indian to be a good Christian. Ten years later the *Relation* spoke of the battle between Jesus Christ and Satan over control of a land that the devil had ruled for so long. The source of the evil was their social freedom, reported the *Relation*, their polygamy and inability to remain in committed monogamous relationships. The missionary demand for monogamy was an obstacle to conversion. Brebeuf could have added the integrated nature of Indian religion and the difficulty of learning the Indian languages to his list of reasons why relatively few Indians became Christians. Brebeuf's remarks contrast sharply with writings of other Jesuits who worked with the Native Americans in Central and South America. José Urquijo has written about how each Jesuit writer had a particular objective in writing, thus accounting for both condemnations and praises.[9]

Jesuit accounts of Sinaloa were equally unflattering to the Indians. Pérez de Ribas's classic statement about life among the Indians of seventeenth-century Sinaloa exalts the labors of the European Jesuits while diminishing the civility of the native groups along the northwest coast of Mexico.[10] He paints a picture of starving, naked "savages," bound by tribal affinity, scraping an existence from the inhospitable landscape. The picture is probably accurate.[11] Pérez's account matches what the Jesuit Annual Letters from Mexico had to say about the Indians. While Pérez goes into detail about Indian social habits, housing, hunting, clothes, religion, population decline, and government (very little on language), the Annual Letters from Mexico with a more cosmopolitan audience in mind focus on the exotic aspects of Indian religion.

The attraction to Christianity in Northwest Mexico was based more on economic and social reasons than a response to Christian spiritual principles.

For example, the Yaquis invited the Jesuit missionaries to their villages in 1610 because they wanted to take advantage of the new crops, plows, and cattle ranching that the Jesuits were introducing and distributing to new converts.[12] New converts in the mountains of Sinaloa were "granted" land for cultivation and access to food in times of famine. The Jesuits were instrumental in finding work for Indians in neighboring silver mines, thus increasing their authority and power. Their own cattle ranches in Sinaloa employed Indian laborers.[13] Among a people ravaged by European killer diseases (half of the Indian population perished in the first decades of Jesuit missionary activity) that disrupted the normal rhythms of food cultivation and gathering, survival through missionary charity was a major incentive for becoming a Christian. In the early days of the mission in Sinaloa new male Indian converts received coats, jackets (for caciques), hats, shoes, and a belt; women received dresses and a petticoat "that their fidelity might be rewarded and others might see how good it was to become a Christian."[14] The Jesuits in Sinaloa did not have to compel most of the Indians to become Christians. The material and economic benefits were evident.

As far as the Indians were concerned, accepting Christianity did not necessarily mean a total abandonment of the old religion. Although the Jesuits argued that *their* gods had abandoned them ("see how the Indians were ravaged by disease and the Europeans were not touched!"), the counter argument "If you want your children to die, then have them baptized,"[15] seemed to have little effect, possibly because the Indians never intended to completely abandon their gods. Syncretism was a law of religious life among the Indians of Mexico—as long as the missionary was not immediately present. Given the dispersion of Indian villages and hamlets on the frontier, the nature of their religion tended toward a blending of both religions. The vigilance of the Jesuit missionary, who depended on informants who either wished to ingratiate themselves or were convinced of the correctness of warning about the continued activity of the shamans, kept the Christian church within acceptable limits of worship.[16] The writings of the Jesuits on the Indians of the Central Valley of Mexico seem much more tolerant of differences. Jesuits in the College of Mexico analyzed Indian medicine, geography, language, history, clothes, and customs.[17]

Missionary methods in seventeenth-century Maryland did not bank on military or social pressure. The existence of a catechism written by Fr. Andrew White and the recently found copy of the Ten Commandments written in the Piscataway language illustrate the initial importance that the Jesuits attached to evangelizing the Indians of the Chesapeake.[18] The Indians welcomed the missionaries as forerunners of potential trading relationships with Maryland settlers, which would have meant protection from the incursions of northern tribes.[19] However, other motivating factors were at work. In the short time that the Jesuits evangelized the Piscataways and other Indian groups around the Chesapeake they managed to convert one hundred thirty Indians. Were they bona fide converts or Christian in name only? The Indians may well have been drawn to the missionaries with the hope of future trading relations but at the same time the spiritual claims of the Jesuits, their rites of baptism, Mass, and formal prayers appealed to the Indians. The Jesuit report of 1639 spoke of the "hope of the Indian harvest."[20] By 1642 over one hundred thirty had been baptized.

The Jesuits chose Port Tobacco as a fixed residence because it gave them relatively easy access to the surrounding Indian villages. The stories related by the Jesuits in their reports from Maryland dwelled on the Indians' astonishment at apparent cures for illnesses. Were the Jesuits more powerful than the shamans the Indians already had? The Jesuit reports do not reveal the immediate Indian reply to the Christian message. The conversion of the entire village of Port Tobacco may well have been the reaction of obedient subjects to their ruler's conversion. Since the Jesuits worked for the most part through interpreters, their reading of the Indians' understanding of the new religion probably was faulty. However, after 1650 local and international politics intervened and the religious conflicts that divided England hindered the Jesuits from further proselytization of the Indians of Maryland.

The initial Jesuit description of potential Indian converts in Maryland was unflattering. "Whoever shall contemplate in thought the whole earth," said the author of the 1639 report from Maryland, "will perhaps nowhere find men more abject in appearance than these Indians."[21] He went on to say that they were unrestrained and inclined to vice, ignorance, barbarism, and wanderering. But they had souls. And to partially balance the portrait, the writer said that they were docile, patient, God-fearing, and worshiped few idols. There was hope for conversions.

One event that strongly impressed the Jesuits was Chief Maquacomen's adoption of European dress. He "exchanged the skins with which he was heretofore clothed for a garment made in our fashion."[22] In New France, Mexico, and in Maryland the gesture of adopting European dress was not merely symbolic. It represented what missionaries considered essential in the process of conversion to Christianity. The Indian should adopt Western law, ritual, and accept as a model the feudal structures of Christianity. Adopting Western dress was an external sign of acceptance. What today would be called inculturation, the process whereby the evangelized culture reexpresses the Christian message in its own terms, was hardly considered. Instead, the missionaries believed that the structures they were imposing on America possessed a worldwide, universal significance that by their very nature would compel adherence. In fact, they did not. What the missionaries brought to America instead represented an alien worldview.

Although the Jesuit missionary experience in North and South America was dissimilar, the common themes that run through both continents indicate that the missionaries brought similar attitudes with them to the New World. Although conversion and baptism were never physically forced on Indians, the threat of an eternal fire engulfing those who refused to become Christian was a less than subtle form of coercion. By developing a system that rewarded those who became Christian, coercion was raised a psychological notch thereby encouraging the non-Christian to join the ranks of the believers. In Julí, as in other mission sites, those who were not members of *cofradías* felt marginalized. A fortiori, those who were not Christian were ostracized.

Repetitious indoctrination, the hallmark of Roman Catholic instruction, could only be experienced by a sedentary agricultural group and not by those who hunted and gathered for sustenance. The missionaries tried to create stable, agricultural communities where they did not exist by convincing governments to allow them to run communities like Julí where no lay Spaniards could live or like the French Jesuit community of Sillery that attempted to erect a European-like Huron village in New France. For the Jesuits, instruction, isolation, and monitoring were easier if small Indian settlements were relocated and combined with others. Better still if the Indian community did not abandon its site in order to hunt. Stable agricultural settlements meant that the European missionaries could plan, instruct, and develop religious structures that would remain for the long term. Numerous conversions, a steady flow of baptisms, confessions, Christian marriages, and adoption of Christian beliefs and rituals were assured only if the Indian could be instructed regularly.

Sometimes the relocation was forced, sometimes not. Indians were often more moved by economic motives than cultural ones. For example, the Mojos Indians of the Upper Amazon voluntarily moved from scattered settlements into European-like villages in order to allow the Jesuit missionaries to act as their protectors and to be able to trade with Spanish towns. The same motives operated in the reductions of Paraguay. Yerba mate grown by the Indians was assured transportation and distribution if the Guaraní clustered in Christian villages. The European missionaries used a variety of incentives to create stable agrarian settlements.

The devil was considered the universal obstacle to conversion. Whether working through the Indian priests of Florida, New France, or New Spain, or through the *huacas* of the Andes, the devil was the convenient reason why the Native American clung to old beliefs. In the absence of other explanations that came much later, the devil was credited with preventing the Indian from enjoying the benefits of Christianity and an eternity in heaven. The devil was believed to be proactive in his battle with the European Christians. Not only did the devil encourage the Native American to reject the new belief system but he also was held responsible for the hardships that the missionaries encountered.

The Western concept of the devil as evil personified only gradually took hold of the Native American mind. Deities had always been conceived of as incorporating good and evil. Hence, the missionary was hard put at the outset of his evangelizing to separate the dualistic properties of each. This may have been the reason behind the Indian's persistent adoration of ancient gods. He could not reject them without doing violence to his cultural world.

Spanish missionaries saw the devil behind the Indian reluctance to wholeheartedly embrace the new religion. Popular religion in sixteenth-century Spain clearly saw the devil everywhere. The Jesuit who had been schooled in the Spiritual Exercises of St. Ignatius was especially inclined to do so. He saw himself struggling with the evil spirits marshaled beneath the banner of Lucifer, which St. Ignatius described in the Second Week of the Spiritual Exercises. The movements in Peru and Mexico against autochthonous religion were not haphazard reactions to native religious forms but a conscious cultural response against the perceived core—the devil—of the indigenous belief system.

A major tool that the Jesuits required for their task of evangelization was a thorough familiarization with the language and customs of the people they evangelized. Some form of language school was set up in each major mission area. The reason for learning the language was the need to communicate accurately to potential converts.

The colonial mission stations served the indigenous population in the Paraguay reductions, in the Andes, in the Amazon, in the *Llanos* of Colombia, in the growing urban areas, and on the rural farms and ranches. The number of conversions made, baptisms administered, and marriages performed were all recorded by those who measured success by numbers, and each year a tally was sent from America to the central Jesuit office in Rome. The number of Indian villages and communities that remained within the Christian fold over long periods of time was an even better measure of success. Every village in the Andes had its patron saint, its fiesta. The townsfolk may have artfully blended the old religion with the new but they were wise enough to keep the latter marginalized.

With the Jesuit missionaries, a new belief system had found its way into the American scene. One religion had not completely replaced the other, but it was close enough to ensure a lasting foothold.

Notes

INTRODUCTION

1. Bernard Lewis, "The Roots of Muslim Rage," *Atlantic Monthly,* September (1990), 47.

2. Johannes Fabian, *Time and the Other. How Anthropology Makes Its Object* (New York: Columbia University Press, 1983), 91.

3. James Clifford, *The Predicament of Culture* (Cambridge: Harvard University Press, 1988), 91–113; Stephen Greenblat, *Renaissance Self-Fashioning: From More to Shakespeare* (Chicago: University of Chicago Press, 1980).

4. Marvin Lunenfeld, ed., *1492: Discovery, Invasion, Encounter: Sources and Interpretations* (Lexington: D.C. Heath, 1991), 37, discusses the ambiguity and inadequacy of the word "encounter."

5. Fawcett Premier Edition, 1959, 175. Confrontation between European and native provides dramatic dialogue. See James Michener, *Hawaii* (New York: Faucett, 1959), 365–68; Hugh Thomas, *Conquest: Montezuma, Cortés, and the Fall of Old Mexico* (New York: Simon and Schuster, 1993), 277–79; Maurice Collis, *Cortés and Montezuma* (London: Faber and Faber, 1963), 129–32; and the character Lieutenant John Dunbar's (Kevin Costner) early encounter with the Sioux in the movie, *Dances With Wolves.*

6. Chinua Achebe, *Things Fall Apart* (New York: Fawcett Publications, 1959), 161.

7. Bernard Cohn, *Colonialism and Its Form of Knowledge* (Princeton: Princeton University Press, 1996), 42.

8. Greg Dening, *Islands and Beaches. Discourse on the Silent Land. Marquesas, 1774–1880* (Honolulu: University Press of Hawaii, 1980), 49.

9. Ida Altman and Reginald D. Butler, "The Contact of Cultures: Perspectives on the Quincentenary," *American Historical Review* 99 (1994):

478–503, report on the most significant studies that appeared around the time of the quincentenary.

10. Henry F. Dobyns, *Their Numbers Become Thinned: Native American Population Dynamics in Eastern North America* (Knoxville: University of Tennessee Press, 1983); Jerald T. Milanich, *Florida Indians and the Invasion from Europe* (Gainesville: University Press of Florida, 1995).

11. Anthony Pagden, *European Encounters with the New World: From Renaissance to Romanticism* (New Haven: Yale University Press, 1993); David E. Stannard, *American Holocaust: Columbus and the Conquest of the New World* (New York: Oxford University Press, 1992); Tzvetan Todorov, *The Conquest of America: The Question of the Other* (New York: Harper and Row, 1984); Fredi Chiappelli, ed., *First Images of America: The Impact of the New World on the Old* (Berkeley: University of California Press, 1976); Dobyns, *Their Numbers Become Thinned;* and Daniel K. Richter and James H. Merrell, eds., *Beyond the Covenant Chain: The Iroquois and Their Neighbors in Indian North America, 1600–1800* (Syracuse: Syracuse University Press, 1987).

12. Both physical and psychological coercion were present.

13. James Axtell, *After Columbus: Essays in the Ethnohistory of Colonial North America* (New York: Oxford University Press, 1988), 42, 47, mentions cases of English settlers opting for Indian life, but the occurrence was more frequent in the post-1865 West.

14. William B. Taylor, "Santiago's Horse," in William B. Taylor and Franklin G. Y. Pease, eds., *Violence, Resistance, and Survival in the Americas: Native Americans and the Legacy of Conquest* (Washington: Smithsonian Institution Press, 1994), 154; William B. Taylor, *Magistrates of the Sacred: Priests and Parishioners in Eighteenth Century Mexico* (Stanford: Stanford University Press, 1996).

15. John M. Ingham, *Mary, Michael, and Lucifer: Folk Catholicism in Central Mexico* (Austin: University of Texas Press, 1986), 190.

16. The European insisted upon what he believed to be essential for maintaining right order. The rest was up to the discretion of local authorities. See Charles Gibson, *The Aztecs under Spanish Rule* (Stanford: Stanford University Press, 1978), 48.

17. Daniel T. Reff, *Disease, Depopulation, and Culture Change in Northwestern New Spain, 1518–1764* (Salt Lake City: University of Utah Press, 1991), 187.

18. Thomas, *Conquest;* and Collis, *Cortés and Montezuma,* make much of this attitude. See Matthew Restall, "The Spanish Conquest Revisited," *Historically Speaking,* 5, no. 5 (May/June 2004): 2–5, for another view.

19. Cited in Gary B. Nash and Julie Roy Jeffrey, *The American People. Creating a Nation and a Society.* Fifth Edition (New York: Longman, 2001), 33.

20. Calvin Martin, *Keepers of the Game: Indian-Animal Relationship and the Fur Trade* (Berkeley: University of California Press, 1978), argues that the fragmentation of Iroquois society was not due to their desire for Western goods but because their overhunting had created a disequilibrium with the beaver spirits.

21. Matthew 28: 19.

22. Luke 15: 24.

23. John Boswell, *Christianity, Social Tolerance, and Homosexuality: Gay People in*

Western Europe from the Beginning of the Christian Era to the Fourteenth Century (Chicago: University of Chicago Press, 1980).

24. John H. Elliott, *Imperial Spain, 1469–1716* (New York: 1963), 95–99.

25. Robert Ricard, *La "conquête spirituelle" du Mexique. Essai sur l'apostolat et les méthodes missionaires des Ordres Mendiants en Nouvelle-Espagne de 1523–24 à 1572* (Paris: Institut D'Ethnologie, 1933), 119–20.

26. Ibid.

27. Stafford Poole, "Some Observations on Mission Methods and Native Reactions in Sixteenth-Century New Spain," *The Americas* 50, no. 3 (1994): 337–49.

28. Louise M. Burkhart, *The Slippery Earth: Nahua–Christian Moral Dialogue in Sixteenth-Century Mexico* (Tucson: University of Arizona Press, 1989).

29. Fernando Cervantes, *The Devil in the New World: The Impact of Diabolism in New Spain* (New Haven: Yale University Press, 1994); Ingham, *Mary, Michael, and Lucifer.*

30. Georges Baudot, "The Devil and His Magic Spells in Nahua Colonial Literature," in *Five Hundred Years After Columbus: Proceedings of the 47th International Congress of Americanists* (New Orleans: Tulane University [Middle American Research Institute], 1994), 129–30.

31. Pío Baroja, "Witchcraft and Catholic Theology," in Bengt Ankarloo and Gustav Hennigsen, eds., *Early Modern European Witchcraft: Centres and Peripheries* (Oxford: Oxford University Press, 1990), 19–44.

32. William A. Haviland, *Cultural Anthropology* (New York: Wadsworth/Thompson Learning, 2002), 164–67; C. Schrire, *Past and Present in Hunter Gatherer Societies* (Orlando, Fla.: Academic Press, 1984).

33. Helen Nader, *Liberty in Absolutist Spain: The Habsburg Sale of Towns, 1516–1700* (Baltimore: Johns Hopkins University Press, 1990), might offer a clue about Spanish bias toward fixed, legal property rights.

34. As the model *confessionario*, I use that of Francisco Pareja, which he wrote for the Timucua Indians of Florida. A copy of the original is in the Rare Book Room of the New York Public Library, Francisco de Pareja, *Confessionario en lengua Castellana y Timuquana con algunos consejos para animar el penitente* (Mexico, 1613). An edition of the text is in Jerald T. Milanich and William C. Sturtevant, *Francisco Pareja's Confessionario: A Documentary Source for Timucuan Ethnography* (Tallahassee: Division of Archives, History, and Records Management, Florida Department of State, 1972). Ricard, *La "conquête spirituelle" du Mexique*, 346, lists *confessionarios* printed in Mexico in the sixteenth century.

35. Milanich and Sturtevant, *Francisco Pareja's Confessionario*, 25.

36. Ibid., 30.

CHAPTER I

1. Brian Fagan, *Ancient North America* (New York: Thames and Hudson, 1995). Brian Fagan, *The Great Journey* (London: Thames and Hudson, 1987); Julian H. Stew-

ard, ed., *Handbook of South American Indians* (New York: Cooper Square Publishers, 1963), 15, 330–63.

2. Calvin Martin, *Keepers of the Game: Indian-Animal Relationship and the Fur Trade* (Berkeley: University of California Press, 1978); Elizabeth Tooker, *An Ethnography of the Huron Indians, 1615–1649* (Washington, D.C.: Bureau of Ethnology, bulletin no. 190, 1964); Manuel M. Marzal, *Estudios sobre religión campesina* (Lima: Pontificia Universidad Católica del Peru, 1977).

3. Genesis 1: 3.

4. "*Nos sauvages ne point sauvages en ce qui regarde les devoirs que la nature mesme nous oblige de rendre aux morts.*" Lucien Campeau, S.J., *III. Monumenta Novae Franciae. Fondation de la Mission Huronne (1635–1637)* (Rome-Québec: Monumenta Historica Societatis Iesu /Les Presses de l'Université Laval, 1987), 388.

5. Ibid.

6. Philippe Aries, *At the Hour of Our Death* (New York: Knopf, 1981), 154.

7. Félix Zubillaga, *Monumenta Antiquae Floridae (1566–1572)*, vol. 3 (Rome: Monumenta Historica Societatis Iesu, 1946), 388.

8. Félix Zubillaga, "P. Pedro Martínez," *AHSI*, 7 (1938), 53.

9. Bernard Cohn, *Colonialism and Its Form of Knowledge* (Princeton: Princeton University Press, 1996), 39.

10. Hubert Jedin, *A History of the Council of Trent*, 2 vols., Translated from the German by Dom Ernest Graf, O.S.B. (St. Louis: Herder Book Co., 1957–1961). is still the best treatment of the council's influence. Norman Tanner, *Decrees of the Ecumenical Councils. Vol. II. Trent to Vatican II.* (Washington, D.C.: Sheed & Ward and Georgetown University Press, 1990) contain its pronouncements. John W. O'Malley, *The First Jesuits* (Cambridge: Harvard University Press, 1993), 321, states that the Society of Jesus was somehow not interested in the reform of the European church. It "was not their concern." Actually it was, even though the Jesuits in America were intent on building a *new* church, not reforming an old one.

11. Tanner, *Decrees*, 666–79.

12. Ibid., 685.

13. Anton C. Pegis, "Molina and Human Liberty," in Gerard Smith, S.J., ed. *Jesuit Thinkers of the Renaissance* (Milwaukee: Marquette University Press, 1939), 75–131. See also E.M. Burke, "State of Pure Nature," pp. 823–824, *New Catholic Encyclopedia*, 2nd Edition, Vol. 11 (Detroit: Thomson-Gale, 2003).

14. George R. Healy, "The French Jesuits and the Idea of the Noble Savage," *William and Mary Quarterly*, 15 (1958): 147.

15. Tanner, *Decrees*, 755–56.

16. Ibid., 703.

17. Ibid., 695–98.

18. Ibid., 666, 685.

19. Alistair McGrath, *Reformation Thought: An Introduction* (Oxford: Basil Blackwell, 1988), 19–21.

20. Patrick Collinson, "The Late Medieval Church and Its Reformation (1400–1600)," in *Oxford Illustrated History of Christianity*, ed. John McManners (New York: Oxford University Press, 1990), 263–66.

21. Anita Mancia, "La controversia con i protestanti e i programmi degli studi teologici nella Compagnia di Gesu," *AHSI*, 54 (1985), explains the theology curriculum of the Jesuits.

22. Healy, "The French Jesuits," 152.

23. Andrew Greeley, "Magic in the Age of Faith," *America*, 10 (1993): 8–14. Although the Jesuits by and large were "urban inspired," their Christianity was rural. See Thomas M. Lucas, *Landmarking: City, Church and Jesuit Urban Strategy* (Chicago: Loyola Press, 1997), 110.

24. Sabine MacCormack, *Religion in the Andes* (Princeton: Princeton University Press, 1993), 87.

25. Irene Flint, *The Rise of Magic in Early Medieval Europe* (Princeton: Princeton University Press: 1991).

26. Greeley, "Magic in the Age of Faith," 8–9.

27. Andrew Greeley, "The Faith We Have Lost," *America*, Vol. 169, no. 9 (1993), esp. 26–27.

28. William A. Christian, *Apparitions in Late Medieval and Renaissance Spain* (Princeton: Princeton University Press, 1981), 37.

29. John Boswell, *Christianity, Social Tolerance, and Homosexuality: Gay People in Western Europe from the Beginning of the Christian Era to the Fourteenth Century* (Chicago: University of Chicago Press, 1980). Not quite a wink, but almost!

30. MacCormack, *Religion in the Andes*, 41.

31. The *Indipetae* section of the Roman Archives of the Jesuits (ARSI) contains several thousand of these letters written by Jesuits between the end of the sixteenth century and the middle of the eighteenth. I have examined the sections for New France, Mexico, and Maryland.

32. See the letter of Juan Carrasco, September 8, 1584, stating that after reading the letters of Xavier, he felt a great desire to undergo similar trials.

33. John T. Noonan, *A Church that Can and Cannot Change: The Development of Catholic Moral Teaching* (Notre Dame: Notre Dame University Press, 2005), discusses the circumstances under which radical changes in church teaching have taken place.

34. Antonio Astrain, *Historia de la Compañía de Jesús en la Asistencia de España*, 4 vols. (Madrid: Est. Tip. "Sucesores de Ribadeneyra," 1913–1925), 753–55.

35. Archivum Romanum Societatis Iesu, Rome, Italy, hereafter cited as ARSI. *Indipetae* 758, no. 199.

36. José de Acosta, *De Procuranda Indorum Salute* (Madrid: Consejo Superior de Investigaciones Científicas, 1984 [1577]); see also Francisco Mateos, ed., *Historia general de la Compañía de Jesús en la provincia del Perú. Crónica anónima de 1600 . . .* (Madrid: Consejo Superior de Investigaciones Científicas, 1944), 191–93.

37. *Indipetae* 757, no. 250, 301.

38. Ibid.

39. Ibid., 301

40. *Indipetae*, 301.

41. Ibid.

42. *Liste de Missionaires Jesuites. Nouvelle France et Louisiane* (Montréal: Colege Sainte-Marie, 1929), 19.

43. Ibid. Antoine was not sent to America.

44. JR 118–20.

45. *Indipetae*, 767.

46. Ibid.

47. These were circulated in France in the *Jesuit Relations*.

48. ARSI, Gall. 110, fols. 54–56.

49. J. Lloyd Mecham, *Church and State in Latin America* (Chapel Hill: University of North Carolina Press, 1966), 36; W. Eugene Shiels, *King and Church: The Rise and Fall of the Patronato Real* (Chicago: Loyola University Press, 1961).

50. John Hemming, *Red Gold: The Conquest of the Brazilian Indians, 1500–1760* (Cambridge: Harvard University Press, 1978); Dauril Alden, *The Making of an Enterprise: The Society of Jesus in Portugal, Its Empire, and Beyond, 1540–1750* (Stanford: Stanford University Press, 1996), 71–73.

CHAPTER 2

1. Rogel to Borja, 10 November 1568, Félix Zubillaga, *Monumenta Antiquae Floridae (1566–1572)* (Rome: Monumenta Historica Societatis Iesu, 1946), 331–33. Hereafter cited as *MAF*.

2. Sedeño to Borja, 6 March 1570, *MAF*, 423–24.

3. Cited in Michael Kenny, *The Romance of the Floridas: The Finding and the Founding* (New York: AMS Press, 1970), 168.

4. Ibid., 169.

5. Ibid., 172.

6. *MAF*, 94–99.

7. Indian groups in Florida at the time of the Spanish invasion are described in Jerald T. Milanich, *Florida Indians and the Invasion from Europe* (Gainsville: University Press of Florida, 1995), 15–103. Also valuable are Randolph J. Widmer, *The Evolution of the Calusa: A Nonagricultural Chiefdom on the Southwest Florida Coast* (Tuscaloosa: The University of Alabama Press, 1988); and Jerald T. Milanich and Samuel Proctor, eds., *Tacachale: Essays on the Indians of Florida and Southeastern Georgia during the Historic Period* (Gainesville: University Press of Florida, 1978).

8. Widmer, *The Evolution of the Calusa*, 29.

9. The scenes of America recorded by artists for European audiences helped to create the image of a fantasy continent peopled by strange creatures and one-eyed monsters. These early images became the foundation of bias and wild imaginings. Jacques de Moyne de Morgues executed the plates in Theodore de Bry, *Brevis Narratio eorum quae in Florida* . . . (1591). Robert F. Berkhofer, "White Conceptions of Indians," in *Handbook of North American Indians*, vol. 15 (Washington: Smithsonian Institute, 1978) analyzes the relationship between images and bias.

10. Jerald T. Milanich and Charles H. Fairbanks, *Florida Archaeology* (New York: Academic Press, 1980), 211; Milanich, *Florida Indians and the Invasion from Europe*, 1–2.

11. David B. Quinn, *North America from Earliest Discovery to First Settlements: The Norse Voyages to 1612* (New York: Harper and Row, 1977), 104.

12. "Relación Anónima," *MAF*, 216.

13. Lewis Hanke, *The Spanish Struggle for Justice in the Conquest of America* (Philadelphia: University of Pennsylvania Press, 1949) is the classic account of Spain's official attitude toward American Indians in the sixteenth century. After 1573 King Philip II of Spain forbade the use of the word "conquest" to describe Spain's activity in America. See Marvin Lunenfeld, ed., *1492: Discovery, Invasion, Encounter: Sources and Interpretations* (Lexington: D.C. Heath, 1991), 189, for the exact wording of what was called the *requirimiento* by which the Spaniards demanded submission of the Indians.

14. "Customs of the Indians of Florida, 1566," in David B. Quinn, ed. *New American World. A Documentary History of North America to 1612* (New York: Arno Press, 1979), II, 539.

15. Ibid. *MAF*, 430.

16. *MAF*, 284.

17. Ibid., 288.

18. Ibid., 331–32.

19. Ibid., 135–36.

20. Ibid., 340.

21. Ibid., 125.

22. Ibid., 288.

23. Ibid., 426.

24. Ibid., 407.

25. Greg Dening, *Islands and Beaches: Discourse on a Silent Land, Marquesas, 1774–1880* (Honolulu: University Press of Hawaii, 1980), 19–20, describes the encounter between native Hawaiian and European in which neither possesses the cultural constellations to understand the other. Much of what Dening says I have applied to the Jesuits and the Florida Indian.

26. *MAF*, 216.

27. Berkhofer, "White Conceptions," 526.

28. *MAF*, 215.

29. *MAF*, 240.

30. Ibid., 280.

31. The mix of religion and society of the Calusa is in Milanich and Proctor, *Tacachale*, 31–36.

32. *MAF*, 282–83.

33. Caption under the sketch of Le Moyne, engraving by Theodore de Bry, *Americae*, part 2, plate 35.

34. Widmer, *The Evolution of the Calusa*, 6–8.

35. *MAF*, 283.

36. Ibid., 285.

37. Ibid.

38. *MAF*, 284.

39. Ibid., 279.

40. Ibid.

41. *MAF*, 280.

42. Christopher Vecsey, ed., *Religion in Native North America* (Moscow: University of Idaho Press, 1990), 187–89.

43. *MAF*, 277.

44. Ibid.

45. Ibid.

46. *MAF*, 289, 338.

47. *MAF*, 278.

48. *MAF*, 287–88.

49. *MAF*, 281.

50. Ibid.

51. Lyon, "Spain's Sixteenth-Century North American Settlement Attempts," 278.

52. *MAF*, 321, 327.

53. Quinn, *North America*, 104.

54. *MAF*, 240.

55. Ibid., 239.

56. Ibid.

57. Before going to Florida Villareal was stationed in the Jesuit college of Córdoba and could have seen there the traditional *Moros y Cristianos* plays. For this type of theatrical presentation in Southern Spain see Robert Ricard, "Les fêtes de "Moros y Cristianos" à Juviles (Prov. de Grenade)," *Bulletin Hispanique*, 48 (1946).

58. *MAF*, 237; Henry F. Dobyns, *Their Numbers Become Thinned: Native American Population Dynamics in Eastern North America* (Knoxville: University of Tennessee Press, 1983), 41–49.

59. *MAF*, 238.

60. Ibid.

61. *MAF*, 423.

62. *MAF*, 607–8.

63. Milanich and Proctor, *Tacachale*, 19–49; John Goggin and William Sturtevant, "The Calusa: A Stratified, Nonagricultural Society (with notes on sibling marriage)," in W. H. Goodenough, ed., *Explorations in Cultural Anthropology: Essays in Honor of George Peter Murdoch* (New York: McGraw-Hill, 1964), 195–97.

64. J. Allen, "Big Circle Mounds," *Florida Anthropologist*, 26 (1948): 17–21; John Goggin, "The Tekesta of South Florida," *Florida Historical Quarterly* 4, no. 18 (1940): 274–80.

65. Berkhofer, "White Conceptions," 526–27.

66. *MAF*, 400.

67. Ibid., 331.

68. Ibid.

69. George R. Healy, "The French Jesuits and the Idea of the Noble Savage," *William and Mary Quarterly*, 15 (1958): 147.

70. Ibid.

71. *MAF*, 283.

72. Ibid.

73. Ibid.

74. Ibid.

75. Cited in Félix Zubillaga, "Métodos misionales de la primera instrucción de San Francisco de Borja para la América Española (1567)," ARSI 12 (1943): 62.

76. *MAF*, 281.

77. Pío Baroja, "Witchcraft and Catholic Theology," in *Early Modern European Witchcraft: Centres and Peripheries*, ed. Bengt Ankarloo and Gustav Hennigsen (Oxford: Oxford University Press, 1990), 19–44.

78. Ruth Martin, *Witchcraft and the Inquisition in Venice, 1550–1650* (Oxford: Basil Blackwell, 1989).

79. *MAF*, 85.

80. *MAF*, 429.

81. Ibid., 430.

CHAPTER 3

1. James Axtell, *After Columbus: Essays in the Ethnohistory of Colonial North America* (New York: Oxford University Press, 1988), 100–101, 111–12.

2. Félix Zubillaga, *Monumenta Mexicana*, vol. 4 (Rome: Institutum Historicum Societatis Iesu, 1956–1981), 13–15. Hereafter cited as *MM*.

3. Ibid., 14–15. The story of the northward expansion of the Mexican frontier is told in Philip Wayne Powell, *Soldiers, Indians, and Silver: The Northward Advance of New Spain, 1550–1600* (Berkeley: University of California Press, 1952).

4. Philip Wayne Powell, "North America's First Frontier," in Powell et al., *Essays on Frontiers in World History* (College Station: Texas A&M University Press, 1983).

5. Peter Gerhard, *The Northern Frontier of New Spain* (Princeton: Princeton University Press, 1982), 272–87.

6. "Memorias para la Historia de Sinaloa," Bancroft Library, University of California, Berkeley, Manuscripts B, 113, is a 918 folio-page collection of the Annual Letters (*Cartas Anuas*) of the Jesuits in the missions of Sinaloa and Sonora. Hereafter, the collection is cited as *CA*. The population estimate is in the Annual Letter for 1593, fol. 25. The most recent and reliable population estimates are in Daniel T. Reff, *Disease, Depopulation, and Culture Change in Northwestern New Spain, 1518–1764* (Salt Lake City: University of Utah Press, 1991), 209–18.

7. Félix Zubillaga, "La provincia jesuítica de Nueva España. Su fundamento económico: siglo XVI," ARSI 38 (1969), 79–80.

8. Ibid., 274.

9. Andrés Pérez de Ribas, *My Life among the Savage Nations of New Spain* (Los Angeles: Ward Ritchie Press, 1968 [1644]), 19.

10. W. Eugene Shiels, *Gonzalo de Tapia (1561–1594): Founder of the First Permanent Jesuit Mission in North America* (New York: United States Catholic Historical Society, 1934), 57–59, contains a contemporary account of the Jesuit's death.

11. *CA*, 21.

12. Ibid.

13. Ibid.

14. The *Anua* of 1593 is given in Shiels, *Gonzalo de Tapia*, 110–11.

15. *CA*, 85.

16. Ibid.

17. *CA*, 86.

18. The fiesta is described in detail in ibid., 87–88.

19. *CA*, 429.

20. Ibid., 403.

21. Ibid., 145.

22. Ibid.

23. Ibid., 745.

24. Ibid., 45.

25. Ibid.

26. Ibid., 41.

27. Ibid., 42.

28. Ibid., 353, 354.

29. Ibid., 930–32.

30. Reff, *Disease, Depopulation, and Culture Change*, 261–63.

31. *CA*, 114.

32. Ibid., 45.

33. Ibid.

34. Ibid., 374–75.

35. Ibid., 699.

36. Report of November 14, 1654, Archivum Romanum Societatis Iesu, Rome, Italy, Mex. 17, fols. 250–71. Hereafter cited as ARSI, Mex.

37. Catalogi Triennales, 1580–1653, ARSI, Mex. 4.

38. "Instrucción Secreta del P. Hernando Cabero Visitador . . . 10 noviembre 1664," ARSI, Mex. 17, fols. 301–3.

39. ARSI, Mex. 17, fol. 300.

40. ARSI, Mex. 3, fol. 225. The third part of the Catalogi Triennales lists individual Jesuits, their national origins, health status, proficiency in studies, and perceived talents. Unknown is the criteria used for these judgments. Presumably, the local superior had something to say about health and mental status as well as studies in philosophy and theology that were the basis for the evaluation of talents. Although not altogether reliable, these assessments allow one to form some idea about the missionaries posted to Sonora and Sinaloa.

41. María Paz Haro, "Religious Orders, the Indian, and the Conquest," *Encounters* (summer 1992): 20; and Lewis Hanke's classic, *The Spanish Struggle for Justice in the Conquest of America* (Philadelphia: University of Pennsylvania Press, 1949).

42. Lewis Hanke, *Aristotle and the American Indians: A Study in Race Prejudice in the Modern World* (Bloomington: Indiana University Press, 1959), examines the Dominican role in the early defense of the Indian.

43. *MM*, vol. 3: 522.

44. *CA*, 849.

45. Ibid.

46. Ibid., 524.

47. See Robert F. Berkhofer, "White Conceptions of Indians," in *Handbook of North American Indians*, vol. 15 (Washington, D.C.: Smithsonian Institute, 1978), 526, on describing Indians by deficiency.

48. *CA*, 174.

49. Ibid., 666.

50. Ibid.

51. Ibid., 107.

52. Ibid.

53. Ibid., 63.

54. Ibid., 97.

55. Ibid., 578–79.

56. Ibid., 744.

57. The stones on which Gonzalo de Tapia's blood fell were preserved in a box and kept in the Jesuit college chapel in Sinaloa. His right arm with two fingers still in place were brought to the Jesuit college in Mexico City. The chapel and house that he had constructed were preserved as a shrine. The Jesuits maintained that Tapia was killed *in odium fidei*, "out of hatred for the faith," which would have made him eligible to be declared a martyr of the church.

58. *CA*, 699.

59. Eric Wolf, *Sons of the Shaking Earth* (Chicago: University of Chicago Press, 1959), 168.

60. Reff, *Disease, Depopulation, and Culture Change.*

61. James Axtell, *The European and the Indian: Essays in the Ethnohistory of Colonial North America* (New York: Oxford University Press, 1981), 73–77.

62. See Wolf, *Sons of the Shaking Earth*, 168 ff. for other similarities.

63. Roberto Mario Salmon, *Indian Revolts in Northern New Spain. A Synthesis of Resistance* (Lanham, MD: University Press of America, 1990), esp. ch. 1–4.

64. Susan M. Deeds, *Defiance and Deference in Mexico's Colonial North. Indians Under Spanish Rule in Nueva Viscaya* (Austin: University of Texas Press, 2003) examines the social and economic ramifications of Jesuit work in nearby Nueva Viscaya where they became embroiled with Spanish mining and large-scale farming interests. See also Luis González-R, ed., *Revoltes des Indiens Tarahumars (1626–1724): Traduction du latin, introduction, commentaires* (Paris: Institut des Hautes Etudes de L'Amerique Latin, 1969), LIII–LV.

65. Axtell, *After Columbus*, 111.

66. Oakah L Jones, Jr., *Nueva Viscaya. Heartland of the Spanish Frontier* (Albuquerque University of New Mexico Press), 1988, 101.

CHAPTER 4

1. Peter Gerhard, *A Guide to the Historical Geography of New Spain* (Cambridge: Cambridge University Press, 1972), 27–28.

2. L. Clark Keating, *The Extirpation of Idolatry in Peru*. Translated and edited by L. Clark Keating (Lexington: University of Kentucky Press, 1968).

3. Robert Ricard, *La "conquête spirituelle" du Mexique: Essai sur l'apostolat et les méthodes missionaires des Ordres Mendiants en Nouvelle-Espagne de 1523–24 à 1572* (Paris: Institut D'Ethnologie, 1933), 165.

4. Hanns Prem, *Milpa y Hacienda. Tenencia de la tierra indígena y española en la Cuenca del Alto Atoyac, Puebla, México* (Weisbaden: Franz Steiner Verlag, 1978).

5. Andrés Pérez de Ribas, *My Life among the Savage Nations of New Spain* (Los Angeles: Ward Ritchie Press, 1968 [1644]).

6. The account of the resettlement program is in a collection of documents in the Bancroft Library, University of California, Berkeley, Manuscripts B 113, fols. 164–340.

7. Ibid., 160–61.

8. Ibid., 301.

9. Ibid., 198.

10. Ibid., 261, 267.

11. Ibid., 196.

12. Ibid., 745.

13. Ibid., 45.

14. Ibid.

15. Ibid., 42.

16. Daniel T. Reff, *Disease, Depopulation, and Culture Change in Northwestern New Spain, 1518–1764* (Salt Lake City: University of Utah Press, 1991), 262, notes how simple care can have positive effects on the ill person. Also *Cartas Anuas*, Bancroft Library, University of California, Berkeley, 273, 294, 246. Hereafter cited as *CA*.

17. *CA*, 192, 193.

18. Eduardo Williams, "The Stone Sculpture of Ancient West Mexico," *Ancient Mesoamerica*, 2 (1991): 181–92, examines the use and importance of such sculptures.

19. *CA*, 192.

20. Ibid., 193.

21. Ibid., 294.

22. Ibid., 273.

23. Ibid., 294.

24. Ibid., 206.

25. Ibid., 294.

26. Ibid., 528.

27. Ibid., 384–403.

CHAPTER 5

1. Franklin Pease G.Y., "La cultura en el Peru en los tiempos de la evangelización," *Revista Peruana de Historia Eclesiástica*, 3 (1994): 216.

2. Karen Spalding, *Huarochiri. An Andean Society under Inca and Spanish Rule* (Stanford: Stanford University Press, 1984), is a comprehensive account of the evolution of the village from pre-Inca through the Spanish colonial period. See also Sa-

bine MacCormack, *Religion in the Andes* (Princeton: Princeton University Press, 1993).

3. *Monumenta Peruana*, vol. 1, 134. Hereafter cited as *MP*.

4. Francisco Mateos, ed., *Historia general de la Compañía de Jesús en la provincia del Perú. Crónica anónima de 1600 . . .* , vol. 1 (Madrid: Consejo Superior de Investigaciones Científicas, 1944), 46; Antonio Astrain, *Historia de la Compañía de Jesús en la Asistencia de España*, vol. 4 (Madrid: Est. Tip. "Sucesores de Ribadeneyra," 1913–1925), 545–46.

5. Two major studies of Julí are Armando Nieto Vélez, "Jesuitas en el mundo andino: las reducciones de Juli," *Revista Peruana de Historia Eclesiástica*, 3 (1994): 129–44, and A. Echánove, "Origen y evolución de la idea jesuítica de "Reducciones" en las misiones del Virreinato del Peru," *Missionalia Hispánica*, 12 (1955): 95–144. Both show that Julí influenced how the Jesuits would proceed in their mission work in America for the next 190 years.

6. *MP*, vol. 1, doc. 52.

7. Rector of the *Doctrina* of Julí to Juan de la Plaza, 1 Aug. 1576, *MP*, vol 2, 356.

8. José de Acosta's report of 1577, ARSI, Peru 12, fol. 21.

9. Toledo's regulations are outlined in Roberto Levillier, *Gobernantes del Perú*, vol. 4, 48–208.

10. Mateos, *Historia general*, 407.

11. The chronicler acknowledges the rumors of exploitation. *Murmurado no poco* is the phrase he uses to describe the resentment. Ibid., 407.

12. Charles Stanish, et al., *Archaeological Survey in the Juli-Desaguadero Region of Lake Titikaka Basin, Southern Peru. Review Draft* (Chicago: Field Museum, [no date]), gives detailed raised-field sites near Julí. The survey also summarizes the ethnohistorical research done on the region.

13. Clifford T. Smith, William M. Denevan, and Patrick Hamilton, "Antiguos camellones de la región del Lago Titicaca," in *La tecnología en el mundo andino*, ed. Heather Lechtman and Ana María Soldi, 25–50 (México: Universidad Nacional Autónoma de México, 1981), 36–41; Stanish et al., *Archaeological Survey*, fig. 31.

14. Smith, Denevan, and Hamilton, "Antigues camellones," 44; Vásquez de Espinosa, *Compendio*, 474.

15. Noble David Cook, *Demographic Collapse: Indian Peru, 1520–1620* (New York: Cambridge University Press, 1981).

16. John Hyslop, *Inka Settlement Planning* (Austin: University of Texas Press, 1990), 287.

17. See Nicholas P. Cushner, *Jesuit Ranches and the Agrarian Development of Colonial Argentina, 1650–1767* (Albany: State University of New York Press, 1983), 32–33, for a discussion of the function and consequences of large structures on the Latin American landscape.

18. Mason, *Ancient Civilizations of Peru*, 69–70.

19. Mateos, *Historia general*, 409.

20. The account of the epidemic is in the Jesuit Annual Letter of 1604, ARSI, Peru 12, fol. 337.

21. ARSI, Peru 13, fol. 112.

22. Daniel T. Reff, *Disease, Depopulation, and Culture Change in Northwestern New Spain, 1518–1764* (Salt Lake City: University of Utah Press, 1991).

23. John Hyslop, *The Inka Road System* (New York: Academic Press, 1984), 133–34.

24. ARSI, Peru 12, fol. 286. This sum represents food, clothing, and specie distributed in 1603.

25. *MP*, vol. 6, 717.

26. ARSI, Peru 12, 136-37.

27. Mateos, *Historia general*, 409.

28. In 1603 the Annual Letter mentioned the excellent music heard in the churches of Julí. Instruction was given in two instruments. One instrument mentioned was the *viguela de arco*, an oval-shaped instrument with five cords played with a bow. A second instrument was the *orlos*, which was similar to an oboe. ARSI, Peru 12, fol. 286.

29. *MP*, vol. 2, 624–25; *MP*, vol. 3, 96–97; also the Annual Letter of 1597 written by Pablo José de Arriaga, ARSI, Peru 12, fols. 136–37.

30. *Cédula* of July 19, 1589, Lilly Library (Bloomington, IN), Latin American Manuscripts, Peru, Box 1581–1589; see the list of Peruvian epidemics spanning the sixteenth and seventeenth centuries in Cook, *Demographic Collapse*, 60–61.

31. Reff, *Disease, Depopulation, and Culture Change*, 243.

32. See the account of *cofradía* activity in ARSI, Peru 12, fol. 337.

33. ARSI, Peru 13, fol. 112.

34. *MP*, vol. 2, 619; *MP*, vol. 3, 97.

35. Mateos, *Historia general*, 401.

36. José Toribio Medina, *La imprenta en Lima* (Santiago de Chile: Impreso y Grabado en Casa del Autor, 1904–1907), 3. For the role of the Jesuits in early Lima printing, see Hensley C. Woodbridge and Lawrence S. Thompson, *Printing in Colonial Spanish America* (Troy, N.Y.: Whitson Publishing Company, 1976), 41–46. Page 134 contains a reproduction of the title page of the 1584 Lima version, printed by Antonio Ricardo, of the *Doctrina Christiana y Catecismo para Instrucción de los Indios*, and page 136 shows how the Quechua and Aymara texts were arranged.

37. ARSI, Peru 12, fol. 136. Arriaga also uses in his letter the term *doctrina* as a place, roughly equivalent to the modern term "parish." The word *doctrina* used as a place conveyed different meanings in the Spanish colonial missionary world. In the Philippines, for example, a doctrina was a remote Christian village having no resident priest.

38. Mateos, *Historia general*, 406.

39. Amalia Castelli, "Tunupa: Divinidad del Altiplano," *Etnohistoria y Antropología Andina (Primera Jornada del Museo Nacional de Historia)*, (Lima, 1978): 202.

40. Gary Urton, *At the Crossroads of Earth and Sky. An Andean Cosmology* (Austin: University of Texas Press, 1981).

41. See the remarks of Cobo on marriage and relationships in *Inca Religion and Customs by Fr. Bernabé Cobo* (Austin: University of Texas Press, 1990), 204–10.

42. A number of these Works of Mercy became specific obligations assumed by *cofradías*.

43. ARSI, Peru 12, fol. 337v.

44. Rodrigo de Cabredo in Annual Letter of 1603, ARSI, Peru 12, fol. 287.

45. Pedro Borges," La extirpación de idolatría en Indias como método misional (Siglo XVI)," *Missionalia Hispánica*, 15 (1957): 193.

46. Bernabe Cobo, *Inca Religion and Customs*. Translated and edited by Roland Hamilton and John Howland Rowe (Austin: University of Texas Press, 1991); [Pablo José Arriaga] L. Clark Keating, *The Extirpation of Idolatry in Peru*. Translated and edited by L. Clark Keating (Lexington: University of Kentucky Press, 1968); John Holand Rowe, "Inca Culture at the Time of the Spanish Conquest," *Handbook of South American Indians* (New York: Cooper Square Publishers, 1963), 15, 183–330; Frank Saloman and George Urioste, trans., *The Huarochiri Manuscript. A Testament of Ancient and Colonial Andean Religion* (Austin: University of Texas Press, 1991); Manuel M. Marzal, *Estudios sobre religion campesina* (Lima: Pontificia Universidad Católica del Peru); and Franklin Pease G.Y., *El dios creador andino* (Lima: Mosca Azul Editores, 1973) are a few of the standard volumes on the subject.

47. Different regions had different names for the Creator God. Wiracocha and Pariacaca were common names of the Creator God in other accounts.

48. This account of native religious beliefs was written by the Jesuit provincial, Rodrigo de Cabredo, in 1603. In all probability he compiled the account from reports sent to him by Jesuit mssionaries in Julí. ARSI, Peru 12, fol. 287.

49. Marzal, *Estudios sobre religión campesina*, 111.

50. Pease, *El dios creador andino*, 14.

51. Marzal, *Estudios sobre religión campesina*, 112; 147. Other missionaries and popular preachers of the time commented on this convergence. Marzal, *Estudios sobre religión campesina*, 111.

52. José de Acosta, *De Procuranda Indorum Salute* (Madrid: Consejo Superior de Investigaciones Científicas, 1984 [1577]), 423.

53. Pease, *El dios creador andino*, 54.

54. Cobo, *Historia*, II, 160.

55. Cobo, *Historia*, II, 166; Marzal, *Estudios sobre religión campesina*, 117.

56. Duviols, *La lutte*, 37.

57. *MP*, 113.

58. The Council of Lima in 1553 ordered that native priests be rounded up and locked up in one place so they couldn't infect other Indians. Rubén Vargas Ugarte, *Los Concilios Limenses* (Lima: 1952), II, 340.

59. *MP*, vol. 2, 356-57.

60. *MP*, vol. 6, 707.

61. ARSI, Peru 12, fol. 337v.

62. Ibid.

63. ARSI, Peru 12, fol. 9. This letter appears to be the Annual Letter for 1570. The wording cited is "*y entre ellos algunos hijos de principales que de temor y verguenza los tenían encubiertas.*"

64. Ibid., fols. 9–9v.

65. Cobo, *Inca Religion*, 170.

66. Luis Millones, "Religion and Power in the Andes: Idolatrous Curacas of the Central Sierra," *Ethnohistory* 26, no. 3 (summer 1979): 243–62.

67. ARSI, Peru 12, fol. 390.

68. Ibid.

69. Ibid., fol. 390v.

70. One Indian fortune teller in Julí was frequently visited by Spaniards. "Misión de Julí, 1611," ARSI, Peru 13, fol. 113.

71. The restriction on Spaniards may have been held more in the breech. The Jesuit documents frequently refer to Spaniards living in Julí and participating in day-to-day activity.

72. Alejandro Camino, Jorge Recharte, and Pedro Bidegaray, "Flexibilidad calendárica en la agricultura tradicional de las vertientes orientales de los Andes," in Heather Lechtman and Ana María Soldi, eds., *La tecnología en el mundo andino* (México: Universidad Nacional Autónoma de México, 1981), 169–194.

73. *MP*, vol. 2, 367.

74. Norman Meiklejohn, *La iglesia y los Lupaqas durante la colonia* (Cuzco: Centro de Estudios Rurales Bartolomé de las Casas, 1988), 191–246.

75. See the letter of the Indian caciques of Chucuito to King Philip II, Sept. 12, 1597, *MP* vol. 6, 443–51.

76. Ibid., 449.

77. Steve Stern, "The Rise and Fall of Indian-White Alliances: A Regional View of 'Conquest' History," *Hispanic American Historical Review* 61, no. 3 (1981): 461–91.

CHAPTER 6

1. The documentation on the gold mines spans a decade, from 1647 to 1657. Archivo General de las Indias, Seville, Spain, Charcas, 120. Hereafter cited as *AGI*.

2. Five of the most recent are Martín María Morales, "Los comienzos de las reducciones de la Provincia del Paraguay en relación con el derecho indiano y el Instituto de la Compañía de Jesús," *Archivum Historicum Societatis Iesu*, LXVII (1998), 3–129; Rafael Carbonell de Masy, *Estrategias de desarrollo rural en los pueblos guaranies, 1609–1767* (Barcelona: Bosch, 1992); Rubén Saguier Bareiro and Jean-Paul Duviols, eds., *Tentación de la Utopía. La República de los jesuítas en el Paraguay* (Barcelona: Tusquets, 1991); Robert Lacombe, *Guaranis et jésuites: Un combat pour la liberté* (Paris: Société d'Ethnografie, 1993); and Maurice Ezran, *Une colonisation douce: Les missions du Paraguay* (Paris: Harmattan, 1989).

3. Morales, "Los comienzos de las reducciones," 3.

4. William A. Haviland, *Cultural Anthropology* (New York: Wadsworth/Thompson Learning, 2002), 432.

5. Guillermo Furlong, *Misiones y sus pueblos de Guaranies* (Buenos Aires: 1962); Pablo Hernández, *Misiones del Paraguay: Organización social de las doctrinas guaranies de la Compañía de Jesús* (Barcelona: G. Gili, 1913).

6. The founding is described in the Jesuit Annual Letter of 1626, edited by Jaime Cortesão, *Jesuítas e bandeirantes no Guaira (1549–1640)* (Rio de Janeiro: Biblioteca Nacional, 1951), 235–40.

7. Guillermo Furlong Cardiff, *Cartografía jesuítica del Río de la Plata* (Buenos Aires: Tallares S.A. Casa Jacobo Peuser, 1936), Número XXXVI.

8. John Patrick Donnelly, "Antonio Possevino's Plan for World Evangelization," *Catholic Historical Review*, 75 (1988), 179–98.

9. Chinua Achebe, *Things Fall Apart* (New York: Fawcett Publications, 1959), 184.

10. José de Cardeil, "Carta y Relación de las Misiones de la Provincia del Paraguay," Archivum Romanum Societatis Iesu, Rome, Italy, Paraq. 24, fol. 20. Hereafter cited as *ARSI*.

11. Serafin Leite, *Cartas dos premieros jesuítas do Brasil* (São Paulo: Comissão do IV Centenario da Cidade de São Paulo, 1954), I, doc. 5.

12. Judith Shapiro, "From Tupã to the Land Without Evil: The Christianization of Tupi-Guarani Cosmology," *American Ethnologist*, 14 (1987): 16–27.

13. Branislava Susnik, "*Los Aborígenes del Paraguay.*" *Etnohistoria de los guaranies. Epoca Colonial* (Asunción: Museo Etnográfico "Andrés Barbero," 1979–1980). 165.

14. Antonio Ruiz de Montoya, S.J., *The Spiritual Conquest: Accomplished by the Religious of the Society of Jesus in the Provinces of Paraguay, Paraná, Uruguay, and Tape. A Personal Account of the Founding and Early Years of the Jesuit Paraguay Reductions* (St. Louis: Institute of Jesuit Sources, 1993), 47.

15. Ibid.

16. The word-for-word encounter between Brazilian Native Americans and Europeans that I rely on here is in the Portuguese translation of Yves d'Evreux, *Viagem ao norte do Brasil feita nos annos de 1613 a 1614 . . .* traduzida pelo Dr. Cezar Augusto Marques (Maranhão: 1874).

17. Ibid., 286.

18. Ibid., 300.

19. Ibid., 286–97.

20. Ibid., 286.

21. Ibid., 268.

22. When the Europeans set up their chapel, they made sure that the altar was decorated with a large number of images that they had carried with them from France. Ibid., 297.

23. Alfred Métraux, "Les migrations historiques des Tupi-Guarani," *Journal des la Société Américanistes de Paris*, nouvelle série (1927), 1–45; Shapiro, "From Tupã to the Land Without Evil," 131.

24. Cortesão, *Itapua*, 36–37.

25. Ibid., 39.

26. Cortesão, *Jesuítas e bandeirantes*; Morales, "Los comienzos de las reducciones," 32–39.

27. Morales, "Los comienzos de las reducciones," 38.

28. Mercedes Avellaneda, "La alianza militar jesuíta-guaraní en la segunda mitad del siglo XVII y los conflictos suscitados con las autoridades locales," in *Jesuítas: 400 Años en Córdoba* (Córdoba: Congreso Internacional. Tomo I, 1999), 84–85.

29. "Respuesta al exortatorio . . . 1664," Cortesão, *Itatin*, 275–85.

30. Royal Cedula of November 1, 1608, in Pablo Pastells, S. J., *Historia de la Compañía de Jesús en la Provincia del Paraguay . . . según los documentos originales del Archivo General de Indias*, vol. 1 (Madrid: Librería General de Victoriano Suárez, 1912–1946), 143, 140.

31. "Breve Relación de las misiones del Paraguay . . . ," ARSI, Paraq. 14.

32. ". . . se visten en mandándeselo." Ibid.

33. Carta Anua, May 17, 1609, ARSI, Paraq. 8, 6–7.

34. Susnik, *Etnohistoria de los guaranies*, 122.

35. Ibid., 18.

36. Ibid., 19.

37. Ibid., 20–21. The fight between Jesuits and settlers was bitter and long. Morales believes that the Jesuits came to Paraguay with biased views of the Spanish settlers. Isolating the Guaraní from the evil Spaniards led to the segregation policy that eventually became official. Taking the high moral ground, they considered themselves the only protectors of the Indians against the Spaniards in Santa Fe and Villarica. Morales, "Los comienzos de las reducciones," 47–49, passim.

38. The standard examination of the issue is Enrique de Gandía, *Francisco de Alfaro y la condición social de los Indios* (Buenos Aires: 1939). Also see Silvio Zavala, *Origenes de la colonización en el Río de la Plata* (Mexico: Editorial de El Colegio Nacional, 1977), esp. chapter 2, "El tratamiento de los Indios por los pobladores," 117–428.

39. "Clausula de una carta del P. Marcial de Lorenzana para el P. Diego de Torres, 1610," ARSI, Paraq. 11, Historia 1610–1695, fol. 70.

40. Ibid.

41. "Suplemento de el Anua pasada del año 1614 de la misión de Guayra," ARSI, Paraq. 8, fols. 142–47.

42. Ibid., 75.

43. "Carta Anua, 1626–1627," in Jaime Cortesão, *Jesuítas e bandeirantes no Guaira* (Río de Janeiro: Biblioteca Nacional, 1951), 209.

44. Ibid., 218–19.

45. Carta Anua 1633, in Jaime Cortesão, *Jesuítas e bandeirantes no Tape (1615–1641)* (Rio de Janeiro: Biblioteca Nacional, 1969), 39.

46. The congregation's reports signed by Francisco Vásquez de Trujillo on June 12, 1632, are in AGI, Charcas 2.

47. Ibid.

48. Report of September 11, 1639 in ARSI, Historia 11, ff. 258–59.

49. Henestrosa to the Crown, September 6, 1641, AGI, Charcas 282.

50. Testimonio, AGI, Charcas 28. The seventeenth-century *padrones* that include population counts for tribute records as well as munitions and arms data are in AGI, Charcas 120. The padrón for Santo Tomé reduction in 1657 includes, (1) a taffeta flag with the Borgoña arms, (2) two cases of ramrods, (3) 32 rifles, (4) four swords, (5) 32 machetes, and (6) 32 wooden shields. The reduction had 3,494 individuals of both sexes and 102 old folk.

51. Pastells, *Historia*, vol. 2, 1028, 438.

52. "Breve noticia de la numerosa y florida Xristiandad Guaraní," [1767], ARSI, Paraq. 14.

53. Morales, "Los comienzos de las reducciones," 4.

54. Nusdorffer to San Lorenzo, January 26, 1747, Archivo General de la Nacion, Buenos Aires, Argentina (hereafter cited as AGNBA), Compañía, 79. Susnik, *Etnohistoria de los guaranies*, 129, points out how the recently baptized of the Guaraní militia frequently went after its former enemies.

55. "Carta y Relación de las Misiones de la Provincia del Paraguay . . . 1747," ARSI, Paraq. 24, fol. 20.

56. Ibid.

57. "Breve Relación de las Misiones del Paraguay . . ." ARSI, Paraq. 14, fol. 3

58. The ceremony is minutely described in the "Breve Relación," ARSI, Paraq. 14.

59. See, for example, Número XLIX, "Mapa de un pueblo de las misiones."

60. Loose map in ARSI, Paraq. 14. See also the recent archaeological excavations of reduction sites in María Alejandra Funes, "Intervenciones arqueológicas en el sector sur del Conjunto Jesuítico-Guaraní de Nuestra Señora de Loreto, provincia de Misiones (Argentina)" in *Jesuítas: 400 Años en Córdoba* (Córdoba: Congreso Internacional, Tomo 2, 1999).

61. Ezran, *Une colonisation douce*, situates the reductions among the attempted utopias from Plato's Republic to the modern kibbutz.

62. What I say here is modeled on commentary apropos of the ninth-century Plan of St. Gall in Basil de Pinto, "The Plan of St. Gall," *America*, 143 (1980): 362. The three-volume edition is Walter Horn and Ernest Born, *The Plan of St. Gall: A Study of the Architecture and Economy of and Life in a Paradigmatic Carolingian Monastery*, 3 vols. (Berkeley: University of California Press, 1979).

63. Magnus Mörner, "The Guaraní Mission and the Segregation Policy of the Spanish Crown," *Archivum Historicum Societatis Iesu*, 30 (1961): 376–83.

64. "Breve Relación," ARSI, Paraq. 14, fol. 7.

65. "Memorial que tubo prevenido el P. Ignacio de Frias para dar al Consejo de Indias deshaciendo la calumnia de negociación, 1694," ARSI, Historia 11, folios 518–19.

66. I summarized the issues several years ago in a brief article " 'Palaces in the Desert': The Jesuits in Paraguay," *America* (February 11, 1978): 94–95.

67. "Carta Anua, 1626," Cortesão, *Jesuítas e bandeirantes no Guaira*, 215–16. "Years ago the Indians traveled 50 or 60 leagues from the pueblos to take the tea from the forests. They used wagons for the seven towns on the eastern side of the Uruguay River. The other towns used rafts on the Uruguay and the Paraná Rivers. The Indians would carry the tea on their shoulders from where it was grown to the rivers." Breve Relación, ARSI, Paraq. 14, fol. 13.

68. The trial and error experiments are in "Breve Relación," ARSI, Paraq. 14, fol. 13.

69. Sánchez Labrador, *Paraguay Natural*, ARSI, Paraq. 17, fol. 359.

70. Ibid.

71. "Breve Noticia de la numerosa y florida Xristiandad Guaraní," ARSI, Paraq. 14, fol. 31.

72. The cédula is dated September 19, 1675, Pastells, *Historia*, II, 101.

73. "Memoria de Yerba que a ydo bajando de las reducciones, 1671–1673," AGNBA, Compañía de Jesús IX, 47/8/4, fol. 66.

74. The edict is in *AGNBA*, Compañía de Jesús IX, 47/8/5, fols. 1–10.

75. Summary of the audiencia laws in ibid., 7/1/1, fol. 570.

76. Royal Order of September 16, 1684. Ibid., 47/8/5, fols. 92–94.

77. Shipping reports to Santiago, Lima, and Potosí are scattered throughout the Jesuit documents in the Argentine National Archives. See for example, AGNBA, Compañía de Jesús IX, 6/10/1, fols. 897–99; as well as 6/10/7.

78. AGNBA, Compañía de Jesús IX, 6/10/1, fol. 945.

79. Ibid., (about 1750) 7/1/1, fol. 425; and ibid. fol. 517.

80. "Asi mismo tomara Vuestra Merced para sí los 4 mil pesos del contrato de la manera y en las condiciones que el . . . y todo lo demás que quedara se ha de emplear en oro de buenos quilates; lo qual se podrá comprar en Chile . . ." "Instrucción que el P. Antonio Miranda, Procurador en este Colegio Máximo del Tucumán a don Andrés Lascano, vecino de la misma Ciudad . . . Córdoba 17 de diciembre 1754," AGNBA, Compañía de Jesús IX, 6/9/10.

81. Memorial of Jaime Aguilar, October 26, 1735, AGNBA, Compañía de Jesús IX, 6/9/7.

82. Rafael Carbonnel de Masy," Les 'réductions' du Paraguay," *Études* 375 (July–August 1991): 102.

83. Ibid., 102. Two head of cattle a year were slaughtered for slaves. Guillermo Furlong, *Bernardo Nusdorffer y su "Novena Parte" (1760)* (Buenos Aires: Ediciones Theoría, 1971), 37.

84. ARSI, Paraq. 14, fol. 11.

85. Breve Relación, ARSI, Paraq. 14, fols. 8-9.

86. Carbonnel de Masy, "Les "réductions" du Paraguay," 106.

87. Estrada, "Antecedentes para la historia del desarrollo."

88. "Visita del P. Prov. Laurenzo Rillo, 20 abril 1728," AGNBA, Compañía de Jesús IX, 7/1/1.

89. Bravo, *Inventario de los bienes*, 662–63.

90. "Razón de los cueros . . . , 1754," AGNBA, Compañía de Jesús IX, 6/10/1, doc. 729; and ibid., 6/9/6.

91. Sánchez Labrador, *Paraguay Natural*, ARSI, Paraq. 17, fol. 294.

92. Ibid, 296. Epidemics in the reductions were continual through the seventeenth and eighteenth centuries. 1614, 1617, 1626, 1629, 1630, 1633, 1635-36, 1718, were exceptionally lethal years. Susnik, *Etnohistoria de los guaranies*, 143, says that the proximity of houses in a reduction was a major factor in spread of disease. The 1636 epidemic was particularly severe in Jesús María, claiming fifteen or sixteen victims a day. Cortesão, *Jesuítas e bandeirantes no Tape*, 149.

93. Sánchez Labrador, *Paraguay Natural*, 430.

94. Cortesão, *Jesuítas e bandeirantes no Tape*, 118.

95. Ibid., 108–9.

96. Cortesão, *Jesuítas e bandeirantes no Tape*, 54.

97. Haviland, *Cultural Anthropology*, 48.

98. Ruiz de Montoya, *The Spiritual Conquest*, 85.

99. Diego de Boroa, Carta Anua of September 28, 1614, in Cortesão, *Itatin*, 15.

100. The *Breve Noticia*, ARSI, Paraq. 14, fols. 27–28 says that each town had a choir of thirty and from the total of three hundred the best singers were chosen for the *Escuela de Música*. On the feastday of Corpus Christi a long procession passed under arches constructed for the occasion, including live tigers, alligators, wolves, warthogs, deer, lions, leopards, and monkeys; dancers performed in front of the Blessed Sacrament as the procession moved through the streets of the reduction.

101. Andrew Greeley, "Why Do Catholics Stay in the Church? Because of the Stories," *New York Times Magazine*, July 10, (1994), 34.

102. Letter of P. Joseph Orregio, August 20, 1636, Cortesão, *Itapua*, 29–30.

103. Carta Anua, ARSI, Paraq. 8, fol. 5.

104. Ibid.

105. Ruiz de Montoya, *The Spiritual Conquest*, 33. Ruiz was a major force behind the arming of the Guaraní in 1640.

106. Ibid.

107. Ibid.

108. Guillermo Furlong, *Bernardo Nusdorffer y su "Novena Parte" (1760)* (Buenos Aires: Ediciones Theoría, 1971), 121.

109. "Ordenes para todas las Reducciones aprobadas por N.P. General Julio Paulo Oliva [1690]," ARSI, Paraq. 12, 173–173v. These orders written by the Jesuit provincials for reductions should not be taken to mean that what was prohibited had at some point actually occurred. But it may have! For example, in 1628 Nicolás Durán forbad the use of "flying rockets" or fireworks during fiestas because the Guaraní houses were made of dried brushweed or straw that could easily catch fire. No record of previous fiesta fires is preserved.

110. See the discussion of the ability of groups to adapt to modern times in Haviland, *Cultural Anthropology*, 464.

CHAPTER 7

1. Georg Kubler, *Art and Architecture in Spain and Portugal and Its Possessions* (New Haven: Yale University Press, 1964), and Pal Kelemen, *Baroque and Rococo in Latin America* (New York: Macmillan, 1951) are classic. Robert J. Mullen, *Architecture and Its Sculpture in Viceregal Mexico* (Austin: University of Texas Press, 1997); Harold E. Wethey, *Colonial Architecture and Sculpture in Peru* (Cambridge: Harvard University Press, 1949); José María Vargas, ed., *Arte Colonial de Ecuador: Siglos XVI–XVII* (Barcelona: Salvat Editores, 1977); Fernando Arellano, *El arte jesuítico en la América española, 1568–1767* (San Cristobal: Universidad Católica del Tachira, 1991); are more recent.

2. Arellano, *El arte jesuítico*; Gauvin Alexander Bailey, *Art on the Jesuit Missions in*

Asia and Latin America, 1542–1773 (Toronto: University of Toronto Press, 1999). Rene Javellana, *Wood and Stone: For God's Greater Glory. Jesuit Art and Architecture in the Philippines* (Manila: Ateneo de Manila University Press, 1991) has examined Jesuit art and colonial churches in the tropical Philippines.

3. John McAndrew, *The Open Air Churches of Sixteenth-Century Mexico* (Cambridge: Harvard University Press, 1965).

4. See examples in Robert Ricard, *La "conquête spirituelle" du Mexique: Essai sur l'apostolat et les méthodes missionaires des Ordres Mendiants en Nouvelle-Espagne de 1523–24 à 1572* (Paris: Institut D'Ethnologie, 1933), 120, passim.

5. Carmelo Saenz de Santa María, *Historia de la educación jesuítica en Guatemala* (Madrid: Consejo Superior de Investigaciones Científicas, 1978), 155.

6. Arellano, *El arte jesuítico*, 196.

7. Gabriel Cevallos García et al., *Arte Colonial de Ecuador. Siglos XVI–XVII* (Quito: Salvat Editores Ecuatoriana S. A. Quito, 1977), 79–93.

8. Ibid., 96; economic reports of the college are in Archivum Romanum Societatis Iesu, Rome, Italy, Quito 11. Hereafter cited as *ARSI*.

9. Recio, "Compendiosa relación de la christiandad de Quito," 261, 264

10. Nicholas Cushner, *Lords of the Land: Sugar, Wine, and Jesuit Estates of Coastal Peru, 1600–1767* (Albany: State University of New York Press, 1980); Nicholas P. Cushner, *Farm and Factory. The Jesuits and the Development of Agrarian Capitalism in Colonial Quito, 16001767* (Albany: State University of New York Press, 1982) and *Jesuit Ranches and the Agrarian Development of Colonial Argentina, 1650–1767* (Albany: State University of New York Press, 1983), examine the great estates run by the Jesuits in America.

11. See Pablo Macera's discussion of this in *Mapas coloniales de haciendas cuzqueñas* (Lima: Universidad Nacional Mayor de San Marcos, 1968), xi, xii.

12. The maps in ibid. have sketches of the main hacienda building as well as associated structures.

13. "Libro de Officio del P. Procurador," in APA (San Miguel), passim.

14. Kelemen, *Baroque and Rococo*, 193.

15. "Preceptos," Biblioteca de Salamanca, Salamanca, Spain. Hereafter cited as BS.

16. David Mitchell, *The Jesuits: A History* (London: Macdonald, 1980), 135, 139.

17. Bailey, *Art on the Jesuit Missions in Asia and Latin America*, 49, 50–51.

18. See the pictures and sketches of the Reductions in Robert H, Jackson, www2.h-net.msu.edu/~latam/powerpoints/JesuitMissions.pdf

19. The two best works on the reductions and their goals are Guillermo Furlong, *Misiones y sus pueblos de Guaranies* (Buenos Aires: Tip. Editora, 1962), and Pablo Hernández, *Misiones del Paraguay: Organización social de las doctrinas guaranies de la Compañía de Jesús* (Barcelona: G. Gili, 1913).

20. Collection of letters from the general in Rome APA, no pressmark.

21. Cushner, *Lords of the Land*, 177–78, and the sources cited therein.

22. See ibid., 176–80 for a discussion of the wealth of the Jesuits.

23. See the controversies in Luis Martin, *The Intellectual Conquest of Peru: The*

Jesuit College of San Pablo, 1568–1767 (New York: Fordham University Press, 1968), 36–38; and chapter 3, of this book.

24. Mario Scaduto, "Il Teatro Gesuitico," *AHSI* 36 (1967); Justo García Soriano, "El teatro del Colegio en España," *Boletín de la Real Academia Española* 16 (1927); K. Skelly, "El teatro en la América Hispana durante el siglo XVI," *RCEH* 7 (1982); and Nigel Griffen, *Jesuit School Drama: A Checklist of Critical Literature* (London: Grant and Cutler, 1976) are basic. An excellent overview is William H. McCabe, *An Introduction to Jesuit Theater: A Posthumous Work* (St. Louis: Institute of Jesuit Sources, 1983). A recent study of the theater in Latin America is Manuel Antonio Arango, *El teatro religioso en la América Española* (Barcelona: Pulvill Libros, 1997).

25. McCabe, *An Introduction*, 11–18.

26. Arango, *El teatro religioso*, 25–27; Juan de Tobar, the Mexican Jesuit, wrote a detailed description of what he calls the indigenous theater that took place in a patio, a *"pequeño teatro,"* thirty feet square honoring indigenous gods. Tobar, *Tratado de Ritos*, 110; Ricard, *La "conquête spirituelle" du Mexique*, 234–28, describes the *"Le Theatre Édifiant"* that the Franciscan missionaries in Mexico used so effectively in the sixteenth century.

27. Garcilaso de la Vega, *Los Comentarios Reales*, Bk. 2, Ch. 28.

28. Bernabe Cobo, *History of the Inca Empire* (Austin: University of Texas Press, 1979), book 14, chapter 18; Martin, *The Intellectual Conquest*, 47.

29. By the end of the eighteenth century, Lima was active with professional acting companies. Leonard, *El teatro en Lima, 1790–1793*; also Arango, *El teatro religioso*, 75–85.

30. "Decuria de Santa María Egipciaca," in Rubén Vargas Ugarte, ed., *De Nuestro Antiguo Teatro: Colección de Piezas Dramáticas de los siglos XVI, XVII, y XVIII. Introducción y notas de Rubén Vargas Ugarte* (Lima: Biblioteca Histórica Peruana, Tomo IV, 1943), 27–39.

31. "Blessed Virgin," *New Catholic Encyclopedia*, vol. 1, 192.

32. "Decuria," 28.

33. Ibid., 29.

34. For males playing female roles in Jesuit productions see McCabe, *An Introduction to the Jesuit Theater*, 178–80.

35. Ibid., 29–30.

36. Ibid., 32.

37. Ibid.

38. McCabe, *An Introduction to the Jesuit Theater*, 144, discusses the specific Jesuit contributions to their theater.

39. "Decuria," 32.

40. Ibid., 36.

41. Ibid., 38.

42. Ibid.

CHAPTER 8

1. See Bruce Trigger, *The Children of Aataensik: A History of the Huron Peoples to 1660*. 2 vols. (Montreal: McGill-Queens University Press, 1976), 609; and Lucien Campeau, *Catastrophe démographique sur le Grand Lacs. Les premieres habitants du Québec* (Montréal: Ed. Bellarmin, 1986). Indian population is also discussed in Henry F. Dobyns, "Commentary on Native American Demography," *Ethnohistory*, 31 (1989): 299–307; William Starna, "Mohawk Iroquois Population. A Revision," *Ethnohistory*, 27 (1980): 371–82; and Alfred W. Crosby, "Virgin Soil Epidemics as a Factor in the Aboriginal Depopulation of America," *William and Mary Quarterly*, 33 (1976): 299.

2. See Garnier's comments on the joy that the death of children brought to him in 1638. *Monumenta Novae Franciae: Les grandes épreuves (1638–1640)* (Rome–Montréal: Institutum Historicum Societatis Iesu / Les Editions Bellarmin, 1989), 4: 24 (hereafter cited as *MNF 4*); also *Monumenta Novae Franciae: Recherche de la paix (1644–1646)* (Rome-Montréal: Institutum Historicum Societatis Iesu, 1992), 6: 554 (hereafter cited as *MNF 6*); and Lalemant's comments in Reuben Gold Thwaites, ed., *The Jesuit Relations and Allied Documents: Travels and Explorations of the Jesuit Missionaries in New France, 1610–1791*, 73 vols. (Cleveland: Burrows Bros., 1896–1901), 19: 91–93 (hereafter cited as *JR*).

3. Drunkenness and debauchery were "the divinities of this land," *JR* 53: 142. For numerous references to Jesuit objections to the liquor trade, see R. C. Dailey, "The Role of Alcohol Among North American Indian Tribes as Reported in the Jesuit Relations," *Anthropologica* 10 (1968): 45–59. See also J. F. Nolan, "The Liquor Problem and the Jesuit Mission in New France," *Acta et Dicta*, 3 (1911–1914): 91–141; and Jerrold Levy and Stephen J. Kunitz, *Indian Drinking. Navajo Practices and Anglo-American Theories* (New York: John Wiley and Sons, 1974).

4. *JR* 6: 253; *JR* 46: 103.

5. Dailey, "The Role of Alcohol," 54.

6. A. F. C. Wallace, "Dreams and the Wishes of the Soul: A Type of Psychoanalytic Theory Among Seventeenth Century Iroquois," *American Anthropologist*, 60 (1959): 234–48.

7. See Lafiteau's Memorial, *JR* 67: 39–47.

8. Nicholas P. Cushner, *Jesuit Ranches and the Agrarian Development of Colonial Argentina, 1650–1767* (Albany: State University of New York Press, 1983), 80–82, 153–54.

9. Each mission village or *reducción* had common land but private plots were worked as well.

10. James P. Ronda, "The Sillery Experiment: A Jesuit–Indian Village in New France, 1637–1663," *American Indian Culture and Research Journal* 3, no. 1 (1979): 1–18.

11. Ibid., 6.

12. Christian Morissoneau, "Huron of Lorette," in *Handbook of North American Indians*, vol. 15, 389–93.

13. *JR* 61: 169. Detailed description of the construction of the Loretto mission village is in *JR* 60: 27–75.

14. Ronda, "The Sillery Experiment," 13.

15. James P. Ronda, " 'We Are Well as We Are': An Indian Critique of Seven-teenth Century Christian Missions," *William and Mary Quarterly*, 34 (1977).

16. William J. Eccles, "The Fur Trade in the Colonial Northeast," in *Handbook of North American Indians*, vol. 15, 324. Also the same author, *The Canadian Frontier, 1534–1760* (Albuquerque: University of New Mexico Press, 1983), 110–120.

17. Calvin Martin, *Keepers of the Game: Indian-Animal Relationship and the Fur Trade* (Berkeley: University of California Press, 1978), argues that the Indians were motivated by less materialistic motives.

18. Nancy Bonvillain, "Missionary Role in French Colonial Expansion: An Exam-ination of the Jesuit Relations," *Man in the Northeast*, 29 (1985), 1–13, puts too much credence in Jesuit rhetoric about the political benefits of missions. Anti-Jesuit feeling at court prompted Jesuits in Paris to overemphasize the great service the missions were accomplishing for French expansion. This was secondary to their primary goals.

19. Eccles, *The Canadian Frontier*, 79. See also Marcel Trudel, *The Beginnings of New France: 1524–1663* (Toronto: McClelland and Stewart, 1973) for the early missions.

20. Trigger, *The Children of Aataensik*; George Hunt, *The Wars of the Iroquois: A Study in Intertribal Trade Relations* (Madison: University of Wisconsin Press, 1940); and Kenneth Morrison, *The Embattled Northeast: The Elusive Ideal of Alliance in Abenaki-Euramerican Relations* (Berkeley: University of California Press, 1984), illustrate the contradictions and conflicts that the Jesuits involved themselves in during the seven-teenth and eighteenth centuries. Politics, economics, and evangelization crisscrossed and impacted on each other.

21. LeJeune's trip is carefully edited in Lucien Campeau, S.J., ed., *Monumenta Novae Franciae. Établissement a Québec (1616–1634)* (Rome–Québec: Monumenta His-torica Societatis Iesu/ Les Presses de l'Universitè Laval, 1979), 2: 667–728 (hereinaf-ter cited as *MNF* 2). Francis Parkman, *The Jesuits in North America in the Seventeenth Century: France and England in North America*. Part Second. (Boston: Little, Brown, 1914), 110–28, discusses the trip at length. Guy La Flèche, *Le missionaire, l'apostat, le sorcier: Relation de 1634 de Paul LeJeune* (Montréal: Presses de l'Université de Mon-tréal, 1973) uses LeJeune's trip as a microcosm of Jesuit missionary experience in Canada. The English translation of LeJeune's account is in Thwaites, ed., *The Jesuit Relations*. The entire set of *The Jesuit Relations* is available online at www .collectionscanada.ca/jesuit-relations/h19-230-e.html. The set is preceded by an excel-lent series of essays on the Jesuits in Canada and *The Jesuit Relations*.

22. *JR* 7:77.

23. Ibid., 93.

24. Ibid., 107.

25. Ibid., 113.

26. Ibid.

27. Ibid., 109.

28. Ibid.

29. Ibid., 111.

30. Ibid., 113.

31. For a discussion of the shaman's role in Indian society see the items listed in

Christopher Vecsey, ed., *Religion in Native North America* (Moscow: University of Idaho Press, 1990), 187–89; also the many references in Ake Hultkrantz, *Conceptions of the Soul Among North American Indians: A Study in Religious Ethnology* (Stockholm: Ethnographical Museum of Sweden, 1953).

32. *JR* 7:121.

33. Ibid., 137.

34. Ibid., 174–77.

35. Ibid., 185.

36. What follows is based primarily on Elizabeth Tooker, ed., *Native North American Spirituality of the Eastern Woodlands: Sacred Myths, Dreams, Visions, Speeches, Healing Formulas, Rituals and Ceremonials* (New York: Paulist Press, 1979) and the same author's *An Ethnography of the Huron Indians, 1615–1649* (Washington, D.C.: Bureau of Ethnology, Bulletin number 190, 1964).

37. Martin, *Keepers of the Game.*

38. Ibid., 3, states that the Jesuits "encouraged" the fur trade. On page 101, the Jesuits "however reluctantly, appear in general to have promoted the trade," as if this were a shameful deed. It would have been surprising if they didn't encourage the fur trade since it was the major link between France and potential Indian converts. On the other hand, the Jesuits had good reason to oppose the trade (which they never did) because it promoted contact with the liquor distributors, provided the Indians with European models of vice, and took them away from their villages for protracted periods of time.

39. James Axtell, *The European and the Indian: Essays in the Ethnohistory of Colonial North America* (New York: Oxford University Press, 1981), 245–315, discusses the impact of Europeans on Indian culture and vice versa.

40. Garnier to his father, 28 April 1638, *MNF* 4, 39.

41. Ibid.

42. *MNF* 4, 77–78.

43. The essay titled "Edifying Narratives" makes this point about military metaphors. See *www.collectionscanada.ca/jesuit-relations/h19-200-e.html*

44. Allan Greer, *The Jesuit Relations: Natives and Missionaries in Seventeenth-Century North America* (Boston/New York: Bedford/St. Martin's, 2000), 146–54.

45. Eastman, *The Soul of the Indian,* IX

46. Essay titled "Description of the New World," www.collectionscanada.ca.

47. The best biography of Marquette is Joseph P. Donnelly, *Jacques Marquette, S.J. 1637–1675* (Chicago: Loyola University Press, 1968). See also Raphael Hamilton, *Marquette's Explorations: The Narratives Reexamined* (Madison: University of Wisconsin Press, 1970).

48. Herbert Eugene Bolton, *Rim of Christendom: A Biography of Eusebio Francisco Kino, Pacific Coast Pioneer* (New York: Macmillan, 1936) is Kino's primary biography. Burrus has edited many of Kino's writings (see note 50).

49. Hamilton, *Marquette's Explorations,* describes forays in search of Indian groups.

50. Ernest Burrus, *Kino and Manje: Explorers of Sonora and Arizona. Their Vision*

of the Future. A Study of Their Expeditions and Plans with an Appendix of Thirty Documents (Rome: Jesuit Historical Institute, 1971), 57–64, discusses the motivation of Kino's explorations.

51. Ruth Lapham Butler, ed., *Journal of Paul du Ru. February 1 to May 8 1700. Missionary Priest to Louisiana* (Chicago: The Claxton Club, 1934).

52. *JR* 50: 267.

53. *JR* 55: 105–15.

54. Herbert Eugene Bolton, "The Mission as a Frontier Institution in the Spanish American Colonies," *American Historical Review*, 23 (1917), used the phrase "frontier institution" in his classic article, arguing that the Franciscan, Dominican, and Jesuit missions extended, held, and developed the frontier.

55. Russell Charles Ewing, "The Pima Uprising of 1751: A Study of Spanish-Indian Relations on the Frontier of New Spain," in *Greater America: Essays in Honor of Herbert Eugene Bolton* (Berkeley: University of California Press, 1945), 259–80.

56. Butler, *Journal of Paul du Ru*, 54.

57. Burrus, *Kino and Manje*, 62.

58. John Parry, *The Age of Reconaissance* (London: Weidenfeld and Nicolson, 1963).

59. Ibid.

60. Butler, *Journal of Paul du Ru*, 11.

61. In the introductory dedication of Gonzalo Fernández de Oviedo, *Historia general y natural de las Indias* (Santo Domingo: 1539–1548).

62. Hamilton, *Marquette's Explorations*, 197.

CHAPTER 9

1. Parker's letter is printed in Robert Emmett Curran, ed., *American Jesuit Spirituality: The Maryland Tradition 1634–1900* (New York: Paulist Press, 1988), 56. Letters from other English Jesuits volunteering for missions are on 57–61.

2. Ibid.

3. Thomas H. Clancy, "The First Generation of English Jesuits" *ARSI* 57: 113 (1988): 146.

4. Raymond J. Layhey, "The Role of Religion in Lord Baltimore's Colonial Enterprise," *Maryland Historical Magazine*, 72 (winter 1977): 492–511, demonstrates the religious linkages between Baltimore's attempts to found a colony on Newfoundland and his Maryland enterprise.

5. William Hand Browne, ed., *Archives of Maryland* (72 vols.) (Baltimore: Maryland Historical Society, 1883–1916), 3: 16.

6. David B. Quinn, "Introduction: Prelude to Maryland" in David B. Quinn, ed., *Early Maryland in a Wider World* (Detroit: Wayne State University Press, 1982), 23.

7. Bossy, "Reluctant Colonists: The English Catholics Confront the Atlantic" in Quinn, *Early Maryland*, 162. Bossy also suggests that investment for the Maryland enterprise was largely supplied by the Jesuits. "It was, in short, not just a Catholic venture, but a specifically Jesuit one."

8. Vitelleschi's letter is reprinted in Thomas Hughes, *History of the Society of Jesus in North America: Colonial and Federal* (4 vols.) (Cleveland: Burrows Brothers, 1907–1917), 1: 246–47.

9. Ibid., 247–48.

10. "Conditions Propounded by Lord Baltimore" in Clayton Coleman Hall, ed., *Narratives of Early Maryland, 1633–1684* (New York: Charles Scribner's Sons, 1925), 91–101.

11. Gerald P. Fogarty, *The Maryland Jesuits, 1634–1833* (Baltimore: Maryland Province of the Society of Jesus, 1976), 10.

12. Hall, "Instructions to the Colonists," *Narratives*, 16.

13. The classic account of the colonists' voyage is "A Briefe Relation of the Voyage unto Maryland, by Father Andrew White, 1634," Hall, *Narratives*, 29–45. A more recent excellent general history that treats thoroughly the colonial beginnings is Robert Brugger, *Maryland, A Middle Temperament, 1634–1980* (Baltimore: Johns Hopkins University Press, 1988). Edwin Warfield Beitzell, *The Jesuit Missions of St. Mary's County, Maryland* (Sponsored by the St. Mary's County Bicentennial Commission, 1976; privately printed) is a mine of information on the Jesuit missionaries in colonial Maryland.

14. Hall, *Narratives*, 73.

15. Ibid., 42.

16. "A Relation of Maryland," ibid., 76.

17. Ibid., 118.

18. Christian F. Feest, "Nanticoke and Neighboring Tribes," in Bruce Trigger, ed., *Handbook of North American Indians: Northeast* (Washington, D.C.: Smithsonian Institution, 1978), 15: 240–52.

19. Joseph P. Donnelly, S.J., *Thwaites' Jesuit Relations: Errata and Addenda* (Chicago: Loyola University Press, 1967), 1–26, explains that the Jesuit Relations from New France were not official reports to Rome but primarily intended for public consumption.

20. A major collection of Jesuit correspondence and records is now located in the Special Collections division of the Georgetown University Library, Washington, D.C. Letterbooks, farm ledgers, bills of lading, and some personal correspondence constitute most of this collection. It was originally housed in the Jesuit Province Archives in Baltimore, so it is catalogued as Maryland Province Archives.

21. Hall, *Narratives*, 118.

22. Ibid., 119.

23. Ibid., 126.

24. Darrett B. Rutman and Anita H. Rutman, "Of Agues and Fevers: Malaria in the Early Chesapeake," *William and Mary Quarterly*, 3rd ser., 33 (1976): 31–60; Daniel Blake Smith, "Mortality and Family in the Colonial Chesapeake," *Journal of Interdisciplinary History*, 8 (1978): 403–37.

25. "From the Annual Letter of 1640," Hall, *Narratives*, 137.

26. Ibid.

27. Archives of Maryland 3: 165–66 (hereafter cited as *AM*). A detailed descrip-

tion of Ingle's raid is in Sally Smith Booth, *Seeds of Anger: Revolts in America 1607–1771* (New York: Hastings House, 1977), 43–47.

28. AM 3: 166–69.

29. J. Moss Ives, *The Ark and the Dove: The Beginnings of Civil and Religious Liberties in America* (New York: Cooper Square Publishers, 1969), 16–17.

30. David W. Jordan, "Maryland's Privy Council, 1637–1715" in Aubrey C. Land, Lois Green Carr, and Edward Papenfuse, eds., *Law, Society, and Politics in Early Maryland* (Baltimore: Johns Hopkins University Press, 1977), 69.

31. AM 10: 12.

32. Fogarty, *The Maryland Jesuits*, 14.

33. AM 1: 246.

34. Brugger, *Maryland*, 21–22.

35. Fr. George Hunter's Day book records that in 1764 sixteen students paid twelve shillings per month for schooling and in 1765 fifteen paid the same for a school year that ran from June to the following June. Five more students were added for terms of three and four months bringing the total to twenty students. The school was probably Newtown. Hunter's day book is in MPA 174 (B).

36. Ibid.

37. The published annual reports that the Jesuits sent to Rome paint a general picture of their activities in Maryland from 1634 to 1681. Hall, *Narratives*, 118–44.

38. AM 5: 309–10.

39. AM 15: viii–x.

40. Ibid., 389–91.

41. Ibid., 5: 130–31.

42. Ibid., 15: 388–91.

43. Ibid., 46: 531.

44. Brugger, *Maryland*, 148.

45. AM 50: 201–02.

46. Ibid., 28: 355.

47. Ibid., 52: 387–88.

48. Ibid., 55: 509–12.

49. Ibid., 55: 512.

50. Lewis's poem is in MPA 2 W 16.

51. Mosley's letters have been edited by Edward I. Devitt, "Letters of Father Joseph Mosley, 1757–1786" in *The Woodstock Letters*, vol. 25 (1906), 54.

52. Ibid., 39.

53. Ibid., 42.

54. Ibid., 54.

55. Ibid., 55.

56. Clemens, "Economy and Society on Maryland's Eastern Shore" in Land, Carr, and Papenfuse, eds., *Law, Society, and Politics in Early Maryland*, 164.

57. Devitt, "Letters of Father Joseph Mosley," 25: 49.

58. Ibid.

59. Mosley's Day Book which is titled "Day Book. Bohemia Manor 1764. St. Jo-

seph's Talbot County," MPA 174 B, records the purchase made on March 17, 1765. In December of 1764 a Mr. Doyne had visited Mosley and offered him one thousand acres of his land called Tinnasarah for ten shillings an acre. Apparently he knew that the Jesuit was in the market for a farm.

60. AM 50: 422.

61. "Regulations of 1751," MPA 57 (1).

62. Ibid.

63. Ibid.

64. "Bohemia [Manor] Day and Ledger Book, 1735–1761," MPA 49 (1), fol. 94.

65. Jesuit land investment, estates, and the role of their landholdings in the rural economy are examined in Nicholas P. Cushner, *Lords of the Land: Sugar, Wine, and Jesuit Estates of Coastal Peru, 1600–1767* (Albany: State University of New York Press, 1980).

66. "Mr. Wm. Hunter's Tytle to St. Inago's . . ." MPA, 100 T 1, is a thorough account of the origins of Jesuit property in Maryland.

67. A monumental study on Western attitudes toward death and the ease with which the Christain faithful thought that donating property and money to the church was a good activity is Philippe Aries, *At the Hour of Our Death* (New York: Knopf, 1981), 437–87.

68. "Bohemia [Manor] Day and Ledger Book, 1735–1761," MPA 49 (1).

69. Records of tobacco sales and distribution from Jesuit farms are in MPA 46 (5).

70. "Day Book. Bohemia Manor 1764," MPA 174 B.

71. "Bohemia [Manor] Day and Ledger Book, 1735–1761," fol.73.

72. Ibid., fol. 103.

73. By this time wheat and corn had become the major products of Bohemia Manor. Around 1710 the decline of tobacco prices in the Chesapeake region caused farms to diversify their crops. However, tobacco was grown on the other Jesuit farms, especially Portobacco. See Gloria Main, "Maryland and the Chesapeake Economy, 1670–1720," in Aubry C. Land, Lois Green Carr, and Edward C. Papenfuse, *Law, Society, and Politics in Early Maryland* (Baltimore: Johns Hopkins University Press, 1977); also Gloria Main, *Tobacco Colony. Life in Early Maryland, 1650–1720* (Princeton: Princeton University Press, 1982).

74. "Bohemia [Manor] Day and Ledger Book, 1735–1761," MPA 49 (1).

75. "St. Thomas Manor," MPA 46 (4).

76. Mosley mentions the kind of foods he had grown accustomed to; the purchases made by Jesuit farm managers and recorded in the farm books are the basis for this list.

77. Devitt, "Letters of Father Joseph Mosley, 1757–1786," *The Woodstock Letters* 25: 51.

78. MPA 25 (9).

79. MPA 57 (1).

CHAPTER 10

1. Hector Macedo, "Recognizing the Unknown: The Discoverers and the Discovered in the Age of European Expansion," *Camões Center Quarterly*, 4 (1992): 8.

2. Louis J. Gallagher, *China in the Sixteenth Century. The Journals of Matthew Ricci, 1583–1610* (New York: Random House, 1953).

3. C. R. Boxer, *The Christian Century in Japan, 1549–1650* (Berkeley: University of California Press, 1951).

4. David E. Mungello, *Curious Land: Jesuit Accommodation and the Origins of Sinology* (Stuttgart: Franz Steiner Verlag, 1985), 36–42, analyzes the European fascination with China.

5. Edward J. Dudley, ed., *The Wild Man Within: An Image in Western Thought from the Renaissance to Romanticism* (Pittsburgh: University of Pittsburgh Press, 1973), describes how the image of the wild man influenced ideas about indigenous America.

6. Joseph P. Donnelly, S.J, *Thwaites' Jesuit Relations: Errata and Addenda* (Chicago: Loyola University Press, 1967), 33–41.

7. Lucien Campeau, S.J., ed., *Monumenta Novae Franciae: Fondation de la Mission Huronne (1635–1637)*. (Rome-Québec: Monumenta Historica Societatis Iesu /Les Presses de l'Université Laval, 1987), 3: 182–404. Hereafter cited as *MNF*.

8. "*Nos sauvages ne point sauvages en ce qui regarde les devoirs que la nature mesme nous oblige de rendre aux morts*" quoted in *MNF* 3: 388

9. José María Urquijo, "El Indio en los escritos de los jesuítas," *Jesuítas. 400 Años en Córdoba. Congreso Internacional* (Córdoba: Universidad Nacional de Córdoba, 1999), II, 239–47.

10. Andrés Pérez de Ribas, *My Life among the Savage Nations of New Spain* (Los Angeles: Ward Ritchie Press, [1644] 1968).

11. Daniel T. Reff, *Disease, Depopulation, and Culture Change in Northwestern New Spain, 1518–1764* (Salt Lake City: University of Utah Press, 1991).

12. Edward H. Spicer, *Cycles of Conquest: The Impact of Spain, Mexico, and the United States on the Indians of the Southwest, 1533–1960* (Tucson: University of Arizona Press, 1962), 58.

13. Evelyn Hu-DeHart, *Missionaries, Miners and Indians: Spanish Contact with the Yaqui Nation of Northwestern New Spain, 1533–1820* (Tucson: University of Arizona Press, 1981).

14. Peter Masten Dunne, *Pioneer Black Robes on the West Coast* (Berkeley: University of California Press, 1940), 191.

15. Ibid., 180.

16. An interesting question is how ancient gods were adored alongside the new deities. See Joseph M. Murphy, *Working the Spirit: Ceremonies of the African Diaspora* (Boston: Beacon Press, 1994), 220–49.

17. Ernest Burrus, "Mexican Jesuit Authors of Indian Materials in Colonial Times," *AHSI*, 53 (1984); and and María Luisa Olsen de Serrano Redondet, "Los jesuítas y las letras," *Jesuítas. 400 Años en Córdoba. Congreso Internacional* (Córdoba: Universidad Nacional de Córdoba, 1999), II, 267–93.

18. The original catechism by White is lost; a copy of his Ten Commandments

written in Piscataway is in the rare book section of the Georgetown University Library.

19. Axtell, "White Legend: The Jesuit Missions in Maryland," *Maryland Historical Magazine*, 81 (1986): 2.

20. Clayton Coleman Hall, ed., *Narratives of Early Maryland, 1633–1684* (New York: Charles Scribner's Sons, 1925), 130.

21. Ibid., 129.

22. Ibid.

Bibliography

ARCHIVES

The primary sources for much of what has been written in this book are found in the central Jesuit Archive in Rome, Italy, and to a lesser extent in local Jesuit and national archives in America. The Jesuit records in Rome are in the Curia Generalis, 5 Borgo Santo Spiritu, Rome 00100 Italy, and are open to any responsible scholar. The archive has well lit reading rooms and provides microfilm and copy service. The *Novae Franciae, Angliae,* and *Mexicanae* province records in the Jesuit Archive contain material on personnel, economic matters, and specific and general reports to the Superior General in Rome. Letters to these provinces from Rome are in the *Epistolae Generalis* section. The catalogues, especially the *Catalogus Rerum* and the *Catalogus Tertius,* are valuable for economic reports and assessments of individual missionaries. The *Indipetae* section has the letters, carefully preserved, written to the General requesting mission posts. Microfilm copies of many of these materials are in the Pius XII Library of St. Louis University. Georgetown University Library has the old Maryland Province records. The *Archivo General de las Indias,* Seville, Spain, also has considerable holdings concerning the Jesuits in America, However, like the materials in the National Archives of Peru and Argentina, they are more economic and official in nature. For the relationship between Jesuit and Native American, the Jesuit Archives in Rome are essential.

BOOKS AND ARTICLES

Achebe, Chinua. *Things Fall Apart*. New York: Fawcett, 1959.

Acosta, José de. *De Procuranda Indorum Salute*. Madrid: Consejo Superior de Investigaciones Científicas, [1577] 1984.

Adelman, Jeremy, and Stephen Aron. "From Borderlands to Borders: Empires, Nation-States, and the Peoples in Between in North American History." *American Historical Review*, 104 (1999): 814–841.

Alden, Dauril. "Indian Versus Black Slavery in the State of Maranhão During the Seventeenth and Eighteenth Centuries." *Bibliotheca Americana*, 1, no.3 (January, 1983).

————. *The Making of an Enterprise. The Society of Jesus in Portugal, Its Empire, and Beyond, 1540–1750*. Stanford, Calif.: Stanford University Press, 1996.

Alegre, Francisco Javier. *Historia de la Provincia de la Compañía de Jesús de Nueva España*. 3 vols., ed. E.J. Burrus and Félix Zubillaga. Roma: Institutum Historicum Societatis Iesu, 1956–60.

Allen, J. "Big Circle Mounds." *Florida Anthropologist*, 26 (1948): 17–21.

Altman, Ida, and Reginald D. Butler. "The Contact of Cultures: Perspectives on the Quincentenary." *American Historical Review*, 99 (1994): 478–503.

Andrés, Melquíades, et. al. *Historia de la teología española*. Vol. 1, Madrid: Fundación Universitaria Española, 1983.

Arango, Manuel Antonio. *El teatro religioso en la América Española*. Barcelona: Pulvill Libros, 1997.

Arellano, Fernando. *El arte jesuítico en la América española, 1568–1767*. San Cristobal: Universidad Católica del Tachira, 1991.

Aries, Philippe. *At the Hour of Our Death*. New York: Knopf, 1981.

[Arriaga, Pablo José] *The Extirpation of Idolatry in Peru*. Translated and edited by L. Clark Keating. Lexington: University of Kentucky Press, 1968.

Astrain, Antonio. *Historia de la Compañía de Jesús en la Asistencia de España*. 4 vols. Madrid: Est. Tip. "Sucesores de Ribadeneyra," 1913–1925.

Avellaneda, Mercedes. "La alianza militar jesuita-guaraní en la segunda mitad del siglo XVII y los conflictos suscitados con las autoridades locales," *Jesuitas: 400 Años en Córdoba*, 6–85. Córdoba: Congreso Internacional. Tomo I, 1999.

Axtell, James. *The European and the Indian: Essays in the Ethnohistory of Colonial North America*. New York: Oxford University Press, 1981.

————. "White Legend: The Jesuit Missions in Maryland." *Maryland Historical Magazine*, 81 (1986): 1–7.

————. *After Columbus: Essays in the Ethnohistory of Colonial North America*. New York: Oxford University Press, 1988.

————. *Beyond 1492: Encounters in Colonial North America*. New York: Oxford University Press, 1992.

Bailey, Gauvin Alexander. *Art on the Jesuit Missions in Asia and Latin America, 1542–1773*. Toronto: University of Toronto Press, 1999.

Bangert, William V. *A History of the Society of Jesus*. St. Louis: Institute of Jesuit Sources, 1972.

——. *A Bibliographical Essay on the History of the Society of Jesus: Books in English.* St. Louis: Institute of Jesuit Sources, 1976.

Bannon, John Francis, ed. *Bolton and the Spanish Borderlands.* Norman: University of Oklahoma Press, 1974.

Baroja, Pío. "Witchcraft and Catholic Theology," *Early Modern European Witchcraft. Centres and Peripheries.* Edited by Bengt Ankarloo and Gustav Hennigsen, 19–44. Oxford: Oxford University Press, 1990.

Baudin, Louis. *Une Theocratie Socialiste: L'Etat jesuite du paraguay.* Paris: Editions Genin, 1962.

Baudot, Georges. "The Devil and His Magic Spells in Nahua Colonial Literature." In *Five Hundred Years After Columbus: Proceedings of the 47th International Congress of Americanists,* 129–130. Compiled by E. Wyllys Andrews V. and Elizabeth Oster Mozillo. New Orleans: Middle American Research Institute, Tulane University 1994.

Beitzell, Edwin Warfield. *The Jesuit Missions of St. Mary's County, Maryland* (Sponsored by the St. Mary's County Bicentennial Commission), privately printed, 1976.

Berkhofer, Robert F. "White Conceptions of Indians." In *Handbook of North American Indians,* vol. 15. Northeast, 522–547. Washington: Smithsonian Institution Press, 1978.

——. *The White Man's Indian: Images of the American Indian from Columbus to the Present.* New York: Knopf, 1978.

Bertonio, Ludovico. *Vocabulario de la lengua Aymara.* Cochabamba: [1612] 1984.

Block, David. *Mission Culture in the Upper Amazon: Native Tradition, Jesuit Enterprise, and Secular Policy 1660–1880.* Lincoln: University of Nebraska Press, 1994.

Blumers, Teresa. *La contabilidad en las reducciones guaranies.* Asunción: Centro de Estudios Antropológicos, 1992.

Bolton, Herbert Eugene. "The Mission as a Frontier Institution in the Spanish American Colonies." *American Historical Review,* 23 (1917): 42–61.

——. *Rim of Christendom: A Biography of Eusebio Francisco Kino, Pacific Coast Pioneer.* New York: Macmillan, 1936.

Bonvillain, Nancy. "Missionary Role in French Colonial Expansion: An Examination of the Jesuit Relations," *Man in the Northeast,* 29 (1985): 1–13.

Booth, Sally Smith. *Seeds of Anger. Revolts in America 1607–1771.* New York: Hastings House, 1977.

Borah, Woodrow. "The Collection of Tithes in the Bishopric of Oaxaca, 1601–1867." *Hispanic American Historical Review,* (November, 1949): 498–517.

—— and Sherburne F. Cook. *Essays in Population History: Mexico and the Caribbean.* Berkeley: University of California Press, 1981.

Borges, Pedro. "La extirpación de idolatría en Indias como método misional (Siglo XVI)." *Missionalia Hispánica,* 14 (1957): 193–270.

Bossy, John. "Reluctant Colonists: The English Catholics Confront the Atlantic." In *Early Maryland in a Wider World,* edited by David Quinn, 149–164. Detroit: Wayne State University Press, 1982.

Boswell, John. *Christianity, Social Tolerance, and Homosexuality: Gay People in Western*

Europe from the Beginning of the Christian Era to the Fourteenth Century. Chicago: University of Chicago Press, 1980.

Boxer, C. R. *The Christian Century in Japan, 1549–1650.* Berkeley: University of California Press, 1951.

———. *Race Relations in the Portuguese Colonial Empire, 1415–1825.* Oxford: Clarendon Press, 1963.

———. *The Portuguese Seaborne Empire, 1415–1825.* London: Hutchinson, 1969.

———. *Race Relations in the Portuguese Colonial Empire, 1415–1825.* Oxford: Clarendon Press, 1963.

———. "The Problem of the Native Clergy in the Portuguese and Spanish Empires from the Sixteenth to the Eighteenth Centuries." In *Studies in Church History.* vol. 6, *The Mission of the Church and Propagation of the Faith.* Edited by Canon Cuming, 85–105. Cambridge: Cambridge University Press, 1970.

Brodrick, James. *The Origin of the Jesuits.* New York: Longmans, 1941.

———. *St. Ignatius Loyola: The Pilgrim Years.* New York: Farrar, Straus, 1956.

Browne, William Hand, ed. *Archives of Maryland.* 72 vols. Baltimore: Maryland Historical Society, 1883–1916.

Brugger, Robert. *Maryland: A Middle Temperament, 1634–1980.* Baltimore: Johns Hopkins University Press, 1988.

Bry, Theodore de. *Brevis Narratio eorum quae in Florida . . .* 1591.

Burghardt, Walter J., S.J. "The Spiritual Exercises as a Foundation for Educational Ministry." Lecture. Creighton University, Omaha, Nebraska, April 19, 1991. http://www.mu.edu/umi/exercise.html.

Burke, E. M. "State of Pure Nature." In *New Catholic Encyclopedia,* 2nd Edition, vol. 11, 823–824. Detroit: Thomson–Gale, 2003.

Burkhart, Louise M. *The Slippery Earth: Nahua–Christian Moral Dialogue in Sixteenth–Century Mexico.* Tucson: University of Arizona Press, 1989.

Burrus, Ernest. "Father Jacques Marquette, S. J.: His Priesthood in the Light of the Jesuit Roman Archives." *Catholic Historical Review,* 41 (1955): 257–271.

———. *Kino and Manje. Explorers of Sonora and Arizona. Their Vision of the Future. A Study of Their Expeditions and Plans with an Appendix of Thirty Documents.* Rome: Jesuit Historical Institute, 1971.

———. and Félix Zubillaga, eds. *Misiones Mexicanas de la Compañía de Jesús, 1618–1745.* Madrid: José Porrúa Turanzas, 1982.

———. "Mexican Jesuit Authors of Indian Materials in Colonial Times." *AHSI,* 53 (1984): 469–503.

Butler, Ruth Lapham, ed. *Journal of Paul du Ru: February 1 to May 8 1700. Missionary Priest to Louisiana.* Chicago: Claxton Club, 1934.

Camino Alejandro, Jorge Recharte, and Pedro Bidegaray, "Flexibilidad calendárica en la agricultura tradicional de las vertientes orientales de los Andes," In *La tecnología en el mundo andino,* edited by Heather Lechtman and Ana María Soldi, 169–94. México: Universidad Nacional Autónoma de México, 1981.

Campeau, Lucien, S.J., ed. *Monumenta Novae Franciae: La première mission d'Acadie (1602–1616).* Vol. 1. Rome–Québec: Institutum Historicum Societatis Iesu, 1967.

———. *Monumenta Novae Francia: Établissement a Québec (1616–1634)*. Vol. 2. Rome–Québec: Monumenta Historica Societatis Iesu/ Les Presses de l'Universitè Laval, 1979.

———. *Monumenta Novae Francia: Fondation de la Mission Huronne (1635–1637)*. Vol. 3. Rome–Québec: Monumenta Historica Societatis Iesu /Les Presses de l'Université Laval, 1987.

———. *Monumenta Novae Franciae: Les grandes épreuves (1638–1640)*. Vol. 4. Rome–Montréal: Institutum Historicum Societatis Iesu / Les Editions Bellarmin, 1989.

———. *Monumenta Novae Franciae: La bonne nouvelle reçue (1641–1643)*. Vol. 5. Rome–Montréal: Institutum Historicum Societatis Iesu / Les Editions Bellarmin, 1990.

———. *Monumenta Novae Francia: Recherche de la paix (1644–1646)*. Vol. 6. Rome/Montréal: Institutum Historicum Societatis Iesu, 1992.

———. *Monumenta Novae Franciae Le Temoignage du sang (1647–1650)*. Vol. 7. Rome/Montreal: Institutum Historicum Societatis Iesu, 1994.

———. "Roman Catholic Missions in New France." In *Handbook of North American Indians*. Edited by Bruce Trigger, 464–71. Vol. 15. *Northeast*. Washington, D.C.: Smithsonian Institution Press, 1978.

———. *Catastrophe démographique sur le Grand Lacs. Les premieres habitants du Québec*. Montréal: Ed. Bellarmin, 1986.

Carbonell de Masy, Rafael. "Les 'réductions' du Paraguay." *Études*, 375 (July August 1991): 101–108.

———. *Estrategias de desarrollo rural en los pueblos guaranies, 1609–1767*. Barcelona: Bosch, 1992.

Castelli, Amalia. "Tunupa: Divinidad del Altiplano." *Etnohistoria y Antropología Andina*, *(Primera Jornada del Museo Nacional de Historia)*, Lima: 1978, 201–204.

Cervantes, Fernando. *The Devil in the New World: The Impact of Diabolism in New Spain*. New Haven, Conn.: Yale University Press, 1994.

Cevallos García, Gabriel, et al. *Arte Colonial de Ecuador. Siglos XVI–XVII*. Quito: Salvat Editores Ecuatoriana S. A. Quito, 1977.

Chevalier, François. *La formation des grandes domaines au Mexique: Terre et Société aux XVIe–XVIIe Siècles*. Paris: Institut d'Ethnologie, 1952.

Chiappelli, Fredi, ed. *First Images of America: The Impact of the New World on the Old*. Berkeley: University of California Press, I, 1976.

Christian, William A. *Apparitions in Late Medieval and Renaissance Spain*. Princeton, N.J.: Princeton University Press, 1981.

Clancy, Thomas H. "The First Generation of English Jesuits." *ARSI*, 57: 113 (1988): 137–162.

Clemens, Paul G. E. "Economy and Society on Maryland's Eastern Shore, 1689–1733." In *Law, Society, and Politics in Early Maryland*, edited by Aubrey C. Land, Lois Green Carr, and Edward Papenfuse, 153–70. Baltimore: Johns Hopkins University Press, 1977.

Clifford, James. *The Predicament of Culture*. Cambridge, Mass.: Harvard University Press, 1988.

Cobo, Bernabe. *Inca Religion and Customs*. Translated and edited by Roland Hamilton and John Howland Rowe. Austin: University of Texas Press, 1991.

Cobo, Bernabe. *History of the Inca Empire.* Austin: University of Texas Press, 1979.

Cohen, Thomas V. "Why the Jesuits Joined, 1540–1600." Historical Papers. *Canadian Historical Association,* (Ottawa, 1974).

Cohn, Bernard. *Colonialism and Its Form of Knowledge.* Princeton, N.J.: Princeton University Press, 1996.

Collinson, Patrick. "The Late Medieval Church and its Reformation (1400–1600)." In *Oxford Illustrated History of Christianity.* edited by John McManners, 233–66. New York: Oxford University Press, 1990.

Collis, Maurice. *Cortés and Montezuma.* London: Faber and Faber, 1963.

Colmenares, Germán. *Las haciendas de los jesuitas en el Nuevo Reino de Granada.* Bogotá, 1969.

Conn, Walter. *Christian Conversion: A Developmental Interpretation of Autonomy and Surrender.* New York: Paulist Press, 1986.

Cook, Noble David. *Demographic Collapse: Indian Peru, 1520–1620.* New York: Cambridge University Press, 1981.

Cortesão, Jaime. *Jesuítas e bandeirantes no Guaira (1549–1640).* Rio de Janeiro: Biblioteca Nacional, 1951.

———. *Jesuítas e bandeirantes no Tape (1615–1641).* Rio de Janeiro: Biblioteca Nacional, 1969.

Costa, Horacio de la. *The Jesuits in the Philippines, 1581–1768.* Cambridge, Mass.: Harvard University Press, 1961.

Crosby, Alfred W. "Virgin Soil Epidemics as a Factor in the Aboriginal Depopulation of America." *William and Mary Quarterly,* 33 (1976): 289–299.

———. *The Colombian Exchange: Biological and Cultural Consequences of 1492.* Westport: Greenwood, 1972.

———. *Ecological Imperialism: The Biological Expansion of Europe, 900–1900.* New York: Cambridge University Press, 1986.

Craine, Eugene R., and Reginald C. Reindorp. *Chronicles of Michoacan.* Norman: University of Oklahoma Press, 1970.

Curran, Robert Emmett, ed. *American Jesuit Spirituality: The Maryland Tradition 1634–1900.* New York: Paulist Press, 1988.

Cushner, Nicholas P. "Slave Mortality and Reproduction on Jesuit Haciendas in Colonial Peru." *Hispanic American Historical Review,* 55 (1975): 177–199.

———. *Lords of the Land: Sugar, Wine, and Jesuit Estates of Coastal Peru, 1600–1767.* Albany: State University of New York Press, 1980.

———. " 'Palaces in the Desert': The Jesuits in Paraguay." *America* (February 11, 1978): 94–95.

———. *Farm and Factory. The Jesuits and the Development of Agrarian Capitalism in Colonial Quito, 1600–1767.* Albany: State University of New York Press, 1982.

———. *Jesuit Ranches and the Agrarian Development of Colonial Argentina, 1650–1767.* Albany: State University of New York Press, 1983.

———."La mortalidad de los esclavos en las haciendas coloniales." In *La iglesia en la economía de América Latina. Siglos XVI al XIX.* Edited by A.J. Bauer, 314–345. México: Instituto Nacional de Antropología e Historia, 1986.

Dailey, R. C. "The Role of Alcohol among North American Indian Tribes as Reported in the Jesuit Relations." *Anthropologica*, 10 (1968): 45–59.

Dalmases, Cándido. *Francis Borgia: Grandee of Spain*. St. Louis: Institute of Jesuit Sources, 1991.

Deagan, Kathleen A. "Spanish-Indian Interaction in Sixteenth-Century Florida and Hispaniola." In William W. Fitzhugh, *Cultures in Contact: The Impact of European Contacts on Native American Cultural Institutions A.D 1000–1800*, 281–318. Washington, D.C.: Smithsonian Institution Press, 1985.

Decorme, Gerard. *La obra de los jesuítas mexicanos durante la época colonial, 1572–1767*. México: Antiqua Librería Robredo de José Porrúa e Hijos, 2 Vols., 1941.

Deeds, Susan M. *Defiance and Deference in Mexico's Colonial North: Indians Under Spanish Rule in Nueva Viscaya*. Austin: University of Texas Press, 2003.

Delanglez, Jean. *The French Jesuits in Lower Louisiana (1700–1763)*. Washington: Catholic University of America Press, 1935.

Dening, Greg. *Islands and Beaches: Discourse on a Silent Land, Marquesas, 1774–1880*. Honolulu: University Press of Hawaii, 1980.

Dennis, Matthew. *Cultivating a Landscape of Peace: Iroquois–European Encounters in Seventeenth-Century America*. Ithaca: Cornell University Press, 1993.

Devitt, Edward I. "Letters of Father Joseph Mosley, 1757–1786." *The Woodstock Letters*, 25 (1906): 129–138.

d'Evreux, Yves. *Viagem ao norte do Brasil feita nos annos de 1613 a 1614 . . .* traduzida pelo Dr. Cezar Augusto Marques. Maranhão: 1874.

Dickason, Olive Patricia. *The Myth of the Savage: And the Beginnings of French Colonialism in the Americas*. Alberta: University of Alberta Press, 1984.

Dirks, Nicholas, ed. *Culture, Power and History: A Reader in Contemporary Social Theory*. Princeton, N.J.: Princeton University Press, 1994.

Dobyns, Henry F. *Their Numbers Become Thinned: Native American Population Dynamics in Eastern North America*. Knoxville: University of Tennessee Press, 1983.

———. "Commentary on Native American Demography." *Ethnohistory*, 31 (1989) 299–307.

Doctrina Christiana y Catecismo para instrucción de los Indios. Madrid: Consejo Superior de Investigaciones Científicas, [Lima, 1584], 1985

Donnelly, John Patrick. "Antonio Possevino's Plan for World Evangelization." *Catholic Historical Review*, 74 (1988): 179–198.

Donnelly, Joseph P. S.J., *Jacques Marquette, S.J. 1637–1675*. Chicago: Loyola University Press, 1968.

———. *Thwaites' Jesuit Relations: Errata and Addenda*. Chicago: Loyola University Press, 1967.

Donohue, J. Augustine. "The Unlucky Jesuit Mission of Bac, 1732–1767." In Charles W. Polzer, *The Jesuit Missions of Northern Mexico*, 465–477. New York: Garland, 1991.

———. *After Kino: Jesuit Missions in Northwestern New Spain, 1711–1767*. Rome: Jesuit Historical Institute, 1969.

Dudley, Edward J., ed. *The Wild Man Within: An Image in Western Thought from the Renaissance to Romanticism*. Pittsburgh: University of Pittsburgh Press, 1973.

Dudon, Paul. *Ignatius of Loyola*. Milwaukee: Bruce, 1949.

Dunne, Peter Masten. *Pioneer Black Robes on the West Coast*. Berkeley: University of California Press, 1940.

——. *Early Jesuit Missions in Tarahumara*. Berkeley: University of California Press, 1948.

Durkin, Joseph T. "Catholic Training for Maryland Catholics," *Historical Records and Studies*, 32 (1941): 70–82.

Duviols, Pierre. *La lutte contre les réligions autochtones dans le Pérou colonial*. Lima: Institut Francais d'Etudes Andines, 1971.

Eccles, William J. "The Fur Trade in the Colonial Northeast," In *Handbook of North American Indians*, edited by Bruce Trigger, 324–34, vol. 15, *Northeast*. Washington, D.C., Smithsonian Institution Press, 1978.

Eccles, W. C. *The Canadian Frontier, 1534–1760*. Albuquerque: University of New Mexico Press, 1983.

Echánove, A. "Origen y evolución de la idea jesuítica de "Reducciones" en las misiones del Virreinato del Peru." *Missionalia Hispánica*, 12 (1955): 95–144.

——. "Origen y evolucion de la idea jesuítica de "Reducciones" en las misiones del Virreinato del Peru. La residencia de Julí, patrón y esquema de reducciones." *Missionalia Hispánica*, 13 (1956): 497–540.

Egaña, Antonio de. "La visión humanística del indio americano en los primeros jesuitas peruanos (1568–1576)." In *Studi Sulla Chiesa Antica E Sull'Umanismo*. Rome: Gregorian University, 1954.

Elliott, John H. *Imperial Spain, 1469–1716*. New York: 1963.

——. "Renaissance Europe and America: A Blunted Impact." In *First Images of America: The Impact of the New World on the Old*, edited by Fredi Chiapelli, 11–23. Berkeley: University of California Press, 1976.

Ewing, Russell Charles. "The Pima Uprising of 1751: A Study of Spanish–Indian Relations on the Frontier of New Spain." In *Greater America: Essays in Honor of Herbert Eugene Bolton*, 259–80. Berkeley: University of California Press, 1945.

Ezran, Maurice. *Une colonisation douce: Les missions du Paraguay*. Paris: Harmattan, 1989.

Fabian, Johannes. *Time and the Other. How Anthropology Makes Its Object*. New York: Columbia University Press, 1983.

Fagan, Brian. *The Great Journey*. London: Thames and Hudson, 1987.

——. *Ancient North America*. New York: Thames and Hudson, 1995.

Feest, Christian F. "Nanticoke and Neighboring Tribes." In *Handbook of North American Indians*. Edited by Bruce Trigger, 240–252, vol. 15, *Northeast*. Washington, D.C.: Smithsonian Institution Press, 1978.

Fitzhugh, William W. *Cultures in Contact: The Impact of European Contacts on Native American Cultural Institutions A.D. 1000–1800*. Washington, D.C.: Smithsonian Institution Press, 1985.

Five Hundred Years After Columbus. Proceedings of the 47th International Congress of Americanists. Compiled by E. Wyllys Andrews V and Elizabeth Oster Mozillo. New Orleans: Middle American Research Institute, Tulane University, 1994.

Flint, Irene. *The Rise of Magic in Early Medieval Europe.* Princeton, N.J.: Princeton University Press, 1991.

Fogarty, Gerald P, S.J., Joseph Durkin, and Robert Emmett Curran, eds. *The Maryland Jesuits, 1634–1833.* Baltimore: Maryland Province of the Society of Jesus, 1976.

Funes, María Alejandra. "Intervenciones arqueológicas en el sector sur del Conjunto Jesuítico–Guaraní de Nuestra Señora de Loreto, provincia de Misiones (Argentina)." *Jesuitas: 400 Años en Córdoba, Congreso Internacional,* Tomo 2. Córdoba: Universidad Nacional de Córdoba, 1999.

Furlong, Guillermo. *Cartografía jesuítica del Río de la Plata.* Buenos Aires: Tallares S. A. Casa Jacobo Peuser, 1936.

———. *Misiones y sus pueblos de Guaranies.* Buenos Aires: 1962.

———. *Bernardo Nusdorffer y su "Novena Parte" (1760).* Buenos Aires: Ediciones Theoría, 1971.

Gagliano, Joseph, and Charles Ronan. *Jesuit Encounters in the New World: Jesuit Chroniclers, Geographers, Educators, and Missionaries in the Americas, 1549–1767.* Rome: Biblioteca Instituti Historici S.I., 1997.

Gandía, Enrique de. *Francisco de Alfaro y la condición social de los Indios.* Buenos Aires: 1939.

Ganson, Barbara. *The Guaraní under Spanish Rule in the Río de la Plata.* Stanford, Calif.: Stanford University Press, 2003.

García Navarro, Luis. *Sonora y Sinaloa en el siglo XVII.* Sevilla: Escuela de Estudios Hispano–Americanos, 1967.

García Soriano, Justo. "El teatro del Colegio en España," *Boletín de la Real Academia Española,* 16 (1927).

Garcilaso de la Vega. *Los Comentarios. Reales,* Bk. 2, Ch. 28.

Gerhard, Peter. *A Guide to the Historical Geography of New Spain.* Cambridge: Cambridge University Press, 1972.

———. *The Northern Frontier of New Spain.* Princeton, N.J.: Princeton University Press, 1982.

Gibson, Charles. *The Aztecs under Spanish Rule.* Stanford, Calif.: Stanford University Press, 1978.

Goddard, Peter. "Converting the *Sauvage:* Jesuit and Montagnais in Seventeenth–Century New France." *Catholic Historical Review,* 84 (1998): 219–239.

Goggin, John. "The Tekesta of South Florida." *Florida Historical Quarterly,* 4: 18 (1940): 274–280.

———. and William Sturtevant. "The Calusa: A Stratified, Nonagricultural Society (with notes on sibling marriage)," In *Explorations in Cultural Anthropology. Essays in Honor of George Peter Murdoch,* edited by W.H. Goodenough, 179–219, New York: McGraw–Hill, 1964.

González–R, Luis. ed. *Revoltes des Indiens Tarahumars (1626–1724): Traduction du latin, introduction, commentaires.* Paris: Institut des Hautes Etudes de L'Amerique Latin, 1969.

Greeley, Andrew. "The Faith We Have Lost," *America,* no. 9 (1993): esp. 26–27.

———. "Magic in the Age of Faith," *America,* no. 10 (1993): 8–14.

———. "Why Do Catholics Stay in the Church? Because of the Stories," *New York Times Magazine*, July 10, 1994.

Greenblat, Stephen. *Renaissance Self-Fashioning: From More to Shakespeare.* Chicago: University of Chicago Press, 1980.

Greer, Allan. *The Jesuit Relations. Natives and Missionaries in Seventeenth-Century North America.* Boston/New York: Bedford/St. Martin's, 2000.

Griffen, Nigel. *Jesuit School Drama: A Checklist of Critical Literature.* London: Grant and Cutler, 1976.

Guglieri Navarro, Araceli. *Documentos de la Compañía de Jesús en el Archivo Histórico Nacional.* Madrid: Editorial Razón y Fé, 1967.

Hall, Clayton Coleman, ed. *Narratives of Early Maryland, 1633–1684.* New York: Charles Scribner's Sons, 1925.

Hamilton, Bernard. *Religion in the Medieval West.* London: Edward Arnold, 1986.

Hamilton, Raphael. *Marquette's Explorations: The Narratives Reexamined.* Madison: University of Wisconsin Press, 1970.

Hanke, Lewis. *The Spanish Struggle for Justice in the Conquest of America.* Philadelphia: University of Pennsylvania Press, 1949.

———. *Aristotle and the American Indians: A Study in Race Prejudice in the Modern World.* Bloomington: Indiana University Press, 1959.

Harris, Steven J. "Mapping Jesuit Science: The Role of Travel in the Geography of Knowledge." In *The Jesuits: Cultures, Sciences, and the Arts, 1540–1773,* 212–240. Toronto: University of Toronto Press, 1999.

Haro, María Paz. "Religious Orders, the Indian, and the Conquest," *Encounters* (summer, 1992): 20–27.

Haviland, William A. *Cultural Anthropology.* New York: Wadsworth/Thompson Learning, 2002.

Healy, George R. "The French Jesuits and the Idea of the Noble Savage." *William and Mary Quarterly,* 15 (1958): 143–67.

Hemming, John. *Red Gold: The Conquest of the Brazilian Indians, 1500–1760.* Cambridge, Mass.: Harvard University Press, 1978.

Hernández, Pablo. *Misiones del Paraguay: Organización social de las doctrinas guaranies de la Compañía de Jesús.* Barcelona: G. Gili, 1913.

Hoffmann, Paul. *A New Andalucia and a Way to the Orient: The American Southeast during the Sixteenth Century.* Baton Rouge: Louisiana State University Press, 1990.

Holborn, Hajo. *A History of Modern Germany: The Reformation.* New York: Alfred A. Knopf, 1959.

Honour, Hugh. *The New Golden Land. European Images of America from the Discoveries to the Present Time.* New York: Pantheon Books, 1975.

Horn, Walter, and Ernest Born. *The Plan of St. Gall: A Study of the Architecture and Economy of and Life in a Paradigmatic Carolingian Monastery.* 3 vols. Berkeley: University of California Press, 1979.

Hu-DeHart, Evelyn. *Missionaries, Miners and Indians: Spanish Contact with the Yaqui Nation of Northwestern New Spain, 1533–1820.* Tucson: University of Arizona Press, 1981.

Hughes, Thomas. *History of the Society of Jesus in North America: Colonial and Federal.*
    2 Vols. London: Longmans, Green, 1908–1917.
Hultkrantz, Ake. *Conceptions of the Soul Among North American Indians: A Study in
    Religious Ethnology.* Stockholm: Ethnographical Museum of Sweden, 1953.
Hunt, George. *The Wars of the Iroquois: A Study in Intertribal Trade Relations.* Madison:
    University of Wisconsin Press, 1940.
Hyslop, John. *The Inka Road System.* New York: Academic Press, 1984.
———. *Inka Settlement Planning.* Austin: University of Texas Press, 1990.
Ingham, John M. *Mary, Michael, and Lucifer: Folk Catholicism in Central Mexico.* Aus-
    tin: University of Texas Press, 1986.
Ives, J. Moss. *The Ark and the Dove: The Beginnings of Civil and Religious Liberties in
    America.* New York: Cooper Square Publishers, 1969.
Jacobsen, Jerome V., S.J. *Educational Foundations of the Jesuits in Sixteenth Century
    New Spain.* Berkeley: University of California Press, 1938.
James, William. *The Varieties of Religious Experience.* New York: Harper, 1914.
Javellana, Rene. *Wood and Stone: For God's Greater Glory. Jesuit Art and Architecture in
    the Philippines.* Manila: Ateneo de Manila University Press, 1991.
Jedin, Hubert. *A History of the Council of Trent,* 2 vols. Translated from the German by
    Dom Ernest Graf, O. S. B. St. Louis: Herder, 1957–1961.
Jesuitas. 400 años en Córdoba. Congreso Internacional 21 al 24 de setiembre de 1999. Cór-
    doba: Universidad Nacional de Córdoba, 1999.
Jones, Jr., Oakah L. *Nueva Vizcaya: Heartland of the Spanish Frontier.* Albuquerque:
    University of New Mexico Press, 1988.
Jordan, David W. "Maryland's Privy Council, 1637–1715." In *Law, Society, and Politics
    in Early Maryland,* edited by Aubrey C. Land, Lois Green Carr, and Edward Pa-
    penfuse, 65–87. Baltimore: Johns Hopkins University Press, 1977.
Kelemen, Pal. *Baroque and Rococo in Latin America.* New York: Macmillan, 1951.
Kenny, Michael. *The Romance of the Floridas: The Finding and the Founding.* New York:
    AMS Press, 1970.
Kingdon, Robert. *Transition and Revolution: Problems and Issues of European Renais-
    sance and Reformation History.* Minneapolis: Burgess, 1974.
Konrad, Herman W. *A Jesuit Hacienda in Colonial Mexico: Santa Lucía, 1576–1767.*
    Stanford, Calif.: Stanford University Press, 1980.
Kubler, Georg. *Art and Architecture in Spain and Portugal and Its Possessions.* New Ha-
    ven, Conn.: Yale University Press, 1964.
Lacombe, Robert. *Guaranis et jésuites: Un combat pour la liberté.* Paris: Société
    d'Ethnografie, 1993.
Lafaye, Jacques. "Une lettre inédite, du XVIe siècle, relative aux Collèges D'Indiens de
    la Compagnie de Jésus en Nouvelle Espagne." *Annales de la Faculte des Lettres
    D'Aix,* (38: 1982): 9–21.
La Flèche, Guy. *Le missionaire, L'apostat, le sorcier: Relation de 1634 de Paul LeJeune.*
    Montréal: Presses de l'Université de Montréal, 1973.
Larkin, John A. "The Macabebe Scouts and Their Reputation." *Singsing,* 1 (2004): 16.
Layhey, Raymond J. "The Role of Religion in Lord Baltimore's Colonial Enterprise."
    Maryland Historical Magazine, 72 (winter, 1977): 492–511.

Leite, Serafim. "Terras que deu Estácio de Sá ao Colegio do Rio de Janeiro." *Brotéria*, 20 (1935).

———.*Cartas dos premieros jesuítas do Brasil.* São Paulo: Comissão do IV Centenario da Cidade de São Paulo, 1954.

———. *História da Companhia de Jesus no Brazil,* 10 vols. Lisbon: Instituto Nacional do Livro, 1938–50.

Leonhardt, P. Carlos. *Documentos para la Historia Argentina: Tomo XIX Iglesia. Cartas anuas de la Provincia del Paraguay, Chile y Tucumán de la Compañía de Jesús (1609–1614).* Buenos Aires: Talleres S.A. Casa Jacobo Peuser, 1927; Tomo XX (1615–1637), 1929.

Lértora Mendoza, Celina A. "Los jesuítas y la introducción de la ciencia moderna en América colonial." In *Jesuitas. 400 años en Córdoba. Congreso Internacional.* vol. 2, 229–244. Córdoba: Universidad Nacional de Córdoba, 1999.

Levy, Jerrold and Stephen J. Kunitz. *Indian Drinking: Navajo Practices and Anglo–American Theories.* New York: John Wiley and Sons, 1974.

Lewis, Bernard, "The Roots of Muslim Rage," *Atlantic Monthly,* September (1990): 47–54.

Lewis, Clifford M. and Albert J. Loomie. *The Spanish Jesuit Mission in Virginia 1570–1572.* Chapel Hill: University of North Carolina Press, 1953.

Liste de Missionaires Jesuites. Nouvelle France et Louisiane. Montréal: Colege Sainte–Marie, 1929.

Lohman Villena, Guillermo. *Historia de la arte dramática.* Lima: 1954.

López de Gómara, Francisco. *Historia general de las Indias* [1551]. Barcelona: Editorial Iberia, 1954.

Lowery, Woodbury. *The Spanish Settlements within the Present Limits of the United States: Florida 1562–1574.* New York: Russell and Russell, 1959.

Lucas, Thomas M. *Landmarking: City, Church and Jesuit Urban Strategy.* Chicago: Loyola Press, 1997.

Lunenfeld, Marvin, ed. *1492: Discovery, Invasion, Encounter: Sources and Interpretations.* Lexington: D. C. Heath: 1991.

Lyon, Eugene. *The Enterprise of Florida: Pedro Menéndez de Aviles and the Spanish Conquest of 1565–1568.* Gainesville: University Press of Florida, 1976.

MacCormack, Sabine. *Religion in the Andes.* Princeton, N.J.: Princeton University Press, 1993.

Macedo, Hector. "Recognizing the Unknown: The Discoverers and the Discovered in the Age of European Expansion." *Camões Center Quarterly,* 4 (1992): 8–13.

Macera, Pablo. *Mapas coloniales de haciendas cuzqueñas.* Lima: Universidad Nacional Mayor de San Marcos, 1968.

Maeder, Ernesto. "La población de las Misiones de Guaranies (1641–1682): Reubicación de los pueblos y consequencias demográficas." *Estudios Iberoamericanos,* 15 (1989): 49–68.

———., ed. *Cartas Anuas de la Provincia jesuítica del Paraguay, 1632–1634.* Buenos Aires: Academia Nacional de la Historia, 1990.

Main, Gloria. "Maryland and the Chesapeake Economy, 1670–1720." In *Law, Society,*

and Politics in Early Maryland, Edited by Aubry C. Land, Lois Green Carr, and
    Edward C. Papenfuse. Baltimore: Johns Hopkins University Press, 1977.
————. Tobacco Colony: Life in Early Maryland, 1650–1720. Princeton, N.J.: Princeton
    University Press, 1982.
Mancia, Anita. "La controversia con i protestanti e i programmi degli studi teologici
    nella Compagnia di Gesu." AHSI 54 (1985): 3–43.
Markham, Sidney. Architecture and Urbanization in Colonial Chiapas, Mexico. Philadel-
    phia: American Philosophical Society, 1984.
Martin, A. Lynn. The Jesuit Mind: The Mentality of an Elite in Early Modern France.
    Ithaca, N.Y.: Cornell University Press, 1988.
Martin, Calvin. Keepers of the Game: Indian–Animal Relationship and the Fur Trade.
    Berkeley: University of California Press, 1978.
Martin, Luis. The Intellectual Conquest of Peru: The Jesuit College of San Pablo, 1568–
    1767. New York: Fordham University Press, 1968.
Martin, Ruth. Witchcraft and the Inquisition in Venice, 1550–1650. Oxford: Basil Black-
    well, 1989.
Marzal, Manuel M. Estudios sobre religión campesina. Lima: Pontificia Universidad Ca-
    tólica del Peru, 1977.
Mason, J. Alden. The Ancient Civilizations of Peru. New York: Pelican, 1988.
Mateos, Francisco, ed.. Historia general de la Compañía de Jesús en la provincia del Perú.
    Crónica anónima de 1600 . . . Madrid: Consejo Superior de Investigaciones Cientí-
    ficas, 1944.
McAndrew, John. The Open Air Churches of Sixteenth–Century Mexico. Cambridge,
    Mass.: Harvard University Press, 1965.
McCabe, William H. An Introduction to Jesuit Theater: A Posthumous Work. St. Louis:
    Institute of Jesuit Sources, 1983.
McDonough, Peter. Men Astutely Trained: A History of the Jesuits in the American Cen-
    tury. New York: Free Press, 1992.
McGrath, Alistair. Reformation Thought: An Introduction. Oxford: Basil Blackwell, 1988.
McNally, Robert E. The Council of Trent, the "Spiritual Exercises," and the Catholic Re-
    form. Philadelphia: Fortress Press, 1970.
Mecham, J. Lloyd. Church and State in Latin America. Chapel Hill: University of
    North Carolina Press, 1966.
Medina, José Toribio. La imprenta en Lima. Santiago de Chile: Impreso y Grabado en
    Casa del Autor, 1904–17.
Meiklejohn, Norman. La iglesia y los Lupaqas durante la colonia. Cuzco: Centro de Es-
    tudios Rurales Bartolomé de las Casas, 1988.
Meissner, William W. Ignatius of Loyola: The Psychology of a Saint. New Haven, Conn.:
    Yale University Press, 1992.
Metraux, Alfred. "Les migrations historiques des Tupi–Guarani." Journal de la Societe
    des Americanistes de Paris 19 (1928): 1–45.
Michener, James. Hawaii. New York: Faucett, 1959.
Milanich, Jerald T. Archaeology of Precolombian Florida. Gainesville: University Press of
    Florida, 1994.

Milanich, Jerald T., and William C. Sturtevant. *Francisco Pareja's Confessionario: A Documentary Source for Timucuan Ethnography*. Tallahassee: Division of Archives, History, and Records Management, Florida Department of State, 1972.

Milanich, Jerald T., and Charles H. Fairbanks. *Florida Archaeology*. New York: Academic Press, 1980.

———— and Samuel Proctor, eds. *Tacachale: Essays on the Indians of Florida and Southeastern Georgia during the Historic Period*. Gainesville: University Press of Florida, 1978.

———— and Susan Milbrath, eds. *First Encounters: Spanish Explorations in the Caribbean and the United States, 1492–1570*. Gainesville: University Press of Florida, 1989.

Milanich, Jerald T., *Florida Indians and the Invasion from Europe*. Gainsville: University Press of Florida, 1995.

Miller, Henry M. "Baroque Cities in the Wilderness: Archaeology and Urban Development in the Colonial Chesapeake." *Historical Archaeology*, 22 (1988): 57–73.

Millones, Luis. "Religion and Power in the Andes: Idolatrous Curacas of the Central Sierra." *Ethnohistory*, 26 no. 3 (summer, 1979): 243–62.

Mitchell, David. *The Jesuits: A History*. London: Macdonald, 1980.

Monumenta Ignaciana. Scripta de S. Ignacio. Rome: Institutum Historicum Societates Iesu, 1904.

Morales, Martín María. "Los comienzos de las Reducciones de la Provincia del Paraguay en relación con el derecho indiano y el Instituto de la Compañía de Jesús." *AHSI*, 67 (1998): 3–129.

Morissoneau, Christian. "Huron of Lorette." In *Handbook of North American Indians*, edited by Bruce Trigger, 389–93, vol. 15, Northeast. Washington, D.C.: Smithsonian Institution Press, 1978.

Mörner, Magnus. *The Economic and Political Activities of the Jesuits in the La Plata Region: The Hapsburg Era*. Stockholm: Institute of Ibero–American Studies, 1953.

————. "The Guaraní Mission and the Segregation Policy of the Spanish Crown." *AHSI*, 30 (1961): 376–383.

Morrison, Kenneth. *The Embattled Northeast: The Elusive Ideal of Alliance in Abenaki–Euramerican Relations*. Berkeley: University of California Press, 1984.

Mullen, Robert J. *Architecture and Its Sculpture in Viceregal Mexico*. Austin: University of Texas Press, 1997.

Mungello, David E. *Curious Land: Jesuit Accommodation and the Origins of Sinology*. Stuttgart: Franz Steiner Verlag, 1985.

————. *The Forgotten Christians of Hangzhou*. Honolulu: University of Hawaii Press, 1993.

Murphy, Joseph M. *Working the Spirit: Ceremonies of the African Diaspora*. Boston: Beacon Press, 1994.

Murphy, Thomas, S. J. *Jesuit Slaveholding in Maryland: 1717–1838*. New York: Routledge, 2001.

Nader, Helen. *Liberty in Absolutist Spain: The Habsburg Sale of Towns, 1516–1700*. Baltimore: Johns Hopkins University Press, 1990.

Nash, Gary B, and Julie Roy Jeffrey. *The American People: Creating a Nation and a Society*. Fifth Edition. New York: Longman, 2001.

Netanyahu, B. *The Origins of the Inquisition in Fifteenth Century Spain*. New York: Random House, 1994.

Nicolas, Antonio T. de. *Power of Imaging: Ignatius de Loyola. A Philosophical Hermeneutic of Imagining Through the Collected Works of Ignatius de Loyola. With a Translation of These Works*. Albany: State University of New York Press, 1986.

Nieto Vélez, Armando. "Jesuitas en el mundo andino: las reducciones de Julí." *Revista Peruana de Historia Eclesiástica*, 3 (1994): 129–44.

Nolan, J.F. "The Liquor Problem and the Jesuit Mission in New France." *Acta et Dicta*, 3 (1911–1914): 91–141.

Noonan, John T. *A Church that Can and Cannot Change. The Development of Catholic Moral Teaching*. Notre Dame: Notre Dame University Press, 2005.

Olsen de Serrano Redondet, María Luisa. "Los jesuítas y las letras." *Jesuítas. 400 Años en Córdoba. Congreso Internacional*. II, 267–93. Córdoba: Universidad Nacional de Córdoba, 1999.

O'Malley, John W. *The First Jesuits*. Cambridge: Harvard University Press, 1993.

———, et al. *The Jesuits: Cultures, Sciences, and the Arts, 1540–1773*. Toronto: University of Toronto Press, 1999.

Pagden, Anthony. *The Fall of Natural Man: The American Indian and the Origins of Comparative Ethnology*. New York: Cambridge University Press, 1982.

———. *European Encounters with the New World: From Renaissance to Romanticism*. New Haven, Conn.: Yale University Press, 1993.

Page, Carlos A. *Manzana jesuítica de la ciudad de Córdoba*. Córdoba: Universidad Nacional de Córdoba, 1999.

Parkman, Francis. *The Jesuits in North America in the Seventeenth Century: France and England in North America*. Part Second. Boston: Little, Brown, 1914.

Parry, John. *The Age of Reconaissance*. London: Weidenfeld and Nicolson, 1963.

Pastells, Pablo, S.J. *Historia de la Compañía de Jesús en la Provincia del Paraguay . . . según los documentos originales del Archivo General de Indias*. 6 vols. Madrid: Librería General de Victoriano Suárez, 1912–1946.

Pease G. Y., Franklin. *El dios creador andino*. Lima: Mosca Azul Editores, 1973.

———. "La cultura en el Peru en los tiempos de la evangelización." *Revista Peruana de Historia Eclesiástica*, 3 (1994): 207–217.

Pegis, Anton C. "Molina and Human Liberty," In Gerard Smith, S.J., ed. *Jesuit Thinkers of the Renaissance*. Milwaukee: Marquette University Press, 1939.

Pérez de Ribas, Andrés. *My Life among the Savage Nations of New Spain*. Los Angeles: Ward Ritchie Press, [1644] 1968.

Phelan, John Leddy. *The Millenial Kingdom of the Franciscans in the New World*. Berkeley: University of California Press, 1970.

Pinto, Basil de. "The Plan of St. Gall." *America*, 143 (1980): 362–363.

Polgar, László. *Bibliografie sur l'histoire de la Compagnie de Jésus, 1901–1980*. 2 vols. Rome: Institutum Historicum S.I., 1981–1986.

Polzer, Charles W. *Rules and Precepts of the Jesuit Missions of Northwestern New Spain*. Tucson: University of Arizona Press, 1976.

———. *The Jesuit Missions of Northern Mexico*. New York: Garland, 1991.

Poole, Stafford. "Some Observations on Mission Methods and Native Reactions in Sixteenth–Century New Spain." *The Americas,* 50 (1994): 337–349.

Powell, Philip Wayne. *Soldiers, Indians, and Silver: The Northward Advance of New Spain, 1550–1600.* Berkeley: University of California Press, 1952.

———. "North America's First Frontier, 1546–1603," In *Essays on Frontiers in World History.* Edited by Philip Wayne Powell et al. College Station: Texas A&M University Press, 1983.

Prem, Hanns. *Milpa y Hacienda. Tenencia de la tierra indígena y española en la Cuenca del Alto Atoyac, Puebla, México.* Weisbaden: Franz Steiner Verlag, 1978.

Quinn, David. *North America from Earliest Discovery to First Settlements: The Norse Voyages to 1612.* New York: Harper and Row, 1977.

———. ed. *New American World. A Documentary History of North America to 1612.* New York: Arno Press, 1979.

———. "Introduction: Prelude to Maryland." In *Early Maryland in a Wider World.* edited by David Quinn, 11–29. Detroit: Wayne State University Press, 1982.

Rahner, Karl, and Paul Imhoff. *Ignatius of Loyola.* New York: Collins, 1979.

Reff, Daniel T. *Disease, Depopulation, and Culture Change in Northwestern New Spain, 1518–1764.* Salt Lake City: University of Utah Press, 1991.

Restall, Matthew. *Seven Myths of the Spanish Conquest.* New York: Oxford University Press, 2003.

———. "The Spanish Conquest Revisited." *Historically Speaking* (5 May/June 2004): 2–5.

Ricard, Robert. *La "conquête spirituelle" du Mexique: Essai sur l'apostolat et les méthodes missionaires des Ordres Mendiants en Nouvelle–Espagne de 1523–24 à 1572.* Paris: Institut D'Ethnologie, 1933.

———. "Sur les fêtes de "Moros y Cristianos" au Mexique." *Journal de la Sociètè des Américanists,* 30 (1938): 375–376.

———. "Les fêtes de "Moros y Cristianos" à Juviles (Prov. de Grenade)." *Bulletin Hispanique,* 48 (1946): 263–264.

[Ricci, Matthew]. *China in the Sixteenth Century: The Journals of Matthew Ricci: 1583–1610,* translated from the Latin by Louis J. Gallagher, S.J. New York: Random House, 1953.

Richter, Daniel K. and James H. Merrell, eds. *Beyond the Covenant Chain. The Iroquois and Their Neighbors in Indian North America, 1600–1800.* Syracuse: Syracuse University Press, 1987.

Ronda, James P. "The European Indian: Jesuit Civilization Planning in New France." *Church History* 41 (1972): 385–95.

———. "We Are Well as We Are": An Indian Critique of Seventeenth Century Christian Missions." *William and Mary Quarterly* 34 (1977), 66–82.

———. "The Sillery Experiment: A Jesuit–Indian Village in New France, 1637–1663." *American Indian Culture and Research Journal* 3 no.1 (1979): 1–18.

Rowe John Howland, "Inca Culture at the Time of the Spanish Conquest." In *Handbook of South American Indians,* 15, 183–330. New York: Cooper Square Publishers, 1963.

Ruiz de Montoya, Antonio, S.J. *The Spiritual Conquest. Accomplished by the Religious of the Society of Jesus in the Provinces of Paraguay, Paraná, Uruguay, and Tape. A Personal Account of the Founding and Early Years of the Jesuit Paraguay Reductions*. St. Louis: Institute of Jesuit Sources, 1993.

Rutman, Darrett B. and Anita H. Rutman. "Of Agues and Fevers: Malaria in the Early Chesapeake." *William and Mary Quarterly* (3rd. ser.) 33 (1976): 31–60.

Saenz de Santa María, Carmelo. *Historia de la educación jesuítica en Guatemala*. Madrid: Consejo Superior de Investigaciones Científicas, 1978.

Saguier Bareiro, Rubén, and Jean–Paul Duviols, eds. *Tentación de la Utopía. La República de los jesuítas en el Paraguay*. Barcelona: Tusquets, 1991.

Saloman, Frank, and George Urioste trans. *The Huarochirí Manuscript. A Testament of Ancient and Colonial Andean Religion*. Austin: University of Texas Press, 1991.

Scaduto, Mario. *Storia della Compagnia di Gesu in Italia*. Rome: Edizioni "La Civilta Catolica," 1964.

———. "Il Teatro Gesuitico." *ARSI*, 36 (1967): 194–215.

Schrire, C. *Past and Present in Hunter Gatherer Societies*. Orlando, Fla: Academic Press, 1984.

Schurhammer, Georg. *Documenta Indica: Epistolae S. Francisci Xaverii aliique scripta ejus*. Nova editio. 2 vols. Rome: Monumenta Historica Societatis Iesu, 1944–45.

———. *Francis Xavier: His Life, His Times. Vol 1. Europe 1506–1541* (trans. M. Joseph Costelloe). Rome: Jesuit Historical Institute, 1973.

Schusky, Ernest L., and T. Culbert. *Understanding Culture*. Englewood Cliffs, N.J.: Prentice Hall, 1967.

Shapiro, Judith. "From Tupã to the Land Without Evil: The Christianization of Tupi–Guarani Cosmology," *American Ethnologist* 14 (1987): 126–139.

Shiels, W. Eugene. *Gonzalo de Tapia (1561–1594): Founder of the First Permanent Jesuit Mission in North America*. New York: United States Catholic Historical Society, 1934.

———. *King and Church: The Rise and Fall of the Patronato Real*. Chicago: Loyola University Press, 1961.

Silver, Timothy. *A New Face on the Countryside: Indians, Colonists, and Slaves in South Atlantic Forests, 1500–1800*. Cambridge: Cambridge University Press, 1990.

Simpson, Lesley Byrd. *Studies in the Administration of the Indians in New Spain*. Berkeley: University of California Press, 1934.

Skelly, K. "El teatro en la América Hispana durante el siglo XVI." *Revista Canadiense de Estudios Hispánicos* 7 (1982).

Smith, Clifford T., William M. Denevan, Patrick Hamilton. "Antiguos camellones de la región del Lago Titicaca." In *La tecnología en el mundo andino*, edited by Heather Lechtman and Ana María Soldi, 25–50. Ciudad Universitaria, México: Universidad Nacional Autónoma de México, 1981.

Smith, Daniel Blake. "Mortality and Family in the Colonial Chesapeake." *Journal of Interdisciplinary History* 8 (1978): 403–437.

Spalding, Karen. *Huarochiri. An Andean Society under Inca and Spanish Rule*. Stanford, Calif.: Stanford University Press, 1984.

Spicer, Edward H. *Cycles of Conquest. The Impact of Spain, Mexico, and the United States on the Indians of the Southwest, 1533–1960.* Tucson: University of Arizona Press, 1962.

Stanish, Charles, et. al. *Archaeological Survey in the Julí–Desaguadero Region of Lake Titikaka Basin, Southern Peru. Review Draft.* Chicago: Field Museum: n.d.

Stannard, David E. *American Holocaust: Columbus and the Conquest of the New World.* New York: Oxford University Press, 1992.

Starna, William. "Mohawk Iroquois Population: A Revision." *Ethnohistory* 27 (1980): 371–382.

Stern, Steve. "The Rise and Fall of Indian–White Alliances: A Regional View of "Conquest" History." *Hispanic American Historical Review* 61. no. 3 (1981): 461–491.

Steward, Julian H. ed. *Handbook of South American Indians.* New York: Cooper Square Publishers, 1963.

Storni, Hugo, S.J. *Catalogo de los jesuítas de la Provincia del Paraguay (Cuenca del Plata) 1565–1768.* Rome: Institutum Historicum Societatis Iesu, 1980.

———. Jesuítas en el Río de la Plata." *AHSI* 125 (1994): 175–181.

Susnik, Branislava. *Los Aborígenes del Paraguay. Etnohistoria de los guaraníes. Época Colonial.* Asunción: Museo Etnográfico "Andrés Barbero," 1979–1980.

Szilas, Laszlo. "Schule. Bilding, Theater." *ARSI* 61 (19): 212.

Tanner, Norman. *Decrees of the Ecumenical Councils. vol. 2, Trent to Vatican II.* Sheed and Ward and Georgetown University Press, 1990.

Taylor, William B. "Santiago's Horse." In *Violence, Resistance, and Survival in the Americas: Native Americans and the Legacy of Conquest.* Edited by William B. Taylor and Franklin Pease G.Y., 24–42. Washington, D.C.: Smithsonian Institution Press, 1994.

Taylor, William B. *Magistrates of the Sacred: Priests and Parishioners in Eighteenth Century Mexico.* Stanford, Calif.: Stanford University Press, 1996.

Thomas, Hugh. *Conquest: Montezuma, Cortés, and the Fall of Old Mexico.* New York: Simon and Schuster, 1993.

Thornton, John. *Africa and Africans in the Making of the Atlantic World, 1400–1680.* Cambridge: Cambridge University Press, 1992.

Thwaites, Reuben Gold, ed. *The Jesuit Relations and Allied Documents: Travels and Explorations of the Jesuit Missionaries in New France, 1610–1791.* 73 vols. Cleveland: Burrows Brothers, 1896–1901.

Todorov, Tzvetan. *The Conquest of America: The Question of the Other.* New York: Harper and Row, 1984.

Tooker, Elizabeth. *An Ethnography of the Huron Indians, 1615–1649.* Washington, D.C.: Bureau of Ethnology, Bulletin number 190, 1964.

———., ed. *Native North American Spirituality of the Eastern Woodlands: Sacred Myths, Dreams, Visions, Speeches, Healing Formulas, Rituals and Ceremonials.* New York: Paulist Press, 1979.

Trigger, Bruce. *The Children of Aataensik: A History of the Huron Peoples to 1660.* 2 vols. Montreal: McGill–Queens University Press, 1976.

Trudel, Marcel. *The Beginnings of New France: 1524–1663*. Toronto: McClelland and Stewart, 1973.

Urquijo, José M. Mariluz. "Los guaranies después de la expulsión de los jesuítas." *Estudios Americanos* 25 (1953): 323–330.

Urquijo, José María. "El Indio en los escritos de los jesuítas." *Jesuítas. 400 Años en Córdoba. Congreso Internacional*. Córdoba: Universidad Nacional de Córdoba, 1999, II, 239–247.

Urton, Gary. *At the Crossroads of Earth and Sky: An Andean Cosmology*. Austin: University of Texas Press, 1981.

Vargas, José María, ed. *Arte Colonial de Ecuador: Siglos XVI–XVII*. Barcelona: Salvat Editores, 1977.

Vargas Ugarte, Rubén, ed. *De Nuestro Antiguo Teatro. Colección de Piezas Dramáticas de los siglos XVI, XVII, y XVIII. Introducción y notas de Rubén Vargas Ugarte*. Lima: Biblioteca Histórica Peruana, Tomo IV, 1943.

———. *Los Concilios Limenses*. 3 vols. Lima: 1952–1964.

Vecsey, Christopher, ed. *Religion in Native North America*. Moscow: University of Idaho Press, 1990.

Wallace, A.F.C. "Dreams and the Wishes of the Soul. A Type of Psychoanalytic Theory Among Seventeenth Century Iroquois." *American Anthropologist* 60 (1959): 234–248.

Wax, Donald W. "Black Immigrants: The Slave Trade in Colonial Maryland." *Maryland Historical Magazine* 73 (1978): 30–45.

Weaver, Jace, ed. *Native American Religious Identity: Unforgotten Gods*. Maryknoll, N. Y.: Orbis Books, 1998.

West, Robert C. *The Mining Community in Northern New Spain: The Parral Mining District*. Berkeley: University of California Press, 1949.

Wethey, Harold E. *Colonial Architecture and Sculpture in Peru*. Cambridge, Mass.: Harvard University Press, 1949.

Widmer, Randolph J. *The Evolution of the Calusa: A Nonagricultural Chiefdom on the Southwest Florida Coast*. Tuscaloosa: University of Alabama Press, 1988.

Williams, Eduardo. "The Stone Sculpture of Ancient West Mexico." *Ancient Mesoamerica* 2 (1991): 181–192.

Williams, Jerry, and Robert E. Lewis. *Early Images of the Americas: Transfer and Invention*. Tucson: University of Arizona Press, 1993.

Wolf, Eric. *Sons of the Shaking Earth*. Chicago: University of Chicago Press, 1959.

Woodbridge Hensley C., and Lawrence S. Thompson. *Printing in Colonial Spanish America*. Troy, N.Y.: Whitson, 1976.

Young, William. *St. Ignatius' Own Story as Told to Luis Goncalvez de Cámara*. Chicago: Regnery, 1956.

———. *St. Ignatius' Letters to Women*. Chicago: Regnery, 1959.

Zavala, Silvio. *Orígenes de la colonización en el Río de la Plata*. Mexico: Editorial de El Colegio Nacional, 1977.

Zubillaga, Félix. "P. Pedro Martínez (1533–1566): La primera sangre jesuítica en las misiones norteamericanos." *ARSI* 7 (1938): 30–53.

————. *La Florida: La misión jesuítica (156–1572) y la colonización española*. Rome: Institutum Historicum Societatis Iesu, 1941.

————. "Métodos misionales de la primera instrucción de San Francisco de Borja para la América Española (1567)." *ARSI* 12 (1943): 58–88.

————. *Monumenta Antiquae Floridae (1566–1572)*. Rome: Monumenta Historica Societatis Iesu, 1946.

————. *Monumenta Mexicana*. 7 vols. Rome: Institutum Historicum Societatis Iesu, 1956–1981.

————. "La provincia jesuítica de Nueva España. Su fundamento económico: siglo XVI," *ARSI* 38 (1969): 3–169.

———— and Walter Hanisch, *Guía Manual de los documentos históricos de la Compañía de Jesús de los cien primeros volúmenes*. Rome: Institutum Historicum Societatis Iesu, 1971.

Zwinge, Joseph. "The Jesuit Farms in Maryland." *Woodstock Letters* 39 (1910): 374–382; 40 (1911): 65–77, 180–199; 41 (1912): 53–77, 195–222, 275–291; 42 (1913): 1–13, 137–150, 336–352; 43 (1914): 83–89, 194–200.

Index

Huron
 burials, 14, 193–194
 Indians, 149, 165

Illapa, 95
Ingle, Richard, 178–179

Jesuits
 accompanied by translators, 177
 architects, 134, 139
 business transactions, 60, 121
 chapels of, 137–140
 Chinese in Jesuit literature, 192
 complain about Spanish behavior, 45
 criticism of construction, 140–141
 cultural superiority of, 63, 96
 as explorers, 166–169
 farms leased, 187
 goals, 20
 gold mines of, 101
 income from farms, 188
 lands in New France, 152
 learn languages, 56, 87, 163–164, 198,
  166, 198
 methods in Sonora, 52, 62
 Relations, 192, 193, 194
 reparation for missions, 15, 27, 32
 in Sinaloa, 56
 slaves of, 187
 use of military metaphors, 165
 wills, 189
Julí, model for Paraguay, 99

Keoki, 7
Kino, Eusebio, S. J., 166, 167
Kittamaquund, 177
Knott, Edward, S. J., 171

La Compañía church, 135
Lake Ontario, 149
LeJeune, Paul, S.J., 155
LeMercier, François de, S. J., 27
Lewis, John, S.J., 183
Lópe de Vega, 143

López de Azpeitia, Ignacio, S. J., 131
Lorenzana, Marcial de, 110
Lowe, Vincent, 181
Lugo, Francisco de. 25
Luther, Martin, 17

Macedo, Hector, 191
Manitou, 162
Maquacomen, 196
Marquette, Pierre, S. J., 161, 162
Marseta, Simon, S. J., 110
Martin, Calvin, 164
Martinez, Pedro, S. J., 31
Mason, John, 9
Masse, Ennemond, S. J., 154
Mattingly, Garrett, 108
Mendoza, Cristobal de, S. J., 109
Mestigoit, 155, 161
Miller, Parson John, 185
Missionary
 key role, 29
 motivation, 22–27
 see also Jesuits
Mohawk Indians, 150
Molina, Luis de, S. J., 17, 59
Montagnais Indians, 155
Morales, Martín María, S. J., 102
Mosley, Joseph, S. J., 184, 189
Mt. Desert Island, 154
Music
 in Guarani missions, 117
 in Sinaloa, 54

Nazpeces, 76
Native Americans
 adjustments to Europeans, 48
 belief system, 33
 environment, 14
 epidemics among, 85
 resettlement, 67, 71–78;
 society; 33
 sports, 38
 values, 13
 women, role of, 15

Lightning Source UK Ltd.
Milton Keynes UK
UKOW05f2337170617
303569UK00001B/31/P